BALANCE OF POWER
OR HEGEMONY:
THE INTERWAR
MONETARY SYSTEM

LEHRMAN INSTITUTE BOOKS

The Lehrman Institute was founded in 1972 as a private, nonprofit, operating foundation devoted to the analysis of public policy in its broadest aspects, with particular emphasis on the historical roots of contemporary policy questions. The Institute encourages interdisciplinary study—so as to foster a greater awareness of the interpenetration of history, politics, and economics—and also contributes to nonpartisan debate on contemporary policy issues. To these ends, the Institute sponsors annually a program of seminars organized around the works-in-progress of a small number of appointed Research Fellows and also conducts other series of study groups, focusing on major problems in foreign affairs and economic policy. These seminars bring together scholars, businessmen, journalists, and public servants.

Beginning in early 1976, the Institute will arrange to publish certain books under its aegis which will include specially commissioned essays and other monographs which were originally presented as working papers in Institute seminars and which, in the judgment of the Trustees of the Institute, are worthy of presentation to a wider public.

The Lehrman Institute does not take any position with regard to any issue: all statements of fact and expression of opinion in these publications are the sole responsibility of the individual authors. The Institute is not affiliated with, nor does it receive funds from, any educational institution or any agency of the United States Government.

BALANCE OF POWER OR HEGEMONY: THE INTERWAR MONETARY SYSTEM

Benjamin M. Rowland, *Editor*
W. H. Bruce Brittain
David P. Calleo
Harold van B. Cleveland
Judith L. Kooker
Robert J.A. Skidelsky

A Lehrman Institute Book
Published by
New York University Press • New York • 1976

Library of Congress Catalog Card Number: 75-27423

ISBN: 0-8147-7368-0

Library of Congress Cataloging in Publication Data
Main entry under title:
Balance of power or hegemony.
(A Lehrman Institute book)
"Essays . . . originally presented as working papers at the [Lehrman] Institute's International Monetary Seminar which met over an eighteen-month period beginning in the spring of 1973."
Includes bibliographical references.
1. Monetary policy—History—Congresses. 2. International economic relations—History—Congresses.
3. Economic history—1918-1945—Congresses. I. Rowland, Benjamin M. II. Calleo, David P., 1934- III. Lehrman Institute. IV. Series: Lehrman Institute. A Lehrman Institute book.
HG255.B33   332.4′5   75-27423
ISBN   0-8147-7368-0

Manufactured in the United States of America

Contents

List of Contributors

BENJAMIN M. ROWLAND was an undergraduate at Yale and worked as a Peace Corps volunteer in Latin America before receiving his Ph.D. degree in European Studies at The Johns Hopkins School of Advanced International Studies. He was Acting Assistant Professor of European studies at the Johns Hopkins Bologna Center; was one of the first Research Fellows appointed at the Lehrman Institute; and subsequently served as its Staff Research Director as well as Associate Director of the Washington Center of Foreign Policy Research. He is the co-author, with David P. Calleo, of *America and the World Political Economy* (1973) and was a contributor to *Retreat from Empire? The First Nixon Administration (1973)*, edited by Robert E. Osgood et al. Currently he is with the international division of the investment banking firm of Salomon Brothers.

DAVID P. CALLEO received his undergraduate and graduate degrees at Yale, taught there, served as consultant to the U.S. Undersecretary of State for Political Affairs, and is now Professor of European Studies at The Johns Hopkins School of Advanced International Studies in Washington, and Vice-Chairman for Academic Affairs at the Lehrman Institute. He is the author, among other works, of *Europe's Future: The Grand Alternatives* (1965); *Coleridge and the Idea of the Modern State* (1966); *Britain's Future* (1968); *The Atlantic Fantasy: The U.S., N.A.T.O., and Europe* (1970);

and, with Benjamin M. Rowland, *America and the World Political Economy* (1973).

HAROLD VAN B. CLEVELAND received his undergraduate and law degrees at Harvard and subsequently served as Assistant Chief in the Division of Investment and Economic Development, Department of State; Deputy Director and Special Economic Advisor, European Program Division, Economic Cooperation Administration; International Economist and Assistant Director of Research, Committee for Economic Development; and Director of Atlantic Policy Studies at the Council on Foreign Relations. He is currently Vice-president at the Economics Department of the First National City Bank and a Trustee of the Lehrman Institute. He is co-author, with Theodore Geiger, of *The Political Economy of American Foreign Policy* (1955), and author of *The Atlantic Idea and its European Rivals* (1966).

W. H. BRUCE BRITTAIN studied at Carleton University, Ottawa, the London School of Economics, and received his Ph.D. degree in economics from the University of Chicago with a dissertation on "French Balance of Payments, 1880-1913." He is currently with the Economics Department of the First National City Bank and wrote with H. van B. Cleveland the essay "A World Depression?" which appeared in the January 1975 issue of *Foreign Affairs*.

JUDITH L. KOOKER did her undergraduate work at Stanford and received her Ph.D. degree in European Studies at The Johns Hopkins School of Advanced International Studies. She was a Research Associate at the Hudson Institute (European Division) and is currently an International Economist at the Office of International Monetary Affairs, Department of the Treasury. She is the author of *International Monetary Reform: The Issues and Outlook* (1973) and of

French Financial Diplomacy: The Interwar Years (forthcoming).

ROBERT J. A. SKIDELSKY was educated at Brighton College and Jesus College, Oxford, and was subsequently appointed Research Fellow at Nuffield College, Oxford. He has also been a Fellow at the Washington Center of Foreign Policy Research, a Research Fellow of the Lehrman Institute, and is currently Professor of European Studies at the Bologna Center of The Johns Hopkins School of Advanced International Studies. He is the author of, among other works, *Politicians and the Slump* (1967) and *Oswald Mosley* (1975), and is now working on a biography of John Maynard Keynes.

Introduction

Academic studies may be the victims as well as the benefi-
ciaries of their own refined perspectives. An underlying premise of the essays here assembled is that many of the attempts to
understand the current turnings and thrashings of international monetary policy have been distorted by too narrow a
focus. The antidote, we believe, may lie in a broad study of
history.

As the title of this volume—*Balance of Power or Hegemony:
The Interwar Monetary System*—should suggest, the purpose
of our study is not simply to explain the operations of international monetary policy in some narrowly technical sense
—intricate and fascinating as that task may be—but to explore
relationships between monetary order and the sovereign
political entities comprising that order. The methodology of
such a study, although perfectly straightforward on one level,
leads to areas of vehement controversy on another. It would
seem useful, therefore, to underscore some of these contentious matters at the outset.

In the literature of international politics, there is a long-
standing and widely accepted practice of discussing relation-

ships among nation-states in systemic terms. Thus, scholarly studies of the Cold War and its denouement are littered with systems described as bipolar or multipolar, symmetrical or skewed, hegemonic or "pentagonally pluralistic," and so on. But attempting to introduce a comparable typology of "systems" for either descriptive or speculative purposes to the study of international economic relations has typically been less well received. Why has this systemic study of economics been relatively slow to develop? The answer, it seems to me, lies in two broad areas. First, there is the theory and practice of economics itself. For economics, at least in the hands of most Anglo-Saxon practitioners, has had a highly developed systemic bias of its own. According to the prevailing canons of liberal economics, there is only one wholly legitimate mode of international economic order and that is the open international one. Within this theoretical framework, any regional system is held to subtract from the efficiency of the whole; its exclusive nature would be contrary to the axioms of liberal economics and hence not worthy of serious consideration.

It is only a small step from this theoretical preference for economic openness to an equally strong affinity for an international political system dominated by a single power. If countries followed enlightened self-interest, the argument goes, they would hew to liberal economic practices as a matter of course. But in an imperfect world they cannot be counted on to do so. Thus, world economic order requires a hegemon. In this manner, what is frequently referred to as a liberal world view might more accurately be called both liberal and imperial: liberal, because it stresses the importance of open trade and stable exchange rates; imperial, because it maintains, implicitly or explicitly, that few countries enter into such relationships voluntarily and that a "single stabilizer" or "lender of last resort" is essential to its success.[1]

---

[1] For an important recent statement of this viewpoint, see Charles P. Kindleberger, *The World in Depression, 1929-1939* (Berkeley and Los Angeles: University of California Press, 1973).

If scholars are loath to explore alternate modes of international economic order because of certain theoretical economic predilections, that reluctance is understandably reinforced when they reflect on the most recent historical period in which an open system did *not* prevail—namely, the interwar years. The absence of a common world economy, it is said, greatly hampered recovery from the Great Depression and ultimately turned country against country as the scramble for markets and resources ripened into war. This combination of liberal economics and interwar historiography has produced an enduring theory which might be summarized in the following manner. In brief, British monetary supremacy in the nineteenth and early twentieth centuries not only coincided with but was responsible for such peace and plenty as that age enjoyed. Similarly, hegemony is believed to have been the foundation for the great boom in the years following World War II. According to this view, without a hegemonic power, which would, of course, be reflected in a unified monetary system, prosperity vanishes and disaster follows. So it was during the interwar years, it is said, with Britain no longer able and America still unwilling to provide critical leadership. So, by inference, it will be in years to come unless America or another responsible power restores order to the world political economy.

While no theory can pretend to be comprehensive, the above view has come to be challenged in many quarters. First, for a growing number the true origins of the economic malaise culminating in the fall of the dollar in 1971 is seen stemming not from an insufficiency but an overextension of American power. Translated into monetary policy terms, America's difficulties arose not from an inability to stanch the flow of claims on American reserves, but from a kind of economic hubris which led American statesmen to believe that such claims could never be asserted in the first place. This critique, to be sure, is aimed less at the institutions of hegemony than at America's performance as fiduciary. The theory that power was needed to preserve economic order had not so much been proved wrong in this view as perverted into a self-serving rationale for the continuation of a particular regime of power.

Others have carried the critique a stage further. Seeing over-extension and collapse as inherent features of *any* concentration of power, they have tried to imagine a political-economic system whose principle of organization was not imperial but plural. For only in conditions of shared power could one hope to mitigate the dangers of concentration reflected in the dollar's collapse. For a final group, the concern has been less with the shape of a theoretically ideal system than with what is practically possible. Few in this group, even though they might welcome it, foresee a return to the concentration of power which underlay the familiar Bretton Woods system. Instead, the increasing diffusion of power in the world political system is seen to necessitate parallel adjustments in the economic relations of the principal members. In this view, the search for a viable plural economic order is not a matter for idle speculation, but one of urgent necessity—a belated adaptation to the real changes that have already taken place.

Whether the world economy needs a leader is the central question to which the essays in this book address themselves. In the introductory essay, Harold van B. Cleveland provides an historical synopsis of the many "monetary systems" the Western world experienced from the pre-World War I gold standard to the Bretton Woods system and beyond. In the process he develops an analytical framework for judging the viability of monetary systems from economic, institutional, and political perspectives. While he views the hegemonic model as the most stable and therefore successful for sustaining an international economy, he is also quick to recognize the weakness inherent in such a system. The so-called Tripartite Monetary system, although in existence only briefly (1936-39) and governed by special political circumstances, suggests to him one possible way of avoiding the excesses (or enjoying the benefits) of both plural and hegemonic models.

Although he would doubtless chafe at the label, Robert Skidelsky's essay on Britain also places him more in the hegemonic than the pluralist camp, certainly with regard to its major premise that a well-functioning international economy requires conscious political leadership. Yet, in espousing that view, he holds out few grounds for optimism. Indeed, as Skidelsky sees it, the British case suggests that misfortune befalls the country that lends its energies and resources to such a task, for it will dissipate its strength and thereby hasten its own decline.

Other essays, such as Judith Kooker's on French—or my own on American—monetary and economic policies during the interwar period, take a more skeptical view toward the necessity of hegemony and seek to explore the conditions whereby a more plural form of monetary order might have succeeded. Thus, among other concerns, Judith Kooker's essay draws attention to the striking parallels between France's critique of the imperial pretensions of sterling in the 1920s and of the dollar in the 1960s, and to the problems of reserve-currency systems in general. My own essay focuses particularly on the keen rivalry between the United States and Britain during the interwar years and speculates on whether the economic and diplomatic costs of that rivalry were indeed worth the benefits of the hegemonic order which followed.

Bruce Brittain's essay on the extent to which economic systems remained integrated during much of the interwar periods leads him to a somewhat different conclusion—namely, that economies tend to remain integrated *in spite of* political conflict. Of all the essays, his viewpoint is perhaps the closest to a classical laissez-faire position, and as such offers an interesting variation on the book's common theme.

The reason for reflecting anew on the interwar period should by now be apparent. Clearly, no one would urge adopting the policies of that unhappy time as models. Rather, differing interpretations of that troubled period and the sources of its malaise might help us to focus on different approaches to the search for a viable political-economic order today. In this spirit, David Calleo's concluding essay outlines the case for regarding the breakdown of interwar political and monetary order not as stemming from the absence of hegemony, but as the unfortunate consequence of an overweening hegemon. Monetary collapse in 1931, according to Calleo's view, flowed not so much from the existence of rival economic centers but from Britain's efforts to recapture a predominating position for its currency—a position, in any case, it never fully enjoyed in the first place.

If a number of the views put forward here are valid, the revisionist implications are far-reaching indeed, not only for the interwar period but for today. If, for example, world order demands a hegemon which, as Cleveland and Skidelsky suggest, ruins itself in providing that necessary leadership, then the main historical events of these years must be read as an inevitably tragic drama, as whole countries sacrifice for the common good. Candidates, of course, are now scarce. Yet if, like Calleo, one can imagine order maintained by a plural, rather than an imperial system, the efforts of countries to exercise control beyond their borders might better be viewed not as an act of self-sacrifice, but of misguided self-serving.

Although any multi-authored group of essays is by definition a collective effort, this volume must be termed more collective than most. A word about the Lehrman Institute, which sponsored the project, is therefore in order.

The Lehrman Institute is an organization concerned with the analysis of public policy in its broadest aspects, while stressing in particular the historical roots of issues with relevance to contemporary policy questions. As its first major in-house project the Institute chose to study the international monetary system from historical as well as analytical perspectives. The essays collected here were originally presented as working papers at the Institute's International Monetary Seminar which met over an eighteen-month period beginning in the spring of 1973.[2] It should not be necessary to say that these essays do not exhaust their subject, for there are clearly numerous legitimate approaches to the study of a field as complex as monetary policy. Even within the framework we set for ourselves, the volume is incomplete in at least one area, for there are no essays on the monetary policy and political economy of the Axis Powers. The omission is doubly unfortunate, for not only did much of the friction preceding World War II revolve around the autarkic policies of the Axis partners, but those policies themselves (insofar as their economic features can be separated from their political and strategic) are increasingly seen by some to have experienced a considerable measure of internal success. But for a volume of these modest proportions, it is perhaps better to leave that immense and polemical topic untouched.

The seminar was especially fortunate to have as its chairman Harold van Buren Cleveland, whose experience as a banker, a diplomat, and a scholar qualify him uniquely not only to write about political economy but to lead others in exploring that elusive subject.

Nicholas X. Rizopoulos, the Institute's Executive Director, and James Chace and May Wu of the Institute's Editorial Advisory Committee all read each of the articles with great care and provided numerous useful suggestions, both editorial and substantive. The authors should also like to thank Betty Gurchick and Carol Rath for their patient typing and retyping of the book's several drafts.

Benjamin M. Rowland

---

[2] These seminars were made possible, in part, through a grant from the Charles E. Merrill Trust, which the Lehrman Institute gratefully acknowledges.

CHAPTER 1

The International Monetary System in the Interwar Period

HAROLD VAN B. CLEVELAND

Although monetary economists have long recognized the importance of "institutions" in their analysis of monetary systems, their interest has seldom extended to the full political setting in which institutions must exist. The following essay is a happy exception. It has the rare distinction of analyzing interwar monetary systems from both political and economic vantage points and, rarer still, of maintaining rigorous analytical standards in the process. In my opinion, it is an example of political economy as it should be written and makes a most fitting introduction to the volume.

An international monetary system may be judged in good order if it makes possible, in participating countries, a high level of employment without much price inflation, with exchange rates that are stable and without extensive use of exchange controls. By this economic criterion, the international monetary system—or systems—of the years between the two world wars were mostly unsuccessful. Compared with the pre-1914 gold standard, or the post-World II dollar standard in its brief heyday from 1959 to 1968, the interwar period was one of international monetary disorder.

To understand this failure and its meaning for our own times, historians should conduct their analyses on three levels. The simplest of the three is the economic. For there exists a well-developed body of monetary theory that can be used to shed valuable light on monetary developments in this period. That theory sees changes in the stock or aggregate supply of money as the main determinant of changes in income, prices, and real output or business activity, as well as in the balance of international payments and exchange rates. From this premise, it follows that knowledge of how the money supply is controlled is the key to understanding monetary and other macroeconomic developments, both domestic and international, whether past, present, or future.

Now, "control" implies institutions through which control is exercised. It implies authority and power to make the institutions do the controllers' bidding. And it implies that the controllers, insofar as they have discretion in shaping monetary policy, are motivated by certain purposes and interests—purposes and interests that may either conflict with, or be in harmony with, those of the monetary authorities of other nations with whom they may share control. Monetary phenomena, then, have institutional and political as well as strictly economic dimensions.

The historical literature on the international monetary system has generally failed to keep all three of these levels of analysis clearly in view. Most histories of the international monetary system have been concerned with institutions and have lacked an explicit and coherent foundation in monetary theory. The leading study on the interwar period, William Adams Brown's monumental work, *The International Gold Standard Reinterpreted, 1914-1934*,[1] invaluable as it is, suffers from this defect. At the other extreme, international monetary history is sometimes written as an abstract, theoretical view of how the system might have worked, or should have worked, with little regard for institutional facts. The typical textbook discussion of the pre-1914 gold standard is vulnerable to this criticism. And with few exceptions, historians of the international monetary system have given only passing attention to the political dimension. Insofar as its aim is methodological, this essay seeks to illustrate how the three dimensions

[1] William A. Brown, *The International Gold Standard Reinterpreted, 1914-1934* (New York: National Bureau of Economic Research, 1940).

of money interacted to determine the outcome in a particularly lively period of monetary history.

Western philosophy, said Alfred North Whitehead, is a series of footnotes to Plato. In like vein, modern monetary systems evolved out of an original monetary system, the gold standard, and all of them have borne the marks of this origin. The gold standard as it existed from about 1880 to 1914 is the archetype of a successful monetary system for the modern world—a world where money consists primarily of legal claims denominated in arbitrary units of a national currency, issued by national banking systems. In such a world, the central problem is how to control the money supply in a manner that is consistent with national interests and with international monetary order. The way the gold standard accomplished this task established a standard of performance that has not been equaled since.

It is therefore useful to think of monetary history since 1914 as the story of how economic, institutional, and political changes altered the conditions that made the gold standard work, thereby creating new problems of national monetary management and international coordination—problems which proved largely unmanageable in the interwar years and are still unsolved today.

We begin the story in the mid-1920s, after the principal currencies—the dollar, the pound, the French franc, and the Reichsmark—had been made freely convertible into gold again. The removal of wartime restrictions on gold exports from the United States in 1919 and the "stabilization" of the three leading European currencies—that is, the restoration of their convertibility into gold at fixed parities—in the years 1924 to 1928 marked the reestablishment, at least in outward form, of the gold standard. But the postwar system differed profoundly from the prewar system, and monetary relations among the leading powers were marked by rivalry and conflict, in place of the harmony that had generally prevailed before 1914.

For a few years, the gold-exchange standard, as the postwar

system came to be known, appeared to function adequately, although Britain's economy stagnated, despite general world prosperity. The new system's inherent defects were revealed in 1929-30, when the U.S. Federal Reserve, abandoning the practice though not yet the theory of the gold standard, went off on a restrictive monetary frolic of its own. The resulting monetary contraction in the United States, aggravated by a protracted banking crisis, spread to the rest of the world via the U.S. balance of payments. Its global deflationary impact was amplified by French monetary policy, by a banking crisis in Germany and by the rapid shrinkage of the sterling and dollar component of international reserves.

The suspension of the gold convertibility of sterling in September 1931 wrote finis to the gold-exchange standard and marked the beginning of a period of severe monetary disorder. This period was characterized by massive deflation of incomes and prices, mass unemployment, and widespread resort to trade restrictions and exchange controls. Punctuated by the suspension of the gold convertibility and the devaluation of the Reichsmark (de facto) in 1931-32, of the dollar in 1933-34 and of the French franc in 1935-36, the early 1930s were also marked by open conflict over monetary policy among the principal powers.

The franc's final capitulation in 1936 and the Tripartite Monetary Agreement in the same year marked the end of this period and the beginning of the third phase of interwar monetary history. The Tripartite Agreement signaled a monetary truce among three of the four monetary powers, the United States, Britain, and France. The system that emerged in this more hospitable political atmosphere was characterized by monetary blocs (a sterling bloc, a franc bloc, a dollar bloc, and a German bloc), with exchange rates between major currencies flexible. With the virtual disappearance of sterling and the dollar from the reserves of the principal powers, gold became again the principal element of central bank reserves, but the system was by no means a reversion to the traditional gold standard. Currencies were not convertible into gold except for official settlements among central banks, and exchange rates among major currencies were not fixed.

By comparison with what preceded it, the post-1936 system worked tolerably well. In part the reason was political: Under the common threat of resurgent German military power, the monetary authorities of Britain, France, and the United States began to work together rather than at cross purposes. The last of the interwar systems also proved to be a harbinger of things to come. As World War II approached, it gradually evolved into a dollar system, foreshadowing the full-fledged dollar standard that would emerge after the war.

The Framework of Economic Analysis

This essay differs from some of the other contributions to this volume in that it is firmly rooted in contemporary monetary theory of the "monetarist" persuasion. This theory is an updated version of the classical quantity theory of money. As noted above, it stresses the causal connection running from changes in a country's money supply to changes in its nominal income or gross national product and its price level. In recent years, it has been successfully used not only to explain changes in income, prices, and economic activity within a country, but also to understand changes in the balance of international payments and in exchange rates, as well as the impact of monetary policy in one country on other countries.

According to monetarist theory, the rate at which a country's money supply grows largely determines the rate of growth of its income. This is because the "demand for money"—the total amount of real purchasing power in the form of cash balances that the community desires to hold—grows at a rather regular rate. If the authorities cause the supply of money (normally defined as currency in circulation and liquid bank deposits) to grow more rapidly than the public's desired level of real cash balances is growing, individuals and firms will try to cut back their cash balances to the desired level. To do so, they will step up their spending on financial assets and on goods and services. For it is inconvenient and unprofitable to hold more wealth in the form of cash than is absolutely necessary for liquidity purposes. Collectively, they will not succeed in reducing the aggregate supply of money; the total supply will be held somewhere in the system. But the public's individual efforts to reduce its real cash balances to the desired levels will increase aggregate spending, which will cause the combined income of the community to rise, business activity to accelerate and, in time, the general level of prices also to rise.

Conversely, if the authorities cause the money supply to grow more slowly, so that the public's real cash balances fall below the desired level, the public will seek individually to rebuild its balances by cutting back its spending, in order to restore the purchasing power of its money holdings to the minimum desired level. In the aggregate, the public will not succeed; the total money supply is determined by the monetary authority. But individual efforts to rebuild cash balances will cause incomes generally to grow more slowly, business activity to decline, unemployment to rise, and inflation eventually to abate or the price level to fall.

Money, according to this view, includes those financial assets—and only those financial assets—that the public wishes to hold primarily as a means of payment and a store of value in highly liquid form. It therefore excludes assets held primarily to earn income—that is, as investments. A necessary consequence of this functional definition of money is that the public's aggregate holdings of money will be determined, not by the public but by the monetary authority. In other words, the public will be willing collectively to hold, in the aggregate, any quantity of money that the monetary authority makes available. This is not true of financial assets that are demanded primarily as investments. If the national treasury, for example, floods the market with government securities, their price will fall—that is, their interest yields will rise—to a level that equates the public's demand for such securities with the new supply. But the market value of money is not affected, in the short run, by the supply. This is not merely because money usually pays little or no interest but because it is demanded as a store of liquidity rather than as an investment. The way the economy adjusts to an excess or deficiency of the supply of money relative to demand is by a change in aggregate spending and the general price level, rather than by a change in the market price of the financial asset—money—itself.

This fundamental distinction between money and other assets is crucial to an understanding of how money works, both domestically and internationally. Failure to grasp it is the source of the view so widely held until recently that "money doesn't matter"—that is, that changes in the supply of money have no determinate or predictable effect on income, business activity, or prices.

In the monetarist view, then, the supply of money is essentially determined by a central bank or other monetary authority, by virtue of its control of the monetary base. The central bank issues currency, and it is also able to determine the level of bank reserves, which in turn determine how much money in the form of bank deposits the private banking system can create on its own. Bank reserves and currency in circulation constitute together the monetary base or "base money"; the relationship or ratio between the base and the money supply—which includes both currency and money in the form of deposits, when held by the nonbank public—is known as the "money multiplier." The central bank controls the monetary base by expanding or contracting its domestic assets—that is, its loans or discounts to banks and to the public, and its holdings of government securities. It also creates or destroys base money by expanding or contracting its foreign assets—that is, its holdings of gold and of financial assets denominated in foreign currencies.

A central bank has, of course, complete control over the

volume of its *domestic* asscts, so far at least as political pressures and the short-term needs of banks for funds to meet legal
reserve requirements allow. But under a monetary system in
which exchange rates are fixed in terms of gold (as under the
gold standard) or in terms of a key currency (as under the
post-World War II dollar standard), a central bank cannot
control directly the volume of its *foreign* assets. For their
volume will rise or fall depending on the condition of the
country's balance of payments—that is, on the amount of gold
or foreign currencies which the central bank buys or sells in
order to maintain its currency at the official parity. This
amount, in turn, is influenced not only by what the home
country's central bank is doing but also by what other central
banks are doing.

More precisely, the balance of payments (the overall balance, not the trade or current balance) depends on whether
the home country's banking system is expanding its domestic
assets (i.e., its outstanding credits) faster, or more slowly, relative to the demand for money at home, than other countries'
banking systems are expanding *their* credit relative to the
demand for money in *their* countries. In short, with exchange
rates fixed, a country's overall balance of payments depends on
whether its monetary conditions are more expansive than the
combined monetary conditions of other countries, or less so. If
more expansive, its international payments will be in deficit; if
less expansive, in surplus.

The net inflow or outflow of funds that constitutes a balance-of-payments surplus or deficit increases or reduces the
banking system's holdings of gold or foreign exchange. Thus, it
also affects the country's monetary base and money supply. In
this sense, under a fixed-rate system, a country's money supply
is not under its sole control. It shares control of its money
supply with other central banks. The manner and degree in
which control is shared depends in part on the economic size
of the country relative to other countries in the system; if the
country is large, it will have more influence over its own money

supply (particularly, in the short run) than if it is small. It also depends on monetary institutions. As we shall see, when a country's currency is widely held and used abroad as "international money," its own monetary autonomy is enhanced and it is able to exert control over other countries' money supplies out of proportion to its own economic size. This is the essence of a "key currency" or "reserve currency" system.

If exchange rates are flexible—that is, free to respond to changes in the supply of or demand for the national currency in foreign exchange markets—matters are quite different. In these circumstances, if the central bank makes the country's money supply grow faster, creating an excess supply of money in the home country relative to monetary conditions abroad, no outflow of funds will ensue. There will be no balance-of-payments deficit. Instead, the value of the home country's currency will fall on the exchanges. It will fall until it convinces operators in the exchange markets that it has moved far enough. At that point operators will be willing to hold increasing amounts of the home currency, rather than convert it into foreign currencies, because they expect its exchange rate to fall no further or even to rise again. The home currency's exchange rate will fall, in short, until it is low enough to make operators indifferent as between holding assets denominated in the home currency and foreign currencies.[2]

---

[2] According to a modern version of the doctrine of purchasing-power parity, this indifference point is reached when the exchange rate has fallen to the point where it will eventually raise the home country's domestic price level sufficiently to increase the domestic demand for money and absorb the initial excess supply of money. Traders in the market are assumed able to judge approximately when the exchange rate has reached this new equilibrium level. Stabilizing speculation would accordingly stabilize the exchange rate at that level. In practice, floating exchange rates seem to behave roughly in accordance with this theory. See "A New View of Exchange-Rate Forecasting," First National City Bank, *Money International* (New York, Nov. 30, 1975), p. 1.

It follows that, to the extent exchange rates are flexible, a country's monetary authority is fully able to control its own money supply. Its balance of payments will be kept in equilibrium by the rise or fall of the exchange rate and by market operators' response to that rise or fall. But if the country is small, the movement of the exchange rate may have a large short-run impact on the domestic price level and on profits and employment in exporting and import-competing industries. For this reason, small countries generally prefer fixed to flexible exchange rates. This, too, is why, in a period like the early 1930s, or at present, when fixed exchange rates among major currencies have broken down, currency blocs form. Smaller countries tend to peg their currencies to the currency of the large country with which they have the closest trade and financial ties.

Let us now put these theoretical tools to work in the real world, starting with a brief analysis of how the original modern monetary system, the pre-1914 gold standard, worked.

How the Gold Standard Worked

Two views of the pre-1914 gold standard may be found in economic texts and the historical literature. One sees the system in purely economic terms as simply an aspect of the market, guided by the unseen hand, owing allegiance to no authority. Central banks, where they existed, controlled the money supply, but only in a mechanical sense. They exercised no discretion. Their behavior was wholly determined by market forces and, perhaps, by certain customary rules. In a lecture delivered in 1932, Jacques Rueff said:

The gold standard governs all the components of our international transactions with faultless effectiveness. Like the price mechanism, of which it is only a specific aspect, it is a forceful but unobstrusive master, who governs unseen and yet is never disobeyed. Nevertheless, it is too wise to oppose the inclinations of men. They are always at liberty to buy according to their preferences, but the monetary mechanism, in its omnipotence, will raise the price of those items whose purchase is contrary to the general interest, until such time as consumers decide of their own free will to stop buying them. The gold standard thus resembles an absolute but enlightened monarch; he does not destroy man's freedom, but employs it for his own ends.[3]

The second view stresses the element of discretion and central control. According to this view, the master of the system was not Rueff's metaphorical monarch, the market, but a flesh-and-blood institution, the Bank of England. The Old Lady of Threadneedle Street exercised her power by virtue of the dominant position of the London money and capital markets in world trade and finance. "During the latter half of the nineteenth century," wrote John Maynard Keynes in 1930, "the influence of London on credit conditions throughout the world was so predominant that the Bank of England could almost have claimed to be the conductor of the international orchestra. By modifying the terms on which she was prepared to lend . . . she could to a large extent determine the credit conditions prevailing elsewhere."[4]

In principle, a gold-based monetary system could be automatic. This would be the case, for example, of a system in which the money supply consisted mainly or entirely of gold. Even a system in which gold and bank notes circulated together and in which there was a well-developed banking system would be automatic—in the sense of involving no discretionary control of the money supply—if bank notes were convertible into gold on demand at a fixed parity by banks of

[3] *The Age of Inflation* (Chicago, 1964), p. 40.
[4] *A Treatise on Money* (1930), *The Collected Writings of John Maynard Keynes*, vol. 6 (London, 1971), p. 274.

issue, and if the ratio between the note issue and the issuing banks' gold reserves was rigidly fixed. The money supply would thus vary in exact proportion with the supply of monetary gold.

Generations of students have learned to think of this as the textbook model of the gold standard. It is far from being an accurate picture of the historical gold standard, however. In his seminal essay, *Monetary Policy Under the International Gold Standard, 1880-1914*, Arthur I. Bloomfield showed that central banks before 1914 normally allowed their gold-reserve ratios to vary over a considerable range. [5] By expanding or contracting their domestic assets, central banks would vary the ratio between their monetary liabilities (deposits and the note issue) and their gold reserves. Discretionary monetary policy, in other words, existed under the gold standard, even though the extent of that discretion was much less before 1914 than it would later become. Nor is there convincing evidence that, in the exercise of their discretion, central banks were governed by hard-and-fast rules of behavior. The rules of the gold-standard game, so beloved of the writers of international economic texts, seem to have been a bit of ideology invented by later generations of bankers and economists attempting to play down the political dimension of monetary policy—and more particularly the special role of the Bank of England—under the gold standard. As Bloomfield observes, the notion that:

[M]onetary policy before 1914, except perhaps in the case of the Bank of England, was essentially "automatic," involving more or less mechanical responses to gold movements and a minimum of discretionary action and judgment ... is a misconception. Not only did central banking authorities, so far as can be inferred from their actions, *not* consistently follow any simple or single rule

[5] A. Bloomfield, *Monetary Policy Under the International Gold Standard, 1880-1914* (New York: Federal Reserve Bank of New York, October 1959).

or criterion of policy, or focus exclusively on considerations of convertibility [of their currencies into gold], but they were constantly called upon to exercise, and did exercise, their judgment on such matters as whether or not to act in any given situation, and if so at what point of time to act, the kind and extent of action to take. . . . [D]iscretionary judgment and action were an integral part of central banking policy before 1914, even if monetary management was not oriented toward stabilization of economic activity in the broader modern sense.[6]

Now, if there was discretion in national monetary management before 1914, we are brought to the question how in these circumstances the gold standard could have worked as well as it did. The question concerns both the system's ability to avoid severe deflation and inflation, and its ability to maintain payments equilibrium and stable gold parities among national monetary systems. Historians agree that in both respects the system was successful far beyond anything experienced since 1914. In the period 1880-1914, price levels in gold-standard countries were generally stable and fluctuations in income and business activity were moderate. The gold parities of the main currencies were seldom if ever in doubt, destabilizing currency speculation was rare and exchange controls were nonexistent.

No leading country was ever forced to abandon gold or to devalue its currency. In general, there was widespread confidence in the ability of the authorities to maintain existing gold parities. Under these conditions, private short-term capital movements proved for the most part an important source of support to official reserves at times of strain.[7]

6 *Ibid.*, p. 25.
7 A. Bloomfield, *Short-Term Capital Movements Under the Pre-1914 Gold Standard*, Princeton Studies in International Finance No. 11 (Princeton, N.J., 1963), p. 29.

The relative stability of incomes and prices before 1914 may be explained simply by the fact that the world's money supply was approximately governed by world gold production. The variations in gold-reserve ratios that central banks allowed were not large enough to permit the total world money supply to grow for long much faster or more slowly than total gold reserves. On the other hand, potential variations in individual countries' gold-reserve ratios were undoubtedly large enough to have caused serious disequilibria to arise between national monetary systems, leading to large payments imbalances, gold movements, and pressure on parities, as a consequence of temporary divergences in the discount rates and monetary policies of central banks. That such disequilibria were rare is shown not only by the stability of parities but also by the limited volume of international gold movement.

Accordingly, there must have been an institutional mechanism that kept central banks' monetary policies—and, more particularly, their discount-rate policies—in line with each other, despite their willingness to depart, temporarily, from customary gold-reserve ratios. The existence of some such mechanism is attested to by the fact that, despite central banks' margin of discretion, their monetary policies seem to have moved in parallel. Before 1914, the central bank's discount rate was the principal instrument of monetary policy. Arthur Bloomfield's study, already referred to, shows that changes by central banks in their discount rates in gold-standard countries were remarkably synchronous. When a central bank changed the rate at which it was willing to discount commercial paper, or to make loans on securities, above or below the rates prevailing in the domestic money market, the bank's domestic assets would fall or rise and so would the country's monetary base. Thus, the positive correlation of discount-rate changes which Bloomfield's study brings out implies a parallelism of monetary expansion or contraction among the countries participating in the gold standard, or at least such of them as had central banks.

Bloomfield also shows that discount-rate changes were

usually made in response to changes in the central banks' gold-reserve ratios. Given a central bank's overriding obligation to safeguard the gold convertibility of the national currency, a substantial fall in its gold-reserve ratio would naturally induce it to raise the discount rate, in order to slow the growth of its liabilities and prevent a loss of confidence in the gold parity. Conversely, if a central bank failed to expand credit (and thus its liabilities) when the gold-reserve ratio improved, it would pass up an opportunity to expand its earning assets. It should be recalled that central banks before 1914 were still essentially commercial banks, apart from their responsibility to safeguard the gold convertibility of the national currency. If, then, we can find an explanation for the tendency of reserve ratios to move in parallel, we shall perhaps discover why the pre-1914 gold standard worked so well.

The clue that unlocks this mystery is the traditional notion that the Bank of England played the coordinating role. It was observed long ago that the Bank of England's discount rate ("Bank rate") seemed to have a controlling influence on Britain's balance of payments, regardless of what other central banks were doing. When Bank rate was raised, a net inflow of funds into Britain would occur, pushing up the pound's exchange rate and pulling in gold. Conversely, when Bank rate was lowered, there would be a net outflow of funds. This occurred *even though other central banks raised or lowered their discount rates along with Bank rate, as they normally did.* The Bank of England's "pull on the exchanges" was stronger than theirs, even though they were all pulling in the opposite direction. As a result, the Bank of England was able not only to dominate the sterling exchanges but also (as Keynes put it) to orchestrate world credit conditions.

This insight is an old one, but the discussion of how the central bank of one country—and by no means the largest—was able to accomplish this remarkable result remains confusing and inconclusive to this day.[8] It cannot be explained by the

---

[8] The inconclusiveness is due partly to lack of data on the

relative size of the British economy and monetary system. In a world consisting of one very large country and a few small countries, monetary conditions in the large country would, with exchange rates fixed, determine monetary conditions in other countries, simply by virtue of the large country's size. Proportionate changes in its money supply would be reflected in more or less equal proportionate changes in the small countries' money supplies. This follows from a proposition of monetary theory: namely, that, with the demand for money given, and exchange rates fixed, changes in a small country's money supply are almost entirely determined by the pace of money creation in the rest of the world. But the British economy was nowhere near large enough to dominate world monetary conditions in this direct sense. Britain's share of world income in 1913 was only about 13 percent.

Thus, to make the traditional hypothesis of British monetary leadership stand up, it is necessary to isolate the particular institutional arrangements by which the Bank of England was able to exert leverage on the monetary base in other gold-standard countries that was quite out of proportion to Britain's economic size. In my view, that leverage was due to the widespread use of the pound as "international money."

The Pound as International Money

Sterling before 1914 was the world's most important "vehicle currency" or means of international payment. The great bulk of Britain's international transactions was invoiced in sterling and much trade between other countries as well. The London commodity exchanges, through which much of the

short-term capital account of the British balance of payments before 1914. The confusion must be attributed largely to an inadequate analytical framework. See Bloomfield, *Short-Term Capital Movements*, op. cit., pp. 71-77, and Peter H. Lindert, *Key Currencies and Gold, 1900-1913*, Princeton Studies in International Finance No. 24 (Princeton, N.J., 1969), pp. 46-57.

world's trade in cotton, wool, and metals passed, were sterling markets. The principal gold market was in London. The London money and capital market, by far the world's largest and most international, was a market for financial claims denominated in sterling.

From sterling's leading role as an international means of payment, it followed naturally that foreigners, including foreign bankš, held a large volume of liquid claims denominated in sterling, including deposits in London banks, Bank of England notes, short-term bills of exchange, and British Treasury bills.[9] Such was the confidence in the parity of the pound that sterling claims were regarded as free of exchange risk and were normally held by foreigners on an uncovered (unhedged) basis. They were accordingly particularly useful both as a means of international payment and as a way of satisfying or helping to satisfy the demand for money abroad, just as foreign-owned dollar deposits in U.S. banks and the Eurodollar market have served as international money in our own times. Foreign banks also held claims on London as part of their liquidity reserves. Thus, sterling claims served as base money abroad, much as today foreign banks' deposits in U.S. domestic banks serve as the reserve base of the Eurodollar system.

For their foreign owners, then, liquid sterling assets functioned as money or near-money. In the case of claims on London held by foreign banks, their monetary nature is underlined by the fact that they consisted mainly of time deposits bearing low interest rates or demand deposits bearing no interest.[10] Some central banks also held liquid sterling assets as official reserves, particularly within the British Empire, although sterling's role as an official reserve currency was more limited before 1914 than it became in the 1920s. But even where, as in France, sterling assets were not held by the central bank, the pound's unquestioned convertibility into gold or

[9] Bloomfield, *Short-Term Capital Movements*, op. cit., p. 72.
[10] Lindert, op. cit., p. 56.

local currencies, as well as its broad utility for international payments, enabled it to function as money in the hands of foreigners and foreign banks, in competition with gold and liquid assets denominated in local currencies.

What was true of the pound was not true of other currencies, however. While the French franc and the Reichsmark seem to have played, in parts of continental Europe, a regional key-currency role similar to that which sterling played in the world at large,[11] the British public did not hold bank deposits or other liquid assets denominated in foreign currencies to anything like the same extent as foreigners held sterling assets. Nor did British banks hold deposits denominated in foreign currencies as part of their liquidity reserves. "British banks kept no substantial amount of deposits abroad as working balances, in view of the fact that the great bulk of Britain's international transactions were settled in sterling. . . . The amount of foreign bills held by London banks and the public generally were all but negligible." [12] The pound, in short, was international money before 1914 in a sense and to a degree that made its position, if not unique, at least predominant.

This difference between the pound and other currencies is probably enough to explain the Bank of England's leverage on the British balance of payments and on monetary conditions in other gold-standard countries. When, for example, the bank of England raised Bank rate, foreign holdings of sterling deposits and other liquid assets would tend to decline, as banks and other lenders in London cut down their lending to foreigners in order to meet the demand for funds at home. For the higher Bank rate would slow the growth of the Bank of England's domestic assets, causing the supply of money in the United Kingdom to fall short of the demand for money. This would cause sterling assets to be repatriated, foreign

[11] *Ibid.*, pp. 16-21.
[12] Bloomfield, *Short-Term Capital Movements*, op. cit., p. 72.

funds to move into London on an uncovered basis in response to rising interest rates, and gold to flow in.[13] Foreign banks' deposits in London would tend to decline and this, along with their losses of gold, would reduce their liquidity and increase their demand for alternative reserve assets in local currency. Thus, foreign banks would raise their rates, compete harder for local deposits, cut back their loans, and seek more credit from the local central bank. But the local central bank could not go far in responding to this demand. With its own gold-reserve ratio now falling, it would have to raise its discount rate defensively—hence, the parallelism of discount-rate changes noted earlier—putting further downward pressure on the local monetary base. In this way, the tightness of credit and higher interest rates in Britain would be transmitted to other countries. Monetary conditions abroad would fall into line with those in Britain.

However, the process would not work the same way if it were the Reichsbank, for example, that made the first move to tighten credit. The unsatisfied demand for money in Germany, resulting from the central bank's restrictive policy, would give rise to an inflow of sterling funds. But—and this is

[13] "So far as concerned interest arbitrage between countries firmly on a gold basis, the exchange risk as a general rule was not covered because of confidence that the exchange rate would move only within narrow limits approximating the gold points. . . . It has been said, so far as Great Britain was involved, that uncovered interest arbitrage was the 'classic kind' of movement of short-term funds under the pre-1914 gold standard, and that the short-run effectiveness of a rise in the Bank of England discount rate depended in substantial part upon the fact that funds moved to London *without* the exchange risk being covered." Idem, p. 42. If the exchange risk to foreigners of holding short-term sterling assets had been considered substantial and had accordingly been hedged (by selling sterling forward or in some other way), the incentive to interest arbitrage would have been greatly reduced or eliminated, and with it the Bank of England's special ability to control the sterling exchanges.

the crucial difference—the outflow of sterling funds to Germany would *not* tighten monetary conditions in Britain much. For the overall British balance of payments would not register a substantial deficit and the British monetary base would not be much reduced. This is because a large part of the additional sterling funds acquired by German residents and banks, instead of being converted into marks, would be redeposited in London. This capital inflow would largely offset the capital outflow caused by the Reichsbank's move. Thus the Reichsbank's restrictive move would not result in a large loss of British gold. And the circular flow of funds from Britain to Germany and back again to London would continue until it had brought monetary conditions in Germany into line with those in Britain again. The reader will not fail to note the similarity of this process to the way the dollar standard works in our own times.

The same difference in monetary leverage between the Bank of England and other central banks would exist in the case of a move to ease credit. If the Bank of England eased first, sterling funds would flow to other countries. This would increase the liquidity of the public and the banks there, pushing down interest rates and inducing central banks to "follow the market" by lowering their discount rates and expanding their domestic assets. The Bank of England would not lose much gold, because foreigners would be willing to hold more sterling deposits and other liquid sterling assets and would accordingly reinvest the funds in London. But if the Reichsbank, for example, made the first move toward ease, the German banking system would lose gold. For British banks and the British public would not be willing to hold more mark deposits. Thus, marks would be converted into sterling, causing the overall German balance of payments to fall into deficit and gold to flow out. Monetary conditions in Germany would fall back into line with those in Britain.

The Gold Standard as a Political System

The success of the gold standard before 1914, then, depended on its political asymmetry. Britain, or more precisely the Bank of England, was not merely *primus inter pares* but also exercised a measure of central control over monetary conditions throughout the gold-standard world. How far this was intentional—whether the mechanisms through which control was exercised were understood at the time—is debatable. But what matters is that control *was* exercised and that it served the purpose of keeping monetary conditions in gold-standard countries consistent with the system's fundamental commitment to the convertibility of currencies, at fixed parities, into gold.

Yet, the political asymmetry should not be exaggerated. The Bank of England's monetary influence abroad was not as unqualified or as universal as the simplified model sketched in the preceding pages might suggest. The model of a completely British-controlled system fits the facts well enough within Britain's own imperial domain. There, British banks were dominant and accustomed to hold a large part of their liquidity reserves in sterling, while local central banks or other monetary authorities also held a large part of all of their official reserves in claims on London rather than in gold. Thus, within the Empire, the gold standard was probably a gold-exchange standard or a key-currency system, as we understand these terms today. The influence of the Bank of England was also felt strongly in Scandinavia, the Netherlands, Japan, Argentina, and a number of other countries around the world that were particularly dependent on British trade, capital, or military protection. Significantly, it was these countries or most of them which, along with most of the British dominions and colonies, joined the sterling bloc after 1931.

On the other hand, two of the largest gold-standard countries, France and the United States, were less subject to

Britain's monetary influence. France's large reserve of gold (second only to Russia's and America's), gave the Bank of France more latitude than many other countries to follow a discount-rate policy inconsistent with the Bank of England's. The French authorities also resorted more frequently than other countries to various "gold devices" to alter the gold export point.[14] Such measures, equivalent to limited flexibility for the franc's exchange rate, served to insulate monetary conditions in France to some extent from British influence. Significantly, the Bank of France's gold-reserve ratio and discount rate were only weakly correlated with Bank rate.[15]

The United States, for its part, was probably less subject to Britain's monetary influence than any European country. Holdings of sterling deposits and other liquid assets in New York and other U.S. cities were doubtless a lot smaller, relative to domestic assets—and to the U.S. monetary base—than in Europe, if only because U.S. foreign trade was much smaller relative to the national income. Internally, too, the U.S. monetary system, which lacked a central bank, was more decentralized than the European monetary systems. It was accordingly less dominated by its principal financial center, New York, where the influence of British monetary policy was doubtless stronger than in the rest of the country. The United States was on the gold standard, so that its monetary base was a function of the gold reserves of the banking system. But the special influence the Bank of England, exerted via changes in the sterling assets of the American public and banks, must have been weaker than in other gold-standard countries.

Nor was London's monetary leverage entirely unique. As already noted, the French franc and the Reichsmark also served in parts of continental Europe as international money.

---

[14] Bloomfield, *Monetary Policy Under the International Gold Standard*, op. cit., p. 52; Keynes, *A Treatise on Money*, op. cit., pp. 286-87.

[15] Bloomfield, *Monetary Policy Under the International Gold Standard*, op. cit., p. 31.

After a careful review of the evidence, Peter H. Lindert says: "The frequent portrayal of London as the only major reserve center before World War I exaggerates somewhat," for France and Germany were also reserve centers.[16] But Germany, and to a smaller extent France, were themselves subject to the one-sided monetary influence of the Bank of England.

In sum, the political structure of the gold standard before 1914 was hierarchial, but hardly hegemonic.[17] Like a feudal monarch, the Bank of England reigned more than she ruled, at least outside the Empire. The Queen's chief vassals, France and Germany, followed her lead to a considerable extent, while also presiding over monetary vassals of their own. The United States, like some remote and powerful barony, was too large and self-contained to be ruled from Threadneedle Street. Later, when the United States had established a central bank and pulled its own monetary domain together, it would become a formidable rival to Britain.

Fundamentally, the ability of the Bank of England to conduct the gold-standard orchestra depended on the doctrine and practice of laissez faire. Except in wartime, control of the money supply was regarded as a private matter, the business of bankers rather than governments. Public opinion took it for granted that central banks and private bankers should follow their own interests, tempered only by a decent regard for the public interest in orderly money markets and stable currencies, convertible into gold. When, during and after World War I,

[16] Lindert, op. cit., p. 76.

[17] As Lindert puts it: "This hierarchy of short-run influence, through which funds moved from lesser to greater financial centers as interest rates rose everywhere, helped to minimize monetary friction among major centers by passing the short-run financial adjustment burden along to the peripheral countries. It provides a striking contrast to the tendency of New York and London to compete for the same mobile funds in later years without either center's having decisive drawing power over funds from continental countries in payments surplus." See op. cit., p. 78.

central banks began to accept regular responsibilities for helping to finance national budgets and to maintain employment and manage demand, the days of the gold standard were numbered. For this modern concept of a national central bank's obligations was bound to clash with the delicate and largely invisible international mechanism that made the gold standard work.

A second environmental factor critical to the success of the system was the inherited monetary equilibrium resulting from generations of its successful operation. The gold standard had evolved gradually from earlier gold–or silver–based monetary systems. For several centuries, the Western world's money supply had consisted primarily of bullion or had been closely tied to bullion except during major wars. Since the supply of gold and silver was limited by nature and technology and was not subject to government manipulation, a bullion-based monetary system was naturally conducive to relative price stability. The importance of this background of equilibrium for the success of the gold standard, can hardly be overestimated. It made the gold parities of leading currencies appear sacrosanct, part of the order of nature, their maintenance a public duty that no right-thinking person would question. It put the mysterious mechanisms that maintained monetary equilibrium out of reach of meddlesome ministers. It sanctioned the air of aloof secrecy that protected central bankers from public scrutiny. Above all, it meant that the system faced no large problems of monetary adjustments that might have tempted governments to disturb its normal functioning.

Small wonder that in a period of money troubles such as our own, nostalgia for the gold standard is a lively force in international monetary politics. Jacques Rueff may have exaggerated when he called the system an aspect of the price mechanism. But from today's perspective, it is hard to quarrel with his admiration for a set of institutions that could accomplish so much so unobtrusively. No monetary system is likely again to prove its equal in satisfying the criterion of international monetary order.

The Gold-Exchange Standard

The architects of the international monetary system that came into being in the mid-1920s intended it to be a restoration of the pre-1914 system. In outward form, it was. The four principal currencies—the pound, the French franc, the Reichsmark, and the dollar—were all convertible into gold again at fixed parities. The right to import and export gold freely, suspended during the war, was restored. Beneath this formal surface, however, the new system differed profoundly from the old, in ways that would prove to be its undoing.

The defining characteristic of the prewar system had been the link between the money supply and the supply of monetary gold. The link existed by virtue of the subordination of credit creation in gold-standard countries to more or less fixed gold-reserve ratios. Under the postwar system, these institutional arrangements were altered fundamentally. The discretionary element in national monetary policies was greatly enlarged. Countries that were formerly content to let the system itself, or the Bank of England, determine their domestic monetary conditions now asserted an independent right to control credit creation for domestic purposes, without adhering to fixed ratios between their central banks' liabilities and gold or total foreign assets. Central banks, in other words, came to practice regularly the offsetting or "sterilization" of gains and losses of foreign assets by expanding or contracting their domestic assets in the pursuit of purely national economic or political ends.[18]

This change inevitably brought national monetary author-

[18] R. Nurkse, *International Currency Experience* (Geneva: League of Nations, 1944), pp. 73-88.

ities into conflict with each other and undermined the coordinating role of the Bank of England. Gold parities were set arbitrarily, to achieve particular national purposes, as in the case of the pound in 1925 and the French franc in 1928. National monetary policies, in sum, had become nationalized and politicized to a degree unimaginable before 1914.

In political terms, there was a fundamental contradiction between the attempt of countries to assert national control of domestic monetary conditions and their decision to make their currencies convertible into gold at fixed parities. The contradiction was not widely appreciated, however, at the time. In 1930 J. M. Keynes wrote:

> I fancy that some advocates of a general return to gold after the war did not fully foresee how great the urge would be towards autonomy and independent action. They conceived that a sort of automatic stability would be attained by everyone voluntarily agreeing, or being practically compelled, to govern his behavior in conformity with the average behavior of the system as a whole. . . . If every central bank were to surrender its right of independent action to the extent of agreeing that it would also regulate its credit policy that no appreciable quantity of gold would ever flow into or out of its vaults—a result which would be sufficiently attained in practice if every central bank were to cause or allow the inflow of gold to produce as much effect as possible on its terms of credit. . . .[19]

Keynes's own proposal for reconciling monetary autonomy and monetary interdependence was to keep the pound off gold and flexible against the dollar, and in this way to divide the monetary system into two great blocs—a sterling bloc, includ-

---

[19] *A Treatise on Money*, op. cit., p. 273.

ing all of Europe and the British Empire (except Canada), and a dollar bloc.[20] But his advice, offered in 1923 before Britain returned to the gold standard, fell on deaf ears. The belief that international monetary order depended absolutely on a return to the gold standard was too firmly rooted to be shaken by an economist's theorizing. But the system that resulted from a return to gold without monetary coordination was bound to fail. It soon proved incapable of assuring either stable parities or full employment.

What gave the gold-exchange standard its name was the accumulation by the Bank of France and other continental central banks of large holdings of sterling and dollar assets as legal reserves. Before 1914, this practice had been largely confined to non-European countries such as Japan and Argentina and to British colonies and dominions. The accumulation by continental central banks of sterling and dollars was natural in the aftermath of inflationary wartime and postwar finance, resulting in a shortage of gold in Europe. As they allowed their exchange rates to depreciate against the pound and the dollar, and got their budgets and domestic credit expansion under control again after the war, the continental countries developed payments surpluses, aided in this respect by a capital inflow from the United States and Britain. As they intervened in the exchange markets to stabilize their currencies against the pound and the dollar, their reserves were replenished in the form of sterling and dollars rather than gold.

Gold did not flow in, because the European currencies were still inconvertible into gold, discouraging private gold arbitrage. And the European central banks were generally unwilling to sell accumulated balances of foreign exchange for gold in the London or New York markets. The former enemy countries were doubtless inhibited from doing so for political

[20] J. M. Keynes, A Tract on Monetary Reform (1923), The Collected Writings, op. cit., vol. 4, pp. 159-60.

reasons, and such gold purchases were officially discouraged by the notion of "gold economy" put forward, mainly at British insistence, at the Genoa monetary conference of 1922. In this period, too, Governor Montagu Norman of the Bank of England was working hard selling the gold-exchange standard in Europe—offering European central banks substantial loans in sterling for the purpose—mainly as a way of rebuilding the City of London's international role.

In sum, the use of sterling and dollars as official reserves was essential to continental Europe's postwar recovery. Given the maldistribution of gold reserves and the inconvertibility of European currencies, there was no other way of restoring the reserve base of the European countries' monetary systems. The only alternative would have been a redistribution to Europe of part of the swollen U.S. gold stock by means of large U.S. government loans to former allies and enemies alike. But in the early 1920s the times were not ripe for a Marshall Plan.

The Actors and their Roles:

(1) *Britain.* If Britain as leader of the prewar system was also its chief political beneficiary, there was rough justice in Britain's being the first to suffer seriously from the postwar system's shortcomings. Britain's chronic depression and persistently high unemployment—throughout the 1920s unemployment averaged about 11 percent and never fell below 9 percent for an entire year—may well have been the bitter fruits of an obsession, shared by the City of London and British officialdom, with restoring the country's prewar financial preeminence.

Within the British establishment, it was never seriously doubted that this objective depended on restoring the pound to its prewar gold parity. In the circumstances, that fact seemed to call for a deflationary monetary policy. And so all through the decade of the 1920s, the Bank of England hewed to a restrictive line. The Bank's domestic assets regularly declined, as did the British monetary base, while the money supply also fell gradually until 1925 and thereafter increased very slowly.[21] The policy probably accounts for the prolonged recession and for much of the unemployment, although the depressed condition of major export industries—coal, textiles, steel, and shipbuilding—due to increased foreign competition after the war, along with the unwillingness of labor to move out of the coal and textile areas, undoubtedly accounts for some of the unemployment. In fact, some economic historians place most of the blame for the 1920s experience on this structural factor.[22] Yet, the competitive weakness of traditional export industries probably would not have caused the general economy to stagnate to the extent it did, if monetary policy had been more expansive.

Was this long continued monetary restraint really necessary? At the time, the majority view was that it was—that the pound was overvalued right through the 1920s, and that tight money was therefore necessary to safeguard the parity. As W. A. Brown put it: "From the moment of the return to gold, the Bank of England was continually resisting a tendency to lose gold." [23] Yet, this reasoning leaves some questions unanswered. Even assuming the pound was overvalued at one time or another in the 1920s,[24] it is not clear why that condition, coupled with tight money, did not lead within a period of two

[21] J. R. Lothian, "A Monetary Interpretation of the United Kingdom in the 1920s," unpublished paper, University of Chicago, 1972.

[22] See, for example, D. H. Aldcroft and H. W. Richardson, *The British Economy, 1870-1939* (London, 1969), p. 55.

[23] Brown, op. cit., p. 603.

[24] Bruce Brittain's examination of price-level relationships among the major countries in this period, corrected for exchange-rate changes, which appears on page 79 of this volume, casts doubt on the proposition that the pound was consistently out of line in terms of domestic purchasing power with the dollar, the French franc, or the Reichsmark during the 1920s.

or three years to a decline in Britain's price level relative to its foreign competitors'—a development which would have restored equilibrium and made it possible for the Bank of England to follow a more expansive domestic line. The question is the more pertinent because the external environment favored such an adjustment; the 1920s were generally a period of rapid real growth and stable or rising prices in continental Europe and the United States.

In fact, however, British prices did not respond much. After falling in 1921 and 1922 along with world prices generally in the wake of the world depression of 1921, the British price level (by the most inclusive measure) was substantially unchanged until the onset of the Great Depression.[25] The failure of British prices to fall may be explained by the heavy geographic concentration of unemployment. Because the unemployed in the depressed regions largely failed to move out and enter into competition with industrial labor for jobs in other areas, the strong downward pressure on wage rates that would normally be associated with so high an average rate of unemployment may have been absent. In fact, as the Macmillan Committee brought out in 1931, nominal wages in British industry in the 1920s proved remarkably sticky, tending to hold the price level up, create unemployment, and frustrate or delay the normal adjustment of prices to tight money and an overvalued currency.

Be that as it may, it is difficult to escape the conclusion that a lower exchange rate, which would have made a lower price level unnecessary, coupled with a more expansive monetary policy, could have substantially mitigated Britain's plight. That a policy of this kind was in fact successful in the 1930s after the pound went off gold, and in a much less favorable international economic climate than that of the 1920s, lends weight to the judgment that the same policy would also have worked a decade earlier.

It may be fair, then, to conclude that Britain's economic

[25] Lothian, op. cit.

welfare in the 1920s was sacrificed on the altar of monetary imperialism. In any event, the sacrifice was in vain. The pound eventually fell anyway, and the weakening of the springs of British economic growth caused by the long period of stagnation reduced the country's capacity to sustain an imperial role.

(2) *France*. In his useful study, *De l'étalon sterling à l'étalon dollar*, Roger Dehem writes:

France's monetary evolution after the war was dominated successively by three myths: (1) Germany will pay for the reconstruction [of France], which made budgetary discipline unnecessary in the short run; (2) monetary rehabilitation consists essentially in the accumulation of a sufficient gold reserve to guarantee [gold] convertibility; (3) the Bank of France cannot submit to an international monetary system ruled by the Bank of England.[26]

These beliefs, or more precisely the second and the third beliefs, epitomize French monetary policy in the period from the de facto stabilization of the franc in 1926 to the franc's final fall from gold in 1935-36. A preoccupation with gold, distrust of the gold-exchange standard as much on political as on economic grounds and, more generally, the defense of France's national monetary autonomy were the dominant themes of French policy in the period, as they have been in our own times. One need only add a dash of Gallic acerbity and eloquence to savor the full flavor of French thought and action in the field of international money. When President Charles de Gaulle said in 1965 that "We consider it is necessary that international trade should rest, as before the two world wars, on an indisputable monetary basis bearing the mark of no particular country . . . gold," [27] he was in the main

[26] Paris, 1972, p. 79.
[27] *The New York Times*, February 5, 1965.

line of French monetary orthodoxy. Like Britain, France was true to its own monetary tradition.

Like Britain, too, France pursued, from 1926 on, a restrictive monetary policy so far as domestic credit was concerned. But unlike Britain, it was the internal purchasing power rather than the external prestige of the national currency the French authorities were concerned about, and the consequences for the French economy were accordingly beneficial. Because the authorities shrewdly held the franc down against the pound and the dollar, instead of trying to restore the pre-1914 parity, France was able to accomplish successfully—even brilliantly —the task of domestic fiscal and monetary *assainissement*, without paying a heavy price in unemployment.

In 1926, the franc was stabilized de facto by pegging it at a rate well below the prewar relationship with the pound and the dollar—a rate the markets accordingly thought likely to rise. For it was generally assumed that the authorities' ultimate intention was to return to gold at the old parity. At the same time, Poincaré's policy of fiscal and monetary austerity was in force. The government's budget was in surplus, and a substantial part of the treasury's revenues were used to repay Bank of France advances, to pile up in inactive accounts in the Bank of France, or otherwise removed from the monetary base. The result was to put downward pressure on the reserves of the French banking system and to stimulate repatriation of funds by the French public and the banks, mainly from London, as well as foreign borrowing. A capital inflow was thus encouraged by higher interest rates in Paris along with the apparent lack of a "downside" exchange risk in converting short-term funds from sterling into francs, because the franc was thought more likely to rise than to fall against the pound.

As the franc was not yet convertible into gold—formal stabilization was delayed until 1928—the Bank of France had to buy sterling in large quantities on the exchanges to keep the franc from rising. Hence, there occurred a rapid rise in the sterling reserves of the Bank of France in this period. This situation served to keep France's monetary base rising, despite the decline in the central bank's domestic assets. Therefore, France managed to combine restrictive fiscal and monetary policies with full employment and rising output. The key was the pegging of the exchange rate at a level the markets believed to be undervalued, along with expansive monetary conditions in the United States and Germany. France's money supply continued to rise and prosperity prevailed.[28]

Nevertheless, the French authorities were not altogether happy with the outcome. They were concerned about the potentially inflationary consequences of pegging the franc, in circumstances where such pegging was bound to attract a large, partly speculative, capital inflow. They were well aware that, given France's domestic monetary policy, the flow would be self-perpetuating. Sterling funds acquired by the Bank of France in pegging the franc would be reinvested in the London money market, whence they would be relent to French borrowers or used to purchase French goods, and so on and on. This feature of a gold-exchange standard was well understood at the time by economic advisors to the Bank of France, such as Albert Aftalion and Jacques Rueff.[29] In the circumstances, the flow had no tendency to reduce the British monetary base or tighten monetary conditions in Britain. For the investment of Bank of France reserves in sterling assets insulated Britain's

---

[28] As W. A. Brown sums it up: "There was within France [after 1926] a deflationary force of large proportions that reduced domestic expenditures, including expenditures on exportable goods, on imports, and on foreign investments, and also a strong motive for the sale of foreign assets temporarily held abroad as a means of replenishing depleted [cash] balances in France. These internal pressures therefore combined to swell the favorable balance of payments of France, but because they were relieved by the pegging of the franc, they did not become strong enough to cause a severe deflation." See op. cit., p. 495. In fact, there was no deflation at all, either in monetary or in income terms.

[29] Ibid., p. 453, note 26. In later years, this mechanism would be largely forgotten, only to be belatedly rediscovered in the late 1960s, when European central banks were chagrined to find that their

gold reserve from the effect of the capital outflow to France. It prevented a movement of gold from Britain to France, which would have tightened monetary conditions in Britain and tended to check the flow of capital and eliminate the upward pressure on the franc.

To the French authorities, there appeared to be an obvious way around the problem—to sell some of the Bank of France's accumulated sterling reserves for gold on the London market. Several objectives would be accomplished simultaneously. By forcing the Bank of England to raise its discount rate and to sell gold, French sales of sterling for gold would tighten credit in Britain and ease the upward pressure on the franc. Sales of sterling would also increase French gold reserves and raise the Bank of France's gold-reserve ratio. In effect, France was proposing to dictate British monetary policy—a dramatic evidence of the change that had occurred in the political structure of international monetary relationships.

In May 1927, the Bank of France began to buy gold for sterling in London. Not surprisingly, the French move provoked a strong reaction. Governor Montagu Norman of the Bank of England demanded that the purchases be stopped. As Governor Emile Moreau of the Bank of France later told the story:

> Mr. Norman sincerely believed he could not raise the Bank of England rate by a full one percent without provoking an uprising in England. If the Bank of France took gold from the Bank of England, it would not thereby restrict credit in London, for the Bank of En-

---

practice of investing dollar reserves in Eurodollar deposits and U.S. Treasury bills tended to maintain or even to swell the world supply of dollars and add to the unwanted upward pressure on their currencies. Rueff, of course, was not one of those who forgot. See his *Balance of Payments* (New York, 1967), chap. 1.

gland would return the sterling to the market. Such purchases would reduce the proportion [gold-reserve ratio] of the Bank and threaten the gold standard in England.[30]

So the Bank of France backed away. When the chips were down, Britain's bargaining power was sufficient to fend off this bold attack on British monetary autonomy. On reparations and other German issues, France needed British support.

The episode marks a turning point in French monetary policy. From then on, the central objective of the Bank of France would be to increase its gold reserve and thereby increase the gold cover of the French currency. The Bank of France continued off and on over the next six years to convert its accumulated holdings of foreign exchange—the largest of any central bank—into gold. Such conversions left France's international reserves and monetary base unchanged (since gold was substituted for sterling or dollars in French reserves), but they reduced the reserves and monetary bases of the countries that lost the gold, thereby exerting a deflationary force on the world's monetary base.

In 1928, when the franc was finally made convertible into gold, French pressure on the world's gold supply and monetary base increased. The franc's new parity, set substantially below the prewar rate, yielded exchange rates with the dollar and the pound that permitted France's balance of payments to remain in surplus. The restrictive domestic monetary policy was continued and a large gold inflow—a veritable golden avalanche, as it was called at the time—developed, swelling French gold reserves and exerting strong downward pressure on the rest of the world's gold reserves. Since France continued to sterilize a part of the gold inflow, the flow was not self-correcting.

The partial sterilization of gold inflows kept down the ex-

---

[30] Quoted in Brown, op. cit., p. 457. For an account of the Moreau-Norman confrontation in 1927, its background and sequel, see Judith Kooker's essay in this volume.

pansive effect of the gold inflow on the French money supply. The money multiplier in France was also low. W. A. Brown notes:

> Large gold imports [after the 1928 stabilization of the franc] could be viewed by France with calm if not with satisfaction for they did not represent a grave danger of inflation. For in France, the small use of checks [i.e., the low ratio of demand deposits to currency in circulation] made possible the absorption of large amounts of gold with a relatively small pyramiding of the superstructure of bank credit and relatively small additions to internal means of payment. Gold imports on a large scale would not inaugurate inflationary forces which, under a differently organized banking system, might have tended to check the inflow.[31]

By the same token, the flow of gold to France probably had a substantial tendency to reduce the world money supply, not only because some of the inflow was sterilized but also because the money multiplier in the countries losing gold was probably higher, on the average, than in France.

In sum, with the return of the franc to gold, the Bank of France became a gold sink. By means of gold purchases and a tight grip on domestic credit creation, as well as by virtue of a low domestic money multiplier, France began to exert a powerful deflationary influence on the world economy. In the short run, the policy worked—for France. In the longer run, the French economy would pay dearly for the general deflation, to which French monetary policy contributed.

(3) *Germany.* Of the four main monetary powers, Germany's monetary experience during the 1920s was by far the most dramatic—and traumatic. The decade began for Ger-

[31] Brown, op. cit., p. 463.

many to the accompaniment of rapidly accelerating inflation. By 1924, Germany's nominal money supply, measured in magnitudes more familiar to astronomers than to economists, had lost much of its real value. People's real cash balances were depleted, business firms were short of working capital, and business activity was depressed.

Hjalmar Schacht, the recently appointed governor of the Reichsbank, faced this situation in the summer of 1924, as the Reichsbank was reorganized under a new statute and the new "gold" Reichsmark, equal in gold value to the prewar mark and convertible into gold, was established. Under its new statute, the Reichsbank was obliged to maintain a 40 percent reserve of gold and foreign exchange against the currency issue, of which at least three-quarters had to be in gold. A few months earlier two other important restrictions on the central bank's freedom of action had been written into the Dawes Plan. One was the obligation to make available foreign exchange to meet reparation payments on the schedule established by the Plan. The other was a prohibition on direct credit to the state.

These conditions created a situation in which monetary expansion and economic recovery in Germany, following the 1924 stabilization, came to depend to an extraordinary degree on an inflow of capital from the United States. Germany's monetary situation in the period following the stabilization was characterized by a large unsatisfied demand for money. Banks were short of reserves, the public had little cash, and business firms lacked working capital to put idle labor and machines to work. But, as a result of the preceding hyperinflation, there was an extreme shortage of financial instruments in the money markets suitable for discounting or open market purchases by the central bank. As a result, the principal means of satisfying the demand for money available to the Reichsbank was to monetize the balance-of-payments surplus—a surplus which was itself a reflection of the severe shortage of funds in the country.

Although the German economy's high real growth rate after 1924 gave rise to a large payments deficit on current account, which was aggravated by the outflow of foreign exchange to pay reparations, the current deficit was more than offset by a massive inflow of private capital, much of it in the form of short-term loans and deposits from the United States. In this period, U.S. monetary policy was generally expansive and U.S. interest rates were well below German rates. Moreover, the New York financial community had confidence in the new German currency and in the new Reichsbank. It was the monetization of this payments surplus that made Germany's recovery miracle possible. But the resulting structure of Germany's balance of payments and the heavy burden of short-term foreign debt made the country unusually vulnerable to any external deflationary pressure—particularly pressure originating in the United States. The whole shaky edifice of German recovery had come to depend too heavily on a large, continuing inflow of U.S. capital.

Had U.S. monetary policy remained on a steady course, Germany could have worked its way out of the situation. In time, the maturity of Germany's foreign debt could have been lengthened out. The German money and capital markets would have developed and matured, increasing the capacity of the Reichsbank to expand the monetary base by domestic credit creation rather than the acquisition of foreign assets. And reparation payments would no doubt have been scaled down or terminated, as they eventually were. Such changes would have reduced Germany's vulnerability to tight money in the United States. But the fates decreed otherwise. The deflationary cyclone moving across the Atlantic struck Germany full force before any of these favorable developments had occurred.

(4) *The United States.* If the practice of holding foreign exchange as official reserves gave the gold-exchange standard its name, if the loosening of the link between gold and credit

rendered the system inherently problematic, it was the establishment in 1913 of the U.S. Federal Reserve System that proved to be the most fateful institutional change in the postwar system. The Federal Reserve's errors of commission and omission were the leading cause of the collapse of the gold-exchange standard as well as of the Great Depression.

Before 1913, the United States had been without a central bank, although the Treasury had performed certain central banking functions including the issue of currency. The possession of a central bank transformed the United States from a passive participant to the leading actor on the international monetary stage. Already the largest of the economic powers by a wide margin, it had, by virtue of that fact alone, more potential capacity to follow an autonomous monetary course and to radiate a correspondingly large monetary influence abroad. The possession of a central bank made that potential actual. From the outset, the Federal Reserve followed a discretionary domestic credit policy that was not tied to its gold reserve or the state of the U.S. balance of payments. Thus, the Federal Reserve became a powerful, active force shaping world monetary conditions, in competition with Britain and France.

The Fed's world monetary influence was not due, as Britain's had been before the war, to the use of the national currency as international money. In the 1920s, sterling was still far ahead of the dollar as a means of international payment and as a currency in which foreigners were accustomed to hold official reserves and private working balances.

The reader is reminded that the Bank of England's ability to influence monetary conditions in other countries before 1914 depended heavily on the fact that foreigners would normally hold a large part of any sterling funds they happened to acquire in sterling deposits and other short-term sterling assets, rather than converting them into other currencies and causing Britain to lose gold. Such holdings were relatively insensitive to interest-rate differentials between London and other money centers, since they served primarily as working balances or reserves rather than as investments. They had, in other words, a monetary character that made it possible for the Bank of England to influence world monetary conditions to a degree far out of proportion to Britain's economic size. By contrast, short-term dollar assets held by foreigners in the 1920s seem to have served less a monetary than an investment function. They were accordingly liable to be moved into or out of dollars, depending on differences in interest rates between New York, London, and continental money markets.[32]

Nevertheless, the sheer size of the U.S. monetary system, together with its swollen gold stock, allowed the Federal Reserve to exert more influence on world monetary conditions than the Bank of England. In this way, the Bank of England's prewar coordinating role was undermined. For the Bank was no longer able to exercise at will a one-sided "pull on the exchanges." If the Fed was pulling the opposite way, the Fed was likely to prevail. As Keynes put it in 1923, arguing against Britain's return to a fixed gold parity:

> With the existing distribution of the world's gold, the reinstatement of the gold standard means that we surrender the regulation of our price level and the handling of the credit cycle to the Federal Reserve Board of the United States.... The Board will be in a position to disregard the Bank. But if the Bank disregards the Board,

[32] "Before the war, the bulk of the foreign deposits held in London and many short-term investments in sterling . . . were held in London as working capital and have, therefore, frequently been referred to in these studies as being the results of Britain's deposit-*compelling* power. Because New York did not fully perform all the functions of an international money market, fewer foreign funds held or employed in New York were of this character. A large proportion were held because New York was *attractive* to foreign short-term capital [i.e., as an investment] and a smaller proportion because they had to be there [i.e., as necessary working balances].

it will render itself liable to be flooded with or depleted of gold as the case may be. It would be rash in present circumstances to surrender our freedom of action to the Federal Reserve Board of the United States.[33]

Keynes's concern may have reflected his awareness of the Federal Reserve's slim qualifications for the world monetary leadership that fate had thrust upon it.

What made the Federal Reserve a bull in the world's monetary china shop was the uncoupling of U.S. monetary policy from the Fed's gold-reserve ratio. Keynes wrote in 1923:

For the past two years, the United States has *pretended* to maintain a gold standard. In *fact*, it has established a dollar standard. . . . The theory on which the Federal Reserve Board was supposed to govern its discount policy, by reference to the influx and efflux of gold and the proportion of gold to liabilities, is as dead as mutton.[34]

After the war, the U.S. gold stock exceeded the minimum legal cover of Federal Reserve notes by a wide margin, and the Federal Reserve was inclined to ignore the effect of domestic credit expansion on the gold stock. Thus, the sharp world boom and inflation of 1919-20 seem to have been due in good part to the rapid expansion of Federal Reserve credit which

---

This was particularly true of balances of foreign central banks, which amounted in 1927 to over a billion dollars, and were largely invested in bankers' acceptances through the agency and with the guarantee of the Federal Reserve banks. It was also true of the foreign funds attracted to the call loan market when the rate was relatively high and of funds coming into New York as a haven of refuge." Ibid., p. 554.

[33] A Tract on Monetary Reform, op. cit., p. 181.
[34] Ibid., p. 155.

was uninhibited by the resulting outflow of gold. The gold outflow expanded the monetary base in other countries, making the boom worldwide. Then, in the spring of 1920, as the gold reserves of the Federal Reserve banks approached the legal minimum, Federal Reserve credit was sharply restricted. The gold movement was reversed and gold flowed into the United States, the inflow swollen by flight capital from a Europe still in monetary and political turmoil. Fearful of inflation, the Federal Reserve proceeded to sterilize a substantial part of the increase in the U.S. gold stock. Between mid-1920 and mid-1922, the gold-reserve ratio was allowed to rise from 44 percent to 78 percent, as the system held down the expansion of domestic credit.[35] The result was the short, sharp world depression of 1921.

The Great Contraction

A great event casts a long shadow before it. The depression of 1921 and its principal cause proved to be harbingers of what would happen when the Federal Reserve embarked on a sustained policy of credit restriction and gold sterilization. Early in 1928, the Federal Reserve began to cut back domestic credit in an effort to damp stock market speculation, and this policy was intensified the following year. The U.S. monetary base stopped growing and, toward the end of 1929, began falling gradually and continued to do so for the following twelve months until it turned up again.

The decline of the U.S. monetary base in 1929-30 would doubtless have led to a business recession in the United States, but what made a recession deepen into the depression that history would call the Great Depression was the protracted U.S. banking crisis. The Fed's pressure on bank reserves, along with the declining value of bank assets (due to falling prices and business failures) caused some banks to fail. As bank

[35] Brown, op. cit., pp. 247-54 and Appendix, Table 2C.

failures spread, there was a stampede of deposit withdrawals, but the Federal Reserve Board and the Administration took no action, allowing hundreds of banks to go the wall. The public's confidence in banks was undermined, and there was a sharp increase in people's preference for holding currency as against bank deposits. This situation tended to pull currency out of the banking system. This reduced the money multiplier. The banks themselves contributed to the reduction of the money multiplier by raising the ratio of their reserves to deposits in order to protect solvency. The ability of the banking system to create money fell much more rapidly than the monetary base. The money supply continued to fall in 1931 and 1932, long after the base had started to rise again.

The U.S. banking crisis could have been arrested in its early stages by a massive injection of reserves into the banking system through open market purchases of government securities by the Federal Reserve, along with some form of deposit insurance—such as now exists—to reassure the public about the safety of its deposits. But the majority of the Federal Reserve banks and the Federal Reserve Board, the Hoover Administration, and most financial leaders had no stomach for such intervention in a process which was accepted in the spirit of laissez faire as natural—even as a beneficial cleansing of a banking system whose troubles were widely attributed not to general economic conditions but to excessive credit expansion and imprudent or incompetent management.

Monetary contraction in the United States in 1930-31 set off a chain of events on the other side of the Atlantic that culminated in a depression in Germany as deep as the one in the United States, with far more destructive political consequences. The German monetary base, as we have seen, was particularly vulnerable to a contraction of credit in the United States. As the Federal Reserve tightened up and the U.S. money supply fell, the flow of U.S. capital to Germany fell off and ceased altogether in 1930-31. Germany's balance of payments went into deficit and the Reichsbank's reserves of gold and foreign exchange declined. The German monetary base fell. And, because of the minimum ratio fixed by law between the Reichsbank's foreign assets and the currency issue, the Reichsbank could not cushion the contraction of the monetary base, due to the loss of foreign assets, by expanding its domestic assets.

Then, in May 1931, came the collapse of the Kreditanstalt Austria's largest commercial bank, followed by the banking crisis in Germany. Money fled Germany as foreigners, fearing that their assets would be frozen or lost when German banks failed, or that the Reichsmark would be devalued, withdrew their funds. Both fears were amply justified. Having failed to obtain the large foreign credits needed to halt the crisis—mainly owing to obstruction from Paris and indifference in Washington—the German authorities were forced, in order to arrest the outflow of funds, to close the banks temporarily and negotiate standstill agreements with foreign creditors. The mark was also devalued de facto by imposing exchange controls and its convertibility into gold was effectively suspended.

Unlike their American counterparts, the German authorities did not allow the banking system nearly to collapse before intervening. Insolvent banks were propped up and the money multiplier in Germany does not appear to have fallen much. But the loss of the Reichsbank's foreign assets was so rapid and the resulting decline of Germany's monetary base so steep that a severe depression was unavoidable. By April 1932, unemployment had reached six million persons, more than a quarter of the labor force, and the days of the Weimar Republic were numbered.

The German currency and banking crisis was followed by a speculative run on the British pound. For, with the mark effectively devalued and the U.S. balance of payments in surplus, the pound looked vulnerable—particularly so in view of Britain's large short-term indebtedness to foreigners and slim gold reserves. Sterling was further weakened by the withdrawals of funds from London by continental banks and firms which needed liquidity, because they feared for the safety of their funds in Germany, or because such funds had been frozen under standstill agreements.[36] Caught between the necessity to adopt restrictive monetary and fiscal measures, if the pound's gold parity was to be saved, and pressure from the Labour Party for a more expansive domestic policy to combat rising unemployment, the British government suspended the gold convertibility of the pound on September 16, 1931, and allowed it to float.

The German crisis and the pound's fall were blamed at the time on speculators. But the necessary condition for these events was the antecedent monetary contraction in the United States. Monetary contraction in the United States inevitably meant payments deficits for the rest of the world, and because the contraction was so rapid and prolonged, a gradual process of balance-of-payments adjustment, working mainly through changes in prices and trade flows but leaving exchange parities intact, proved to be impossible. In the circumstances, currency speculation only speeded up a process that the extreme U.S. monetary contraction had made inevitable.

The pound's quick fall transferred the speculative pressure to the dollar, whose gold parity now looked precarious. European funds poured out of New York, and in three months the United States lost more than 10 percent of its gold stock. The Federal Reserve's response was a further tightening of monetary policy, despite the deepening depression, and this along with the loss of gold put more downward pressure on the U.S. monetary base. In April 1933, the Roosevelt Administration let the dollar float, and then in March 1934 devalued it. With the pound floating and the dollar devalued, it was the turn of France to suffer monetary contraction. France lost gold, the monetary base fell, and the economy slid into depression.

[36] Stephen V. O. Clarke, *Central Bank Cooperation, 1924-31*, (New York: Federal Reserve Bank of New York, 1967), pp. 202-14.

Monetary contraction began later but continued longer in France than in the other leading countries. It continued, indeed, until the franc was finally forced off gold, in 1935-36, by the expansive domestic policies of Leon Blum's Popular Front government.

Finally, the inadequacy of the world's monetary gold in this period contributed importantly to world deflation. At the official price of $20.67 an ounce, the price of gold in the 1920s and early 1930s was too low in terms of national currencies—too low, that is, to attract newly mined gold into monetary reserves. Given that the principal currencies were all tied to gold at a fixed parity, the world's monetary base was thus ultimately linked to a static gold supply. The deflationary potential inherent in the failure of central banks' gold reserves to expand was held in check for a time by the practice followed by central banks in continental Europe and elsewhere of supplementing their gold reserves by holding sterling and dollar assets as foreign reserves which were convertible into gold at a fixed parity. But when sterling and then the dollar came under pressure in 1931, large quantities of these currencies were converted, by private holders and central banks, into gold.

The conversion of foreign holdings of reserve currencies into gold, begun by France in 1927 as a matter of policy, became under the impulse of currency speculation a general phenomenon, whose deflationary impact was added to that of the restrictive domestic credit policies now being pursued simultaneously in the United States, France, Britain, and Germany.

In 1928, holdings of sterling and dollar assets by central banks had constituted more than 40 percent of total central bank reserves. By the end of 1931, the sterling-dollar component of central bank reserves was reduced to an almost nominal level, mainly as a result of private and official conversions of these currencies into gold. Such conversions left the world's supply of monetary gold unchanged, but they wiped out a large part of world reserves, destroying in the process a considerable part of the world's monetary base. Thus, the deflationary potential inherent in gold's undervaluation became actual.

In these varied ways, the workings of an international monetary system based on fixed gold parities and involving the use of reserve currencies helped to spread the U.S. monetary contraction to other countries and, in the process, to amplify its deflationary effects both at home and abroad.

Monetary contraction was responsible not only for the Great Depression but also for the rapid spread of barriers to trade in the early 1930s. As unemployment rose and prices fell, many countries' first response was to raise tariffs. Much of the impetus came from the U.S. Tariff Act of 1930—the notorious Smoot-Hawley Tariff—which triggered a wave of tariff retaliation that spread rapidly around the globe. Then, in 1932, after sterling fell, came a wave of nontariff restrictions—quotas, bilateral clearing, and the like—far more damaging to trade than tariffs. This "new protectionism," as it was called, was mainly an attempt by continental European countries that were unwilling to devalue their currencies to protect their international reserves, domestic money supplies, and employment from the consequences of monetary contraction and depression in the United States. In the case of Germany, Italy, and Japan, there was also a military motive: to reduce vulnerability to blockade in the event of war.

The worst features of commercial policies in the 1930s were associated with the attempts of continental European countries to maintain their gold parities after the two leading currencies—sterling and the dollar—had depreciated. Germany, Italy, and France, countries which clung to the pre-World War I gold parities after 1931, made extensive use of import quotas and export subsidies whereas Britain and the United States made much less use of these extreme forms of trade restriction. In the mid-1930s, for example, more than half of French imports were subject to quota or license, while for Britain the proportion was only 8 percent.[37] Significantly, too, the general reaction of the Western governments against such extraordinary trade barriers may be dated from 1936, the year in which France and the other gold bloc countries finally abandoned the attempt to maintain fixed parities. The Tripartite Monetary Agreement of 1936, in which the United States and Britain accepted the devaluation of the French franc, also contained the first major international declaration of intent to get back to a liberal trading system by taking action "without delay to relax progressively the present system of quotas and exchange controls with a view of their abolition."[38]

Reconstruction and Recovery: The Tripartite System

The monetary traumas of 1931 marked the end of the gold-exchange standard. Economically, it allowed the world's new system. The new system was never taken seriously enough to acquire an official name—perhaps because the financial community still hoped for a return to the gold standard, or because the new system's life was cut short by World War II. We shall repair that neglect by calling it the tripartite system, after the Tripartite Monetary Agreement of September 1936 among the governments of Britain, France, and the United States.[39]

[37] *Commercial Policy in the Interwar Period* (Geneva: League of Nations, 1942), p. 70.

[38] *Ibid.*, p. 80.

[39] The Tripartite Monetary Agreement is the name history has given to parallel declarations by the governments of Britain, France, and the United States, dated September 25, 1936. In November 1936, the governments of Belgium, the Netherlands, and Switzerland advised the U.S. Secretary of the Treasury of their adhesion to the principles of the tripartite declarations. See *Report of the Secretary of the Treasury, Fiscal Year 1936-37*, pp. 258-62.

The tripartite system was a big improvement on the gold-exchange standard. Economically, it allowed the world's monetary base to expand and in this sense was largely responsible for the world's recovery from depression. Politically, it was marked by relative harmony in relationships among monetary authorities and consistency of monetary policies among three of the four leading powers, France, Britain, and the United States. This harmony was not due to a new-found willingness to subordinate national economic interests to the common good but rather to the rise of Nazi Germany, which caused France and Britain to turn to the United States for political support. Acceptance of U.S. monetary leadership was part of the price of that support. In retrospect, the tripartite system may be seen as the beginning of an historical evolution that would issue after World War II in a global dollar standard.

The new system made monetary expansion possible, in part simply because the devaluation of the pound, the franc, and the dollar in terms of gold allowed existing monetary gold stocks to be revalued in terms of local currencies, increasing the world's monetary base. Moreover, the increase in the local currency price of gold was large enough so that gold, which had previously been undervalued relative to the world price level, now became overvalued—the more so as world prices had also fallen. In the case of the dollar, for example, the price of gold was raised by the March 1934 devaluation from $20.67 to $35.00, a 21 percent hike. As a result, gold production began to rise rapidly and most of the increase was attracted by the high official price into the hands of the monetary authorities, providing a continuing source of new base money.[40] Finally, the floating or devaluation of the major currencies freed British and continental monetary authorities from the obligation of defending overvalued parities, so that they were able to ex-

[40] See Bruce Brittain's discussion of this point on page 74 of this volume.

pand domestic credit again, without fear of losing gold.

The relative contributions of gold and domestic credit to the growth of the monetary base differed considerably among the four powers. In the case of the United States, the increase in the Federal Reserve's gold holdings was responsible for the entire increase in the supply of high-powered money from 1933 on. In sharp contrast to its active gold-sterilization policy in the 1920s and early 1930s, the Federal Reserve after 1933 was remarkably passive; in this period, it took virtually no action to expand or contract its domestic assets. Indeed, its only major move during the 1930s was the unfortunate decision to raise reserve requirements sharply in 1936-37, which brought on the 1937 recession.[41] The gold inflow into the United States began immediately after the dollar was devalued and continued almost without interruption until 1941. Up to the devaluation of the French franc in 1936, much of it reflected a reduction in the reserves of France and other gold bloc countries. The inflow of gold was particularly large, owing to the flight of capital from continental Europe in response to a rising fear of war.

In Germany's case, by contrast, where the monetary base and money supply grew more rapidly after 1933 than in the other leading countries, the entire increase was contributed by domestic credit, as the Reichsbank and the German government adopted highly expansive fiscal and monetary policies to reduce unemployment and rearm the nation. It will be recalled that after 1932 Germany had a multiple exchange-

[41] "The Federal Reserve System used its power, particularly during the 1920's, to sterilize gold movements and to prevent erratic changes in high-powered money. After 1933, on the other hand, Federal Reserve credit outstanding was almost constant and the discount rate was not altered from early 1934 to mid-1937. . . . [T]he changes in high-powered money reflected mainly movement in the gold stock. . . ." M. Friedman and A. Schwartz, *A Monetary History of the United States, 1867-1960* (New York: National Bureau of Economic Research, 1963), p. 504.

rate system, buttressed by tight exchange controls. The effect of this system was as if the country had a flexible exchange rate which kept the overall balance of payments in equilibrium, despite the fact that Germany's money supply and price level were rising faster than in the other leading countries. In effect, Germany lived within its own monetary bloc separated from the new system by flexible exchange rates and controls.

In the case of Britain and France, both gold inflow and domestic credit expansion contributed to monetary expansion and economic recovery. Britain was the first and France the last to enjoy the benefits of the new system. The Bank of England's prompt decision in September 1931 to float the pound, revalue its gold stock, and expand domestic credit undoubtedly saved Britain from the depths of depression that Germany and the United States endured. The British economy began to recover more than a year ahead of Germany and the United States. France, along with the other members of the continental gold bloc, clung to their old gold parities long after they had been rendered seriously overvalued by the fall of the pound and the dollar. Thus, the depression in France and the rest of the gold bloc began and ended later than in the other three countries.

Toward a Dollar Standard

When the pound floated in 1931, the British colonies and dominions (except Canada) and a number of other countries that had long been closely associated in monetary and trade terms with Britain (Japan, Argentina, and the Scandinavian countries, for example) also went off gold and pegged their currencies to sterling. In this way, a globe-circling sterling bloc came into existence, which held its official reserves in large part in sterling assets. From 1935 on, the French franc was no longer freely convertible into gold, and on the foreign exchanges it floated against both the dollar and the pound, while the other members of the gold bloc also suspended gold convertibility and pegged their currencies to the French franc.

The United States, after the 1934 devaluation, along with a number of Latin American countries, kept their currencies tied to a fixed gold parity, though no longer freely convertible into gold, while the Canadian dollar, also inconvertible, floated on a managed basis that tended to keep it aligned with the U.S. dollar, much as it does today. Meanwhile Germany had organized a bloc of its own in Central and Eastern Europe along Schachtian lines. Thus, the exchange-rate regime that emerged gradually after 1931 was essentially a system of flexible rates among four monetary blocs whose currencies were no longer freely convertible at fixed parities into gold.

The formal structure of this system was outlined rather sketchily in the Tripartite Monetary Agreement signed on September 25, 1936, by France, Britain, and the United States. The immediate purpose of this agreement was to reassure the French government that if it devalued the franc in terms of gold (the franc was already floating with gold convertibility suspended), the British and American authorities would not react by forcing their own currencies down. The agreement also included technical arrangements whereby balances of the signatories' currencies acquired in the course of their central banks' interventions in the exchange markets would be settled in gold, at a price based on the going exchange value of their currencies relative to the dollar. In this way, the dollar became effectively—though not yet formally —the *numéraire* or standard of value of the new system.[42]

[42] "The price of gold in countries other than the United States was a *resultant* rather than, as it had been before 1931, an *active* factor in establishing exchange rates. Once the dollar price of gold was established, its level in any other country depended simply on that country's exchange rate against the dollar. . . . This is the reason we choose to call the system that came into existence with the creation of the IMF the dollar standard." Louie Tarshis, "The Dollar Stand-

As it evolved, the tripartite system took on other character-istics of a dollar standard. The pound, which had initially been allowed by the British authorities to fall sharply against the dollar in 1932 in what would today be called a clean float, was over the next few years gradually aligned on the dollar at a rate close to its old gold-parity rate. The historical record makes clear that British exchange-rate policy in this period was pri-marily motivated by a desire to stay on the good side of the U.S. authorities in order to avoid possible retaliation and in the light of Britain's deteriorating security position. As Lowell M. Pumphrey has put it:

> The operations of the [British Exchange Equalization] account acquire a clear-cut rationale if interpreted as having been basically influenced over the greater part of the 1932-39 period by the unwillingness of British Trea-sury officials to carry their dollar-sterling operations to the point where they would run into open conflict with the American Treasury. They seem to have believed that the preservation of friendly relations with the American authorities would yield more dividends in the long run than would the pursuit of an inflexible equilibrium policy. . . .[43]

By an "inflexible equilibrium policy," Pumphrey meant, not a fixed rate but its opposite, a clean float. In short, the British authorities aligned the pound on the dollar, even when short-run British economic or monetary interests might have suggested a more flexible policy. In 1939, with war in Europe

---

ard and the Level of International Reserves," in P. David and M. Reder, eds., *Essays in Honor of Moses Abramowitz* (New York, 1974), p. 368. By this criterion, the tripartite system was also a dollar standard.

[43] "The Exchange Equalization Account of Great Britain," *American Economic Review*, December 1942, p. 807.

approaching, this evolution toward a dollar standard was completed when the pound was formally pegged to the dollar.

Pumphrey describes U.S.-British monetary relations in the period from 1932 to the Tripartite Agreement as "passive cooperation," and from then on as "active cooperation . . . accompanied by indications of growing harmony between the [Exchange Equalization] Account and the American Stabilization Fund. The hesitance of the Account in acquiescing in the prevailing dollar-sterling rates disappeared with the deterioration of the international situation after 1936."[44] The franc also gravitated into orbit around the dollar. Until 1938, the French currency was loosely aligned on the pound, but in May 1938, it was formally pegged to the pound, which was in turn aligned on the dollar.

Thus, the tripartite system assumed increasingly the character of a dollar standard, with the other two principal currencies aligned at more or less stable rates on the dollar. Given the great size of the U.S. monetary system and the growing use of the dollar as private international money, this meant that monetary conditions in the United States tended to control conditions throughout the sterling and franc blocs. The dollar was not yet the reserve currency it would later become. With gold somewhat overvalued relative to the world price level and flowing into central bank reserves, there was not yet the condition of a so-called gold shortage that would, after World War II, give rise to large holdings of dollar assets as official reserves. In other respects, however, the tripartite system had evolved by 1939 into an unrecognized form of dollar standard.

Monetary Leadership and Monetary Order

Our brief review of monetary history from 1913 to 1939 has underlined two powerful tendencies in the life of interna-

---

[44] *Ibid.*, p. 811.

tional monetary systems. One is the attraction to governments, their monetary authorities, and the international banking and financial community of fixed or relatively fixed exchange rates. The other is the tendency of international monetary systems to assume a hierarchical form, with the monetary authority of a leading or dominant country acting as a de facto supercentral bank, imposing a certain discipline and coordination on national monetary policies. The functional connection between these two tendencies is obvious. Fixed or stable exchange rates presuppose a large measure of coordination of domestic credit expansion in the countries participating in the system. Coordination presupposes a coordinating agency capable of acting, as it were, supranationally.

Under the pre-1914 gold standard, the Bank of England, owing to the unique role of sterling as international money, was able to perform that function nearly invisibly—and therefore apolitically—because national monetary authorities and banking systems operated largely free of political control. What made the gold standard work was that national monetary authorities were inclined to "follow the market"—and indirectly the Bank of England—rather than to assert independent national objectives of their own.

After 1918, however, this condition was no longer satisfied. Monetary policy had been politicized. Henceforth, to perform a coordinating role, the monetary leader would need to dispose of more monetary influence and political authority than Britain ever possessed, except within its own imperial domain. To recreate international monetary order with stable exchange rates would have required, in the new conditions after World War I, a degree of transnational monetary and political power that can only be described as hegemonic. It presupposed a monetary superpower as well as an international political environment—a threat from an outside power—that would make the other members of the system willing to accept a subordinate monetary status.

The monetary history of the interwar period may be told

—as its chief chronicler, William Adams Brown, told it—as the gradual unfolding of these truths. The gold-exchange system broke down because it sought to combine fixed gold parities with a decentralized and conflicted political structure, in which the four principal actors were unwilling to coordinate their monetary policies voluntarily, and none of them was able unilaterally to coordinate monetary conditions throughout the system. No doubt the breakdown would have been less traumatic and the accompanying depression less severe if national monetary policies—particularly those of France and the United States—had been less perverse, and if Germany's monetary system had been less fragile. But even enlightened national policies could hardly have prevented the breakdown, sooner or later, of a system whose exchange-rate regime was so fundamentally incompatible with its political structure.

In these terms, the system that followed the breakdown—the tripartite system—may be seen as the resolution of this contradiction by reason of the emergence of the United States as a hegemonic monetary power. The completion of that evolution after World War II by the creation of a full-fledged key-currency system based on the dollar confirms the conclusion that fixed exchange rates and monetary leadership stand or fall together.

Another lesson may also be drawn from the interwar experience. If an international monetary system needs central control of credit creation to work well when monetary authorities fix or closely align their exchange rates, it may also work tolerably well without such central control to the extent that exchange rates are allowed to be flexible. And where the political constellation is such as to preclude the full monetary leadership of a dominant power, a more flexible system of this kind may be the best available.

If the political history of the 1930s had been different—if Germany had remained a politically conservative, though a dissatisfied nation instead of the revolutionary power it became, the tripartite system might have retained its initial pluralistic political structure. It might have continued to consist of a dollar bloc, a sterling bloc, and a continental bloc, including Germany, with exchange rates more or less flexible among the blocs, but fixed or relatively more stable within them. There is no way of knowing, with confidence, how well a system of this kind would have worked in the longer run; like all what-if questions about history, this one is unanswerable. Perhaps the conflicts among the leading powers would have been too serious or the quality of their domestic monetary management too poor to allow them to dispense with the dense thicket of trade barriers and exchange controls that grew up as the gold-exchange standard broke down. Yet flexibility of the major currencies would have softened the conflicts of economic interest that gave rise to barriers and controls, by allowing the major powers greater autonomy to control their own domestic monetary conditions.

The relevance of these concluding remarks for our own times is clear. The world now has an opportunity to choose between, on the one hand, continuing dependence on U.S. monetary leadership as the price of relative stability of exchange rates and, on the other hand, a more plural and flexible system, with greater monetary autonomy for the chief actors. How that choice is made will depend on the wisdom and stability of U.S. monetary management in the years to come, and on political developments that may strengthen or weaken Europe's and Japan's sense of political dependence on the United States.

CHAPTER 2

The Relevance of Political Leadership
to Economic Order:
Evidence from the Interwar Period

W. H. BRUCE BRITTAIN

Bruce Brittain's contribution to this volume is the most technically oriented of all the articles and makes the most radical departure from the book's common working hypothesis. For where the other articles debate the relative merits of political hegemony and/or pluralism for world economic order, where they seek explanations, in other words, in the realm of "high politics," Brittain argues that the key to international monetary and economic order is more likely to be found in the low policy realm of national money and credit policies.

Whether or not economic order can survive political disorder is a major issue. Two essays in this volume, one by Harold van B. Cleveland and another by Benjamin M. Rowland, argue that it cannot. In their view, the economic order appropriate to hegemony may be different from what is suitable to a plural political system and vice versa. Attempts to mix the two may be a source of strife. Although there is much to be learned from the interdependencies of politics and economics, my own view is that the notion of a direct relationship between international political and economic order is overstated.

The apparent similarities in the development of political and economic order that are supposed to have characterized the interwar period do not stand up under close examination. If monetary and economic relations could really be read as a metaphor for political developments, there should have been continuous breakdown of economic order as there was a continuous breakdown of political order—at least from 1929 on. But the breakdown of economic order was not continuous. Economic relations deteriorated between 1929 and 1935 but improved thereafter. The economic order that obtained during the period 1936-39 in many ways resembled the period 1920-29. This was hardly the case in international politics. Instead, the evidence of the interwar period suggests that while political hegemony or imperial domination *may* lead to economic order (involving stable currency values and most probably a widely used international reserve currency), economic order may also exist in its absence.

Furthermore, the single sufficient condition for the existence of international order based on widespread use of a key currency with stable exchange rates is the coordination of governmental macroeconomic policies—specifically coordination of domestic monetary policies or domestic money stocks. This coordination of policy need not be imposed by a hegemon. There is enough incentive to achieve stability of international monetary relations to insure that even a political system of many politically equivalent nation-states will produce economic order and stability. Conversely, when coordination is not achieved, instability results, but this need not reflect collapse of political hegemony.

The broad outline of my argument should now be clear. First, the connection between a breakdown of political hegemony in the interwar period and the simultaneous breakdown of international economic order is weak. While the political system slowly disintegrated in the years leading up to 1939, when it finally collapsed, the international monetary system began to recover and demonstrated considerable resilience in the period 1936-39.

Section Two of this paper demonstrates that in several specific senses, 1936-39 was economically as integrated as the period 1926-29; hence, it makes the case for caution in drawing parallels between international political and economic order. Section Three summarizes the connection between diverging monetary policies and the breakdown of international monetary order showing further that domestic economic policies may sometimes diverge when there is a hegemon or converge when there is none. Section Four provides a summary.

The Reemergence of International Economic Order in the Period 1936-39

In contrast to the international political system, which slowly disintegrated in the latter years of the 1930s and finally collapsed into chaos and war in 1939, the international economic system in the period 1936-39 was relatively integrated. In this respect, it was unlike the system which prevailed in 1929-36 and very much like the system that existed between 1926 and 1929. The significant divergence in the trends of the two systems—the one toward and the other away from orderly conditions—demonstrates that international economic order need not coincide with political order and, by corollary, need not be imposed by a hegemonic political power whose existence is one way of establishing that political stability.

The bases of a well-functioning and ordered international monetary system are described in H. van B. Cleveland's essay and need not be repeated in detail. Two conditions are important enough, however, to bear further emphasis, for their presence may be taken as evidence of a highly integrated economic system. First, equivalent rates of aggregate price change when corrected for movements in exchange rates characterize economic order among countries in an economic system. Such equivalence demonstrates that governments are not interfering with the free international flow of goods and services by varying rates of import and export duty, and the equivalence demonstrates that private agents are not erratically changing the distribution of their foreign currency holdings in response to temporary losses of confidence. Second, the economically ordered system is characterized by equivalent rates of monetary growth. This is because diverging monetary growth rates generate pressures on currencies to be either revalued or devalued, and when monetary growth rates are similar (assuming demand conditions to be the same among countries), conditions for exchange-rate stability are established.

Stable exchange rates contribute to economic order, in turn, because they remove two sources of uncertainty. The first is uncertainty about the price of goods that are both traded internationally and produced or consumed by the country in question. The second is uncertainty about consumption prospects when the country in question suffers random changes in output.

As far as price uncertainty is concerned, producers and consumers in a country whose currency fluctuates in unanticipated ways have a difficult planning job—their prices are never secure in foreign markets. While producers sometimes win with a chance increase in the price of their goods, they often lose when the domestic currency appreciates in value, forcing them to drop selling prices in order to stay competitive. A converse situation holds for consumers. The more exchange rates are stabilized the smaller is the problem attached to this form of uncertainty.

Consumption prospects are more certain with stabilized exchange rates, too. This is because temporary falls in output can be met by temporary balance-of-payments deficits. If rates were not stabilized, the attempt to run an overall deficit would be frustrated by exchange-rate depreciation, and the attempt to hold consumption up during a period of falling of output would fail.

The technique used to determine whether these conditions were met during the period 1936-39 (in comparison with the periods 1920-28 and 1929-35) and the specific results are described in the technical appendix. The following chart and discussion summarize the essential evidence. The conclusion is that 1936-39 was more like the period 1920-28 than the period 1929-35.

Chart I compares price levels in the United States, France, the United Kingdom, and Germany. In comparing French and American prices, for example, the level of prices in the United States is divided by the level of prices in France times the value of the dollar in terms of the franc—or the exchange rate between the dollar and the franc. The closer this measure is to one, the more closely tied are prices in the United States and prices in France. This implies that similar goods in the two economies trade at similar prices and that, therefore, the two economies are more integrated than if the measure were away from unity.

Although there are variations in price levels from country to country, there is a fundamental similarity. As a group, France, the United States, the United Kingdom, and Germany were economically interrelated during 1936-39 in much the same way as they were in the period 1920-30. Consider each case separately.

In the case of the United Kingdom, prices corrected for changes in the dollar value of the pound were closely linked to prices in the United States until 1931, diverged significantly from 1931 through 1934, but were again very similar during the period 1935-39. The proximate cause of the divergence in the interim period was the temporary loss of confidence in sterling associated with the French gold purchase policy. This policy, instituted in 1930, called for substitution of all sterling assets held by the Bank of France for gold. Confidence was restored after this crisis passed.

The only other factor that distinguished one period of British-American monetary relations from the other was the fixity of the pound-dollar exchange rate. Between 1919 and 1925 the pound slowly appreciated against the dollar as British authorities sought to reestablish the prewar parity of the pound. The rate floated again in the period 1931-33, but then stabilized for the rest of the decade. In other words, the British price experience was similar to the American price experience and exchange rates were stabilized or fixed in each of the

Chart I

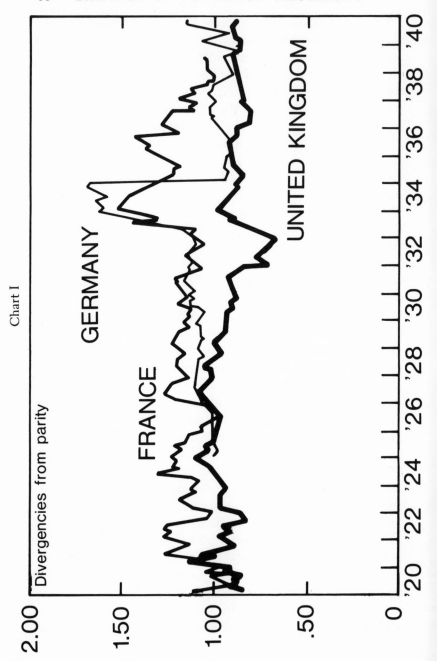

periods 1925-31 and 1934-39. (In terms of British-American price comparison, the period 1934-39 was clearly not one of economic chaos.) Economic order existed on the British-American comparison in those two periods indicating the latter period was relatively stable.

In the case of France, exchange-rate-corrected price levels were similar to those in the United States from 1920 through 1932 and again from 1936 through 1939, after a temporary period of divergence from 1933-35. Fixity or stability of the franc-dollar rate (and similarity of exchange-rate-corrected price movements) also existed in the periods 1926-32 and 1936-39. On the basis of French-American price comparison, then, the period 1936-39 was one of economic order comparable to the period 1926-32 and unlike the intervening period of disorder.

In the case of Germany, the index diverged in the period 1933-34. The period after 1934 differed from the period prior to 1932 in that the mark was not fixed in terms of the dollar. This absence of fixity was indicative of a measure of economic disorder, although the similarity of the aggregate indices before 1933 and after 1934 suggests underlying order.

The closeness of American and German price movements is important, for the evidence of economic order obtained from this comparison cannot be explained away by arguing that 1936 marked the beginning of German political domination by the Americans as may be the case with the French and British examples. Rowland, for example, argues that the Tripartite Agreement of 1936 marked the beginning of French and British political domination at the hands of the Americans. For Germany, the period 1936-39 was one of unparalleled political independence.

A comparison of money stock movements among the same set of countries shows that the economies of these countries were more closely related in the period 1936-39 than in the period 1929-35—a further indication that economic conditions in the years 1936-39 did not mirror political developments in the same period. Further discussion of this issue is left to the appendix.

While the timing of each country's price movements and money supply growth relative to those of the United States is not identical, in each set of comparisons it is clear that the period 1936-39 was characterized by conditions of economic order, very similar to the period 1920-28 and unlike the period 1929-35. But the period 1929-39 as a whole is supposed to be one of disintegrating political relations which had a direct effect on international economic order. This simple correspondence is obviously inadequate. The evidence would seem to indicate that something other than the absence of political hegemony was reflected in the breakdown of the international monetary order in the interwar period.

Policy Divergence as an Explanation of International Monetary Instability

Considerations of political hegemony fail to explain the interwar transition from economic stability to instability and back because they neglect some simple corollaries of monetary theory. Economic order can emerge when monetary policies are either coordinated or uncoordinated. With coordinated monetary policies, exchange rates will be stable and rates of price increase will be identical among countries. With uncoordinated monetary policies, exchange rates will move, but as long as they are left to float freely and as long as the goals of policy are widely known and adhered to, rates of price change will be equalized once account is taken of exchange-rate change.

Economic disorder will emerge when monetary policies are uncoordinated and authorities simultaneously pursue fixed exchange rates. These periods will initially be characterized by diverging rates of price increase and finally by substantial movements of exchange rates when the pressures for rates to move become too great.

To see why this is the case consider that exchange rates can be fixed only if monetary conditions in various nations are coordinated or if nations are willing to have them coordinated through the balance of payments. If money supply growth rates—the indicator of similarity of monetary conditions—are the same in two countries whose growth of money demand is the same, maintaining a fixed rate of exchange between their two currencies is not a problem because both countries will have the same inflation rate. (The inflation rate sets the rate of growth of money supplied equal to the rate of growth of money demanded.) If prices are rising at the same rate in both countries, there will be no change in the relative attractiveness of the goods produced in the two countries. And if the balance of payments between the two remains unchanged, there is no need for the exchange rate to change.

In a fixed rate system, however, different inflation rates cannot be tolerated because one country would always be running a deficit that would tend to lower its rate of monetary growth, raise the rate in the other country, and thereby bring inflation rates together. Thus, monetary conditions have to start off the same or be made the same among countries if rates are to be fixed.

Periods of flexibility can be periods of stability or instability. Stability results when monetary growth rates diverge in systematic ways. Conditions are unstable when monetary conditions diverge in unanticipated ways, introducing uncertainty into the future value of currencies and generally precipitating divergence from purchasing power parity.

Political hegemony, in this argument, is no longer the cause of stability in international monetary relations. Rather, the cause is similarity or dissimilarity in the conduct of monetary policies. Similar conduct establishes the preconditions for order with fixed exchange rates; dissimilar conduct does not destroy those preconditions unless dissimilar rates are pursued. Several combinations are possible. Simple economic self-interest may well be motive enough to generate coordination of monetary policies, stable rates, and economic order. Overriding domestic policy considerations may generate uncoordinated monetary policies compensating exchange-rate movements, and yet, economic stability. Economic instability —characterized by uncoordinated monetary policies and a temporary defense of untenable exchange rates—is probably never the result of conscious policy and is likely to result from governmental error.

The interwar period can be broken down into four subperiods—each of which falls into one of these three catagories. The periods 1919-26 and 1936-39 are periods of economic stability and flexible rates. The period 1927-30 is one of economic stability and stable exchange rates. The period 1931-35 is one of economic instability.

The accompanying graph includes an overlay of these periods on plotting the dispersion of inflation rates—a measure of divergence in monetary conditions—in Germany, France, the United States, and the United Kingdom during the period 1919-39.[1]

Overriding domestic policy goals explain stability with flexible rates during the periods 1919-26 and 1936-39. In the first period, the British desire to return to the prewar parity of the pound in terms of gold dictated deflationary domestic monetary policy to establish domestic British prices that were consistent with a revalued pound. German and French

---

[1] By and large, inflation rates are matters of policy choice; they are determined by public authorities—principally, the central bank, which controls the growth rate of the money supply. Since money demand grows along with the economy's capacity to produce, and as the latter is determined by the labor force, the capital stock and technology—all of which are very slow and regular processes—growth of money demand tends to be fairly stable over time. Since inflation rates change to equate money demand growth with money supply growth and money demand growth is constant over time, changes in the rate of growth of money supply, which imply changes in policy, must be responsible for most changes in inflation.

Chart II

Standard Deviation

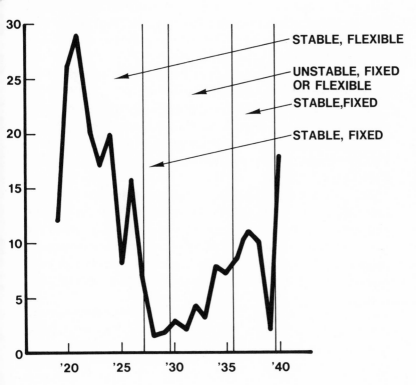

STABLE, FLEXIBLE

UNSTABLE, FIXED
OR FLEXIBLE

STABLE,FIXED

STABLE, FIXED

postwar recovery plans dictated monetary expansion, inflation, and devaluation of their currencies. The U.S. economic
position—unchanged by comparison with the Europeans—
dictated no change in domestic policy.

In the period 1936-39, dissimilarity of policy emerged
between the Germans on the one hand and the French, British, and Americans on the other. Devaluation of the dollar,
franc, and pound in terms of gold led to substantial inflows of
gold to the central banks concerned and the expansion of
French, British, and American domestic money stocks at similar rates. The Germans, however, having broken the link
between growth of the domestic money stock and growth of
international reserves, pursued an independent policy.

Coordination of policy was achieved in the period 1926-30.
This coincides with a period of economic stability and provides no contrary evidence to the assertion that political
hegemony leads to economic stability.

In the period 1930-35, a contractionary monetary policy in
the United States and a difference in policy goals between
Britain and France forced the adoption of flexible exchange
rates and subsequent monetary instability. By 1930, sterling
had gained respectability as an international means of
payment, thus enabling Britain to exert a disproportionate
influence on world monetary affairs. France objected to the
predominant role of sterling and held that the international
monetary system should be based more firmly on gold. But in
1931, the French also demanded that the British buy back
with gold all the British government liabilities that the Bank
of France had accumulated over the years. The British could
not do this. They declared inconvertibility and let the pound
float.[2]

The contractionary monetary policy pursued by the United
States after 1929 probably perpetuated floating and the im-
position of exchange controls. The Great Depression that

[2] For the contradictory view, see Judith Kooker's essay.

resulted from this policy involved substantial deflation of prices and dragged down European countries whose currencies were either directly or indirectly tied to the dollar.

Conclusion

Fixed exchange rates arise when monetary conditions are the same in all countries concerned or when the countries involved are willing to let their balance of payments dictate monetary conditions. This happens only when countries have similar policy goals.

In the interwar period divergences in monetary policy arose as a result of, first, a difference in French and British goals, and, second, a misconceived contraction of the U.S. money stock. British policy was too expansive relative to French policy and American policy was too contractionary relative to all. The strains of inconsistent policy thus caused the dissolution of the international monetary order.

Technical Appendix

Closely tied economies should have closely related rates of price change and closely related money growth rates when exchange rates are fixed. When exchange rates are flexible, rates of change of prices should be closely related when corrected for changes in exchange rates, but there is no necessary correspondence between rates of monetary growth.

More closely tied economies—those with greater proportions of total product being either directly traded or tradable —should experience more similar movements in prices than less closely tied economies.[3]

[3] The following implications are discussed and developed in a more technical fashion, for example, in Johnson, "The Monetary Approach to Balance of Payments Theory," *Journal of Financial and Quantitative Analysis;* and Robert Mundell, *Monetary Theory* (Pacific Palisades, Calif.: Goodyear, 1971).

Even if a country's relationships with the rest of the world are slight, however, there should be long-run equivalence of aggregate rates of price change, if we suppose that underlying cost conditions—relative prices—are unaffected by monetary developments in the longer run. This is because any rise, for example, in the prices of internationally traded goods, will cause domestic producers to produce more traded goods—produce fewer domestic goods—and domestic consumers to consume more domestic goods. This implies excess demand for domestically produced, nontraded commodities and upward pressure on their prices. Now the bigger the domestic sector and the slower the shift of consumption and production, the greater the short-run disparity between movements of domestic and foreign price indices. It follows that more closely related economies will show more nearly equal rates of price increase.

In the case of more closely tied economies observing fixed exchange rates, rates of monetary expansion should also be similar. For example, assume that the demand for money is constant. In this context, if the monetary authority of one country expands the nominal money stock, there will be an excess of money supplied in the economy over the quantity demanded at the existing price. If the economy of the country in question is fully integrated with the rest of the world—that is, it takes its price level from the rest of the world—and monetary authorities elsewhere do not expand their money stocks, that country must run a balance-of-payments deficit, passing some of its monetary expansion to the rest of the world. There is no other way of reducing the excess supply of money. On the other hand, if the economy is not at all integrated with the rest of the world, an excess supply of cash balances can be eliminated through increases in the domestic price level without running a balance-of-payments deficit. In the first case, the movement of money stocks in various countries is synchronized; in the second case, there is no synchronization—except by coincidence. So, more closely related economies have more closely related money stocks.

The degree of closeness or openness among economies should be reflected in the degree of correspondence of their respective price and money stock movements. This degree of correspondence may change over time, however, as trade and exchange controls change, as exchange rates fluctuate randomly, or as the nature of fluctuations—perhaps policy induced—that impinge on the economy changes.

One test of which periods were most open is a regression of the rate of price changes in the U.S. corrected for exchange-rate change on rates of price change in France, Germany, and the United Kingdom. Dummy variables were introduced to distinguish among countries and time periods. The time periods were 1920-29, 1930-35, and 1936-39 for France and the United Kingdom. When the explanatory variable involved German prices, the first time period was divided in two to allow for differences induced by hyperinflation in Germany.

As shown below, the markets of the four countries were relatively integrated in the periods 1920-29 and 1936-39. The tendency to integration was interrupted, however, between 1930 and 1933, when sterling was weak, and again in 1934-35, when the franc was overvalued by purchasing power comparison.

Table I provides a basis for interpreting these results. Part A of the table shows the ratio of the t statistic for the slope coefficient for each country and each of the two time periods 1920-35 and 1936-39 divided by the appropriate t statistic for the first time period, 1920-28.[4] As the standard error of the coefficient's estimate is a measure of dispersion of the observations on the relevant price variable around what is expected, given the rate of change of prices corrected for exchange-rate change in the appropriate country, if the ratio is greater than

---

[4] In the case of Germany, 1925-28.

Definition of Variables

$\overset{*}{P}_{US}$ = observations on quarterly rates of wholesale price change in the United States.
$\overset{*}{P}$ = observations on quarterly rates of wholesale price change in Germany, France, and the United Kingdom.

D_1 = 1 if $\overset{*}{P}$ is an observation for Germany during the period 1920:I-25:I
D_2 =   "   Germany   25:II-29:IV
D_3 =   "   Germany   30:I-35:IV
D_4 =   "   Germany   36:I-39:II
D_5 =   "   United Kingdom   20:I-29:IV
D_6 =   "   United Kingdom   30:I-35:IV
D_7 =   "   United Kingdom   36:I-39:II
D_8 =   "   France   20:I-29:IV
D_9 =   "   France   30:I-35:IV
D_{10} =   "   France   36:I-39:II

$\overset{*}{M}_{US}$ = quarterly rate of U.S. monetary base growth.
$\overset{*}{M}$ = quarterly rate of monetary base growth in Germany, France, and the United Kingdom.

K_1 = 1 if $\overset{*}{M}$ is an observation for France during the period 28:I-35:IV
K_2 =   "   France   36:I-39:IV
K_3 =   "   United Kingdom   28:I-35:IV
K_4 =   "   United Kingdom   36:I-39:IV
K_5 =   "   Germany   28:I-35:IV
K_6 =   "   Germany   36:I-39:IV

Table I

Price Interconnections

A. Standard errors in comparison periods divided by standard error in base period.

(measure of dispersion)

Base Period		Comparison Period (1)	Comparison Period (2)
	25:II to 29:IV	30:I to 35:IV	36:I to 39:II
Germany	1.0	2.0338	.5978
United Kingdom	1.0	2.1766	.6061
France	1.0	.7143	.1259

B. t statistic in comparison period less t statistic in base period

Germany	0	2.1044	−.8188
United Kingdom	0	3.9438	−1.3203
France	0	−1.4510	−4.4400

Regression Results* for Price Interconnection Comparisons

$$\overset{*}{P}_{US} = \quad .0073 \quad + .0134\overset{*}{P}D_1 + .5714 \ \overset{*}{P}D_2 + 4671 \ \overset{*}{P}D_3 + 1.8410 \ \overset{*}{P}D_4$$
$$\cdot \quad (-2.9797) \ (2.0358) \quad (1.2336) \quad (4.1403) \quad (1.2170)$$

$$+ .3374 \overset{*}{P}D_5 + .7971 \ \overset{*}{P}D_6 + .4863 \ \overset{*}{P}D_7$$
$$(3.3519) \quad (7.2957) \quad (2.0316)$$

$$+ .4740 \overset{*}{P}D_8 + .4235 \ \overset{*}{P}D_9 + .1126 \ \overset{*}{P}D_{10}$$
$$(5.0798) \quad (3.6288) \quad (.6398)$$

$\overline{R}^2 = .3270$
D.W. = 1.801
F Statistic for the Regression = 13.19
Degrees of Freedom   = 241

*Rates of change are calculated as quarter to quarter differences of the logs of the purchasing power indices described in Figure 1. The quarterly number is an arithmetic average of three months' data.

Table II

The Monetary Base Interconnection
(t statistic in comparison period less t statistic in base period)

	Base Period	Comparison Period
Germany	0	2.3608
United Kingdom	0	2.6440
France	0	3.0943

Regression Results for Monetary Base Interconnection Comparisons

$$\overset{*}{M}_{US} = \quad .0174 \quad -.0020 K_1 \overset{*}{M} \quad +.3029 \, K_2 \overset{*}{M} \quad -.0044 \, K_3 \overset{*}{M}$$
$$(7.2551) \quad (-.8249) \qquad (2.2694) \qquad (-.8768)$$

$$+.3561 \, K_4 \overset{*}{M} \quad +.0253 \, K_5 \overset{*}{M} \quad +.2308 \, K_6 \overset{*}{M}$$
$$(1.7672) \qquad (.2622) \qquad (2.6230)$$

$\bar{R}^2 \quad = .0637$
D.W. $= 1.6005$

F Statistic for the Regression $= 2.622$
Degrees of Freedom $\quad = 137$

one, the relationship is more exact in the comparison period than in the base period and if it is less than one, the relationship is less exact.

Part B of the table presents the difference in the t statistics in the base period and the comparison period.

The table shows that rates of price change in the United States, the United Kingdom, and Germany were relatively more dispersed on the period 1930-35 than in either of the other periods. It also shows that rates of price increase were similar for those three countries during the first and third periods and dissimilar for all four during the intervening period. The apparent French discrepancy is explained by France's moving so far from purchasing power parity by 1934 (see chart in body of text). The difference in price movements between the United States and France in the later period reflects France's return to purchasing power parity.

A second test relates rates of growth of monetary bases for the United States to monetary base movements in France, Germany, and the United Kingdom for the periods 1928-35 and 1936-39.[5] (The monetary base is money in circulation plus deposits in the commercial banking system with the monetary authority.) Table II shows that there is significant correlation among monetary bases in all four countries in the second period and not in the first. This supports the view that the second period was characterized by greater economic order than the first.

[5] Direct quarterly money stock figures were unavailable except for the United States.

CHAPTER 3

French Financial Diplomacy:
The Interwar Years

JUDITH L. KOOKER

*Depending upon one's vantage point, French mone-
tary policy can be read as a testament either to the
wisdom or the folly of consistent monetary principles.
The parallel between the French critique of Britain's
reserve-currency system in the 1920s and de Gaulle's attack on the overextended dollar of the 1960s is a striking
illustration of how closely the preoccupations of one age
can resemble those of another. Yet, if French policies
and prescriptions of the 1920s speak forcefully to the
dollar's recent excesses, they were surely a disaster when
applied to the depression years of the 1930s. How, then,
does one begin to interpret French monetary policy? It is*

perhaps too easy to fall back on the Keynesian saw about the dangers of pursuing rational policies in an irrational world. For as Judith Kooker's essay illustrates so well, French monetary policies were not only the product of French rationalism, but also of overriding strategic interests, of petty rivalries, national tradition, and a host of other impulses, political and economic. The following essay should help establish history not only as a useful complement but an indispensable prerequisite to the understanding of monetary theory.*

* This essay was written prior to the author's employment at the U.S. Treasury Department and does not reflect the views of the Department.

Historical Considerations

The French Challenge

The French challenge to the international monetary system has been waged for two generations. In the twenties, as well as the sixties and seventies, French statesmen opposed the gold-exchange standard for political and economic reasons. If Gaullist monetary principles are regarded as archaic, then French policy in the interwar period and its long historical consistency have not been well understood. Current French policies derive from a coherent set of political and economic beliefs: *les doctrines monétaires à l'épreuve des faits*. The French themselves claim that their present policies are based on important lessons from actual experience. Without attempting to draw too close a parallel between the interwar and the postwar decades, it is important to examine the French perspective in the light of that historical experience.

The Genoa Resolutions

The French have a long memory in these matters. In his press conference of February 4, 1965, General de Gaulle traced the monetary difficulties of our epoch back to the Genoa Conference of 1922. That conference enshrined the gold-exchange standard, for him the mother error of the international monetary system. At Genoa, the British delegation expressed its concern about a shortage of gold if all countries should try to stabilize simultaneously; hence, it recommended an international convention to "centralize and co-ordinate the demand for gold," and suggested the convention embody "some means of economizing in the case of gold by maintaining reserves in the form of foreign balances, such, for example, as the gold-exchange standard." [1] In the British formulation, gold would be rationed in two ways: Britain and America would hold their reserves in gold and become the gold centers; other countries would be content to hold dollars or pounds instead, using these as the base against which to issue local currency or stabilize their currencies on the exchange market.

The Gold-Exchange Standard in Practice

Even the British admitted that the gold-exchange doctrine was essentially a creation of the British delegation accepted in

---

[1] The gold-exchange standard differs from a pure gold standard in that it permits a central bank to create money not only against gold and claims expressed in the domestic currency, but also against sight obligations payable in foreign currencies legally convertible into gold.

large measure without detailed discussion. In French eyes, the scheme was only to be a temporary expedient to enable a rapid return to convertibility. Yet, like disarmament, it soon became a dogma of Geneva. The League of Nations Financial Committee, which Britain dominated, zealously stabilized the currencies of Austria, Hungary, Estonia, Bulgaria, Greece, and Latvia on the basis of a gold-exchange standard.[2] A modified gold-exchange standard also undergirded the currencies of Germany, Belgium, and Poland. In practice, the gold-exchange system was not based on gold, but on the pound sterling. Convertibility to gold was little more than a theoretical right which few countries dared to exercise.

National Perspectives

In historical perspective, the Genoa proposals aimed at restoring as much as possible of the London-centered financial system which existed prior to 1914. A gold standard which was in effect a sterling standard was important for the City's particular interests as both the Bank of England and City financiers saw those interests. Britain's return to the prewar parity—believed to be essential for restoring the City's central position in international finance—might be hampered if countries used the proceeds of stabilization credits to build up their gold reserves, for most of this gold would be taken from London. It was also considered essential for the system as a whole that countries stabilize as soon as possible. Montagu Norman, the Governor of the Bank of England, and his directors thus worked actively to extend the gold-exchange standard to ease the task of financial management.

For Benjamin Strong, the Governor of the New York Fed-

---

[2] Under the statutes of the new central banks set up in these countries, the "metallic" reserve against which notes were issued included not only gold but also eligible short-term foreign assets, predominantly sterling.

eral Reserve Bank, the proposals had an "ominous sound." First, no one had demonstrated to Strong's satisfaction that there was—or was likely to be—a shortage of gold. More fundamentally, Strong feared the loss of monetary control for the center country whose currency was held by foreigners. His initial misgivings hardened into staunch opposition in 1927 when he witnessed the power the Bank of France exercised over the Bank of England and British monetary policy. In Strong's view, each nation should return to the gold standard and restore its autonomy without any such hazardous dependence on foreign markets. For the American governor the most important objectives were "autonomy and self-reliance and good conduct on sound monetary principles at home." [3]

French objections to the gold-exchange standard fell into several overlapping categories. On the one hand, the French regarded this scheme as a British device to continue a financial role which Britain's debilitated financial position no longer justified. As French economist Edmond Lebée observed:

> This doctrine, which like many others is of Anglo-Saxon origin, reconciles in a singular fashion for the Latins an ardent monetary mystique and the harsh defense of material interests. It is this, as much as its technical advantages, which explains its strange fortune, the transformation of an exotic and provisional expedient into a universal monetary system[4]

French authorities recognized London's paradoxical position. The marvelous network of financial institutions and the desire to remain banker to the world were incompatible with the

---

[3] Stephen V. O. Clarke, *Central Bank Cooperation, 1914-1931* (New York: New York Federal Reserve Bank, 1967), p. 39.

[4] Edmond Lebée, "Le Gold Exchange Standard," in Piétri, Cellier, Lebée, et al., *Les Doctrines monétaires à l'épreuve des faits* (Paris: Alcan, 1932), p. 142.

impoverishment of the nation, the stagnation of export industries, and a declining invisible surplus. The gold-exchange
standard would allow the City to loan abroad even when the
industrial base and invisible earnings which had supported
such loans in the past had disappeared.

On the other hand, the gold-exchange standard was seen as a
threat to French interests in Eastern Europe. The installation
of British supervisors and directors in the new central banks of
these countries and the use of sterling as a reserve currency
threatened to increase British political influence in the area
and diminish that of France. Beyond these particular political
quarrels, the French believed that the gold-exchange standard
made all countries the satellites of the center countries. "The
system," Lebée summarizes, "thus serves as that form of controlled money such as the future dictators prescribe . . . for the
others."5

The French also objected to the gold-exchange standard on
economic grounds for it made domestic monetary management impossible for other countries in the system. Then, as
now, central banks either held their reserves in their own
vaults or returned them to the country of issue to earn interest.
The French regarded the process as inherently inflationary
because the same amount of gold supported two credit
structures: one in the center country where the gold was held,
and one in the gold-exchange country. Unlike a pure gold
standard, withdrawals of capital would thus increase the
money supply of the recipient without diminishing that of the
issuing country. French authorities experimented with the
system from 1926 to 1928 and found it wanting. The gold-exchange standard, the French concluded, left the French
economy at the mercy of British monetary policies. The Bank
of England could force an unwanted monetary expansion in
France by the simple expedient of expanding credit in
London. Massive circular flows of funds added to the problem

5 Ibid., p. 144.

of domestic inflation which French leaders had struggled so hard to control.

Inflation was not an abstract concept for the French, but a real and destructive force that undermined social and political stability. At stake were the sanctity of public and private contracts, the domestic standard of living, and citizens' faith in the ability of their leaders to govern—in short, the political and economic well-being of the nation. As the French saw it, the ultimate danger of the gold-exchange standard was the prospect of uncontrolled credit expansion and collapse. The capacity for monetary expansion—and hence, contraction—was far greater than under the gold standard because of the pyramiding of credit. Moreover, it was not only the gold-exchange countries which suffered, for the center "directing" country was in reality at the mercy of outsiders. Once foreign countries lost confidence in the value of their holdings, they would seek to convert them. The system would ultimately break down, thus making it impossible to reestablish the prewar liberal order which the French themselves were as eager to restore as the British.

The French Outlook

While it is difficult to reduce a national outlook to a few simple propositions, the French position can be said to include at least three principal elements. First, the monetary problem is preeminently political and, as the French never cease to point out, an issue too serious to be left to economists. In the interwar period the favorite British maxim held British monetary policy to be coolly international, as against French finance which was political and national. Although Britain insisted the political and financial spheres could and should be separated, for France the two were inseparably intertwined. In the French outlook, monetary relationships were largely determined by underlying positions of political and military power. No great state could depend on another for its freedom of action in vital internal or external matters.

Second, the French notion of a sound international monetary system is essentially an organic conception, one which emphasizes the need for internal and external equilibrium. With monetary instability—whether inflationary or deflationary excesses—inevitably came social disruption, economic instability, and political unrest. Severe external imbalance —whether in the form of excessive borrowing or lending— threatened to bring on the collapse of not only the irresponsible nations but of the others as well. As noted by French economic historian Alfred Pose: "England had not yet perceived these dangers when from 1922 to 1930 she burdened all the international economic and monetary conferences with her recommendation for the generalization of the regime of the gold-exchange standard, presented as the panacea which would bring an end to monetary disorder." [6]

Third, the French are astonished at the failure of the Western nations to heed the harsh lessons of experience. They had pointed out the dangers of the gold-exchange standard from 1928 through 1931, and their objections to the system hardened considerably after the collapse of sterling in 1931. Although Bretton Woods was heralded by many as the dawn of a new era, French economists saw only the return to a reserve currency system which had proved a disastrous failure in the interwar period. "It will be a subject of astonishment and indignation for history," Jacques Rueff maintains, "to observe that in 1945 the monetary system which had led the world to disaster and despair, which had almost ruined the civilization it belonged to, was reconstituted and generalized." [7]

[6] Alfred Pose, *La Monnaie et ses institutions* (Paris: Presses Universitaires de France, 1942), p. 442.

[7] Jacques Rueff, *L'Age de l'inflation* (Paris: Payot, 1967), p. 12.

This failure to learn from the past, to subject fashionable monetary notions to the test of experience, has been lamented more recently by a former director of the Bank for International Settlements, Roger Auboin:

> Why, especially, do we see at intervals of twenty or thirty years certain of the methods which have always failed in the past become paradoxically fashionable in a new disguise and lead, almost fatally, to the same unfortunate consequences? [8]

However attractive the monetary expedients which nations have adopted in periods of dislocation or crisis may appear, in the French view they inevitably lead to disappointment and crisis. With these general propositions in mind, let us return to France's interwar monetary policies.

The Aftermath of Victory

At the end of World War I, the French economy lay in chaos. Four fierce years of fighting, largely on French territory, had thoroughly disrupted the monetary system, a stable currency, and a balanced, almost self-sufficient, economy. The physical and human losses were staggering, the moral and psychological effects incalculable. Out of a population of 39.6 million people, France had mobilized about 8.4 million people (21 percent of the population). A staggering 1.4 million men were killed or unaccounted for, another 1.1 million were permanently wounded, and there were an estimated 300,000 civilian deaths. The ten northeastern departments, the heartland of French agriculture and industry, lay in ruins. In these circumstances, French leaders advanced three priorities: security against renewed German aggression, the reparation of

[8] Roger Auboin, *Les Vraies Doctrines monétaires à l'épreuve des faits* (Paris: Hachette, 1973), p. 11.

war damages, and the recovery of economic and political power. Differences of national and imperial, political and economic interests were to bring France into conflict with Britain, America, and Germany over all three demands.

The Search for Security

Although British leaders understood France's security needs, Britain's traditional role as mediator of the Continent made them reluctant to commit themselves to a military alliance with France. America, whose official credo since Washington's Farewell Address was aloofness from entangling alliances, would offer only empty promises. For France's postwar leaders—Field Marshal Foch, Premier Clémenceau, and President Poincaré—neither the American-inspired League of Nations nor the continental balance of power advocated by Britain were sufficient guarantees of security. Barring the detachment of the Rhineland from Germany or its dissolution into independent states, only a permanent French or Allied Rhineland occupation would satisfy French security. Lloyd George and Woodrow Wilson countered with a Guarantee Pact in March 1919. In return for a pledge of immediate assistance in the case of renewed German aggression, French leaders agreed to settle for the permanent demilitarization of the Rhineland, but only a fifteen-year Allied Occupation. The Guarantee Pact, however, melted away when the U.S. Senate refused to ratify the Versailles Treaty and the British declared their participation dependent on the Americans. The French found themselves isolated, deceived, and deserted. They had not counted on an international organization but on the military might of the United States joined with that of Britain. They had given up tangible military guarantees, which they alone could administer, for now empty promises from their Allies.

Allied War Debts and German Reparations

Reparations and war debts added a further troubled thread to the web of postwar relations. From the time of the Armistice, France and Britain insisted on a link between reparations and war debts; America's debtors could not be asked to pay more than they received in reparations. Successive American administrations, however, maintained that war debts, an official government obligation, would have to be repaid in full whereas reparations, the spoils of war, were a purely European affair. In any event, initial Franco-British unity on war debts did not extend to reparations. While French statesmen and citizens viewed reparations as a legitimate right, a necessity for the reconstruction of France's economy and a convenient way of keeping Germany weak, British leaders sought to scale down reparations, to finance the defeated nations in need of capital, and to reconstruct their finances. The British were intent on the restoration of the world economy because so much of Britain's wealth had depended on exports and the associated services of banking, shipping, and insurance. For France, who had been almost self-sufficient, the priorities were just the reverse. French statesmen insisted that the French economy and currency must first be restored before France would take an active interest or part in the rehabilitation of other nations.[9]

Conflict over military and reparation policy soon engulfed the full range of Allied affairs. French hopes for continued Allied cooperation were quickly dashed by the dissolution of

[9] As Poincaré reminded the Powers in 1922, "to reconstruct the world ... is first to repair the damages of war for those people who have suffered them ... is first to compensate the victims of an invasion without excuse and of an abominable devastation. . . . To save Europe we intend to begin by assuring the recovery of France." See *Journal Officiel*, Chambre des Députés, June 30, 1922, p. 987.

the Supreme Economic Council, the rapid dismantling of the Allied boards for finance, shipping, and trade, and the abrupt termination of exchange support in 1919. During the war, the pound and the franc had been supported in tripartite stabilization operations at average rates of $4.76 and 17.5¢ respectively (a 10 percent depreciation of the franc). With the termination of allied support, the franc began to collapse. As the franc depreciated about 50 percent by the year's end and 69 percent by the end of 1920, the French became increasingly bitter. Like the proposed Anglo-American security guarantee, the Allied financial support they had counted on had been only another empty promise. Although the French blamed the war, the Germans, and their uncooperative allies for the monetary chaos, the roots of the unfolding crisis can be traced back to inflationary wartime finance, the underdeveloped fiscal system of the Third Republic, and the illusionary budgetary policies of postwar years.

The Financial Drama

The Role of the Bank of France

Napoléon, envious of the Bank of England's guiding role in managing the British economy, established the Bank of France in 1800 and gave it monopoly of note issue in 1803. Despite the Emperor's hopes, the French banking system remained loosely structured with no effective central control. The Bank of France had no powers to engage in open market operations and hence to influence the credit situation directly, and only limited discount facilities. The Bank did not find the discount rate an important weapon and, in times of desired credit restriction, preferred to rely on changes in eligibility requirements or credit rationing. Although free from reserve requirements, the Bank was subject to the *règle de plafond* or maximum note issue established by legislative consent. In practice, it was not the conservative Bank which had to be constrained in its note-issuing power, but importunate governments who took the initiative with the French Chamber time and time again to raise the legal ceiling of the franc as Treasury sums dwindled. In preparation for war, convertibility was suspended by establishing the *cours forcé* and the legal ceiling on the note issue was raised from its 1911 level of FF6.8 billion to FF12 billion in 1914. By the end of 1920, it had reached FF41 billion largely as a result of the FF26.6 billion advanced to the state for wartime expenses. Monetary circulation closely followed the legal limit, increasing more than fivefold from FF6.8 billion to FF37.5 billion by the war's end. The franc, stable since 1803 (at the rate of 19.3¢) initially escaped the consequences of the inflated money supply only because of Allied support operations.

Fiscal Follies

The unanimous aversion of the French to taxes and their almost complete evasion of the same is only too well known. Because citizens refused to declare their income, the old direct taxes—the *Quatre Vieilles* (the four old ladies)—had been levied on such signs of prosperity as the number of doors and windows in a man's house. From 1871 to 1914 over 200 bills for fiscal reform were presented to the French Chamber to no avail. Finally, in 1917, a direct income tax was established, but the inadequacy of tax receipts (estimated at some 10 percent to 12 percent of wartime expenditures) led the government to finance the war by borrowing. Successive ministries managed to raise about 80 billion francs in long-term bonds and only 23.7 billion in taxes; the rest of the costs of the war—estimated at some 150-200 billion francs—were met by external borrowing and the above-mentioned advances from the Bank of France. This disastrous financial balance was hardly improved by the government's shortsighted, almost blind, budgetary policies.

"L'Allemagne paiera!" Finance Minister Lucien Klotz cried

in the spring of 1919. The affirmation soon captured public and private imagination. In 1919, the *Crédit National* was established to float government-guaranteed bonds for reconstruction, with the cost, of course, to be borne by the Germans. The national debt, which had risen from some FF32 billion to FF170.6 billion between 1913 and 1918, increased to FF224 billion in 1920 and some FF428 billion in 1924 in a confusing welter of budgets: the *ordinaire*, balanced, at least on paper; the *extraordinaire*, covered by advances from the Bank of France; and *des dépenses recouvrables*, the most illusory of all, as successive ministries assumed no provisions were necessary since funds expended would be reimbursed by German reparations.

From 1923 to 1926 the monetary crisis increased in severity. Unable or unwilling to carry out a determined fiscal program, successive governments covered the state's mounting expenses by borrowing from the Bank of France. The state's swollen deficits, soaring inflation, and a rapidly depreciating currency all took their economic and political toll. By the spring of 1926, the endless debates in the Chamber—largely concerned with who should bear the burden of the needed financial *assainissement*—had led to mass hysteria, and the flight from the franc could no longer be checked. The Bank of France, which refused to pitch its precious gold resources into the fray, was of little help to a government at wit's end. Prime Minister Aristide Briand ceased pleading with the Bank's directors and appointed his own Committee of Experts in May 1926 to navigate the financial storm. His Committee (mostly industrialists and bankers), recommended a conventional if sound program: There should be no attempt to return to the prewar parity but concertibility should be restored as soon as the budget had been balanced, the balance of payments righted by the repatriation of French capital and foreign credits, and the Bank of France possessed sufficient reserves to guarantee the note circulation.[10] Caillaux, the unfortunate Finance

[10] The program is set forth in *Rapport du comité des experts* (Paris: Imprimerie Nationale, 1926).

Minister, and Briand were thrown out in July 1926 for daring to ask for emergency powers to implement the Committee's recommendations. As the franc plunged to 2¢ and the mobs outside the assembly howled for decisive action, the venerable Poincaré returned on July 21 to save the nation's finances.

The Poincaré Recovery

Confidence returned and the French began repatriating their capital even before Poincaré formulated his fiscal program. To honor state debts, Poincaré created the *Caisse d'Amortissement* armed with the revenues from the state tobacco monopoly; to balance the budget, he imposed severe fiscal measures. He refused to seek foreign loans, and hence avoided having to ratify the war debt accords. France would find and maintain the parity of the franc by itself. Emile Moreau, the Governor of the Bank of France, was willing, however, to approach Benjamin Strong, the Governor of the New York Fed, and Montagu Norman, the head of the Bank of England, on the subject of foreign aid. An initial meeting with Norman convinced Moreau that Norman was no friend of the French; he was "profoundly English . . . imperialistic, wanting world domination for the country he loves. All his monetary alliances are aimed at making sterling the universal instrument of exchange." [11] Nor could the French count on the Americans. Ratification of the war debt accord, Strong reminded Moreau, remained the indispensable condition of American aid.

By August 1926 the repatriation of French capital was sufficient for Moreau to prepare for the return to convertibility. By the law of August 7, 1926, France joined the gold-exchange standard for the first time in its history. This ingenious piece of monetary legislation enabled the Bank of France to purchase gold and foreign exchange at a premium

[11] Emile Moreau, *Souvenirs d'un gouverneur de la Banque de France* (Paris: Librairie de Medici, 1954), p. 49.

(i.e., it sanctioned the franc's depreciation) and, in a more radical departure from French orthodoxy, allowed the Bank to print notes against foreign currency so acquired. From August to December the franc continued to appreciate. When the franc climbed to 4 cents in December, Moreau and his Deputy Governor, Charles Rist, were anxious to stabilize. The disastrous overvaluation of the British pound, which had resulted in crippled export industries, social crisis, and almost permanent unemployment of 10 percent of the labor force, was not to be repeated in France. Poincaré, who, along with the majority of the French, had hoped for a return to the prewar parity, succumbed reluctantly to Moreau's arguments and directed the Bank to stabilize at a rate of 124 francs to the pound in December 1926. De facto stabilization was accomplished.

From January 1927 to October 1927 capital flowed in in unexpected quantity. The French, as well as foreigners, continued to expect a substantial revaluation and were eager to invest in francs. The Bank's foreign exchange reserves, mostly in sterling, climbed from £20 million to over £100 million in May. For Moreau and his advisors, further appreciation of the franc was unthinkable. They were also worried by the inflationary impact of foreign capital inflows. But Poincaré, who had been called in to rule a Chamber elected against him only because of the financial crisis, refused to stabilize legally until after the elections of 1928. Moreau had to find some external means of halting speculation and its inflationary consequences. The Bank of France's sterling holdings provided a convenient instrument.

Central Bank Disputes

In Moreau's opinion, a large part of the speculation was being fed from London. Withdrawing gold from the London market, he reasoned, would force a rise in the Bank of England's discount rate, a contraction in the British money supply, and thereby end the speculative inflows. With these objectives in mind, Moreau began to convert the Bank of France's sterling balances to gold, to the consternation of the British. In hastily arranged conversations, Montagu Norman insisted that the French authorities should take internal measures to stop the speculation. The Bank of France, he pointed out, could *lower* its discount rate, seek to repeal the wartime ban on capital exports, and announce its firm intention to stabilize the franc at its present level. Norman finally warned that, if pressed too far, Britain would be forced off the gold standard to the detriment of all. Determined to prevent further appreciation of the franc and domestic inflation, which he had worked so hard to control, Moreau insisted that he was only playing by the rules of the game: "You have wanted, you Bank of England, to be a clearing place and to locate the world money market in London. You must bear the consequences of your ambitions. We are conforming to orthodoxy in buying gold." [12] The difficulties of the postwar monetary system were all too clear to the French. The defense of the gold-standard in France threatened Britain's fragile financial edifice. But Moreau dared not press the issue as long as the French Treasury had no means of repaying its substantial war debts to the British Treasury. When the Bank of France put pressure on the Bank of England, Moreau sadly concluded, Churchill threatened Poincaré.

The uncooperative attitude of the British authorities was not forgotten. After months of heated debate between the *stabilisateurs* and the *revalorisateurs,* Poincaré agreed to stabilize legally and signed the Governors' stabilization convention. By a stroke of the pen, Moreau and Poincaré would rescue France from its flirtation with the dangerous Anglo-Saxon system. By the terms of the new monetary legislation, the Bank of France would no longer be empowered to issue francs against foreign exchange; foreigners wishing to purchase francs would have to do so with gold. If the Bank of England

[12] Ibid., p. 317.

did not wish to cooperate, the two leaders reasoned, it could be forced to do so by the lever of Britain's slender gold reserves. If sterling holders demanded gold with which to buy francs, Moreau knew Norman would be compelled to raise the discount rate and, if by chance Norman delivered the gold, the natural play of the gold standard would lead to the desired monetary stringency in Britain and increase France's gold reserves in the process. Thus, by the law of June 25, 1928, the parity of the franc was established at 25.52 francs to the dollar and 124.20 francs to the pound. In the text of the law there was no prohibition against holding the foreign exchange already acquired nor a requirement to convert it to gold. The Bank was simply no longer allowed to use the foreign currency as part of its legal reserves. Experience had taught already that it was not worth its weight in gold.

The Domestic Legacy

Although the majority of the French were relieved to have salvaged at least four of their twenty *sous,* the financial crisis left its mark on French internal economic policy. Few understood that devaluation had been the necessary consequence of the nation's disastrous financial and monetary policies. The workers on the Left and the *rentiers* on the Right alike blamed devaluation and not the state-engineered inflation for the reduction in their incomes. All those who had suffered insisted that the franc must never again be devalued lest they be ruined again. As the world plunged into depression, and the British depreciated and the Americans devalued, successive governments would cling stubbornly to the franc's parity, and hence resort to that drastic deflation they had once rejected.

Effects on Foreign Policy

The financial crisis was also to have profound effects on French foreign policy. The French felt that they had recovered from a severe crisis by national will and discipline. Hence, they were to greet their European neighbors' cries for help with little sympathy. The German financial crisis, many French observers believed, was brought on by Germany's own policies, many in express violation of the Versailles Treaty. French monetary and financial authorities also felt that Britain had assumed a more ambitious world role than its resources permitted. If the British would tend to their own shaky economy, instead of trying to rescue the fragile seedlings of Eastern and Central Europe, the pound and the City would not be so dangerously overextended.

The French also saw British pretensions as ultimately damaging to the stability of the French economy itself—a stability financial and political leaders alike were determined to preserve. As long as the government budget had been unbalanced and the deficit financed by borrowing from the Bank of France, the nation suffered from increasing inflation, capital markets were demoralized, and the franc depreciated on the exchange markets. Inflation was not so much a disease of the economy as of the society: The middle classes were impoverished and embittered; successive governments had been routed from office on the inflation issue; public confidence in the ability of French leaders to govern the nation or promote its well-being had been weakened; and parliamentary democracy in France shaken to its roots. Even when the state imposed severe fiscal measures to restore balance, the economy was subjected to imported inflation. French leaders had abandoned the gold-exchange standard precisely because of the fear of inflation and the inability to arrest those inflationary inflows of foreign capital. In the ensuing quarrel across the Channel, British experts pointed to the dangers of "liquidity" shortage in the gold standard, whereas French analysts argued that the gold-exchange standard led to an excess of liquidity and uncontrolled inflation. Although the British continued to urge the Bank of France to keep its sterling reserves (and acquire more), French authorities could not forget their diffi-

culties under a reserve currency regime. Having struggled so
mightily to regain balance, French leaders and monetary
officials alike were doubly sensitive to relinquishing control
over the economy to foreigners. Nor did French economists
have much faith in the exchange stability of French sterling
reserves. Growing British external liabilities were portents,
they believed, to Britain's ultimate insolvency and the
pound's collapse.

Golden Avalanche

At the time of monetary stabilization, the Bank of France's
gold reserves totaled $1,128 million, and its foreign currency
holdings about $1,035 million. Although the Bank had hoped
to be able to liquidate its foreign-exchange holdings rapidly, it
soon discovered it could not realize even a small part of its
holdings without provoking massive gold inflows from Britain.
From 1928 to 1931 gold poured into France in extraordinary
quantities. The Bank converted some $273 million in 1929 but
halted its conversion operations when the British protested,
leaving its foreign-exchange reserves at about $1,040 million.

Despite the termination of official conversion operations,
the golden avalanche continued apace. Gold reserves of about
$1,435 million at the end of 1929 increased to $2,089 million
by the end of 1930 and jumped to an incredible $2,671 million
by the end of 1931. The French share of total world monetary
reserves increased from 8 percent in 1926 to 12-13 percent in
1928, 16 percent in 1929, 19 percent in 1930, and 24 percent by
the end of 1931. France and America, who held some 40
percent of the world's gold, together held approximately
two-thirds of the world's monetary gold.

The Causes of Gold Flows

From 1928 through 1931, British, French, and American
officials and economists engaged in bitter debate on the causes

and consequences of the remarkable gold flows.[13] While consensus was reached on the causes of the golden avalanche into France and America, the consequences—for Britain and the world economy—remained an acrimonious issue. In the case of the United States, gold inflows could be attributed to foreign payments for U.S. goods to sustain national war efforts between 1914 and 1918, and to the financial chaos in Europe in the years 1919 to 1924. Far from viewing the gold inflows as advantageous, the U.S. Federal Reserve Board viewed them as abnormal, temporary, and a menace to financial stability. From 1922 on, the Fed "sterilized" these inflows for three major reasons.[14]

First, much of the gold was only temporarily in the United States, pending the stabilization of European currencies; credit expansion would be foolish since monetary stabilization elsewhere would undoubtedly lead to outflows, exposing the United States to a disruptive cycle of inflation and deflation. Second, since most of the world had not yet returned to the gold standard, gold flows could not serve as a stabilizing force. Third, given the increase in short-term foreign balances in the United States, larger reserves were deemed desirable. Initially sound, the Fed's arguments lost much of their validity once the major European countries had stabilized. Sterilization could be justified only as a means of insulating the American economy from external changes. While the desire to promote domestic stability was understandable, its international effect was to throw the burden of adjustment on other countries, often in the form of severe deflation. The Fed's

[13] The public arguments are presented most clearly in the Royal Institute of International Affairs' *The International Gold Problem: Collected Papers, 1929-1931* (London: Oxford University Press, 1931), and the League of Nations, *Report of the Gold Delegation of the Financial Commission* (Geneva, 1932).

[14] See Federal Reserve Board, *Annual Report for 1923*, pp. 20-22; *Annual Report for 1925*, p. 2; and *Annual Report for 1926*, p. 16.

attempts to reverse the gold inflows by inaugurating an expansionary monetary policy in 1927 backfired; the effect of an easy credit policy was to feed speculation on the New York stock market, drawing American capital—which had previously been invested abroad—and European capital, as well, into the vortex. When the outflow of American foreign investment capital ceased almost entirely after the stock market crash of 1929, the pressure on other countries became unbearable. Faced with the need to pay for imports in the face of severe American commercial restrictions, or to repay previous loans or war debts, many countries had no choice but to pay in gold, subjecting their economies to severe deflationary pressure.

The causes of the gold inflows into France were a bit more complicated, involving both the institutional limitations of the Bank of France and the preferences of French banks. From 1925 on, France regained its traditional balance-of-payments surplus largely because of receipts from tourism, trade spurred by a devalued currency, and reparations payments. Because of this surplus, coupled with the ban on capital export until 1928, French banks came into possession of considerable amounts of foreign exchange. Although the banks initially preferred to earn interest by investing these assets abroad, the reduction in money market rates after 1929 and fears of a liquidity scramble made a renewal of these investments less profitable and less appealing. Repatriation of foreign capital by domestic banks was also motivated by seasonal liquidity needs which the Bank of France was unable to meet. As mentioned earlier, the Bank had no powers to expand the domestic credit situation by open market purchases of securities, and its discount facilities were limited. Moreover, the annual funding operations of the Treasury and *Caisse* often deprived the Paris market of funds during the peak late-summer/early-fall season while these funds piled up idly at the Bank of France. Since only a small part of the consequent pressure on the banks could be met by increased discounts and advances from the central institution, commercial banks felt compelled to repatriate their foreign balances, largely in sterling. French banks sold sterling for francs, the sterling exchange rate fell to the gold export point, and French banks met their liquidity needs by selling gold to the Bank of France. The Bank of France did not liquidate any of its official foreign exchange reserves between June 1929 and September 1931, as shown below.

TABLE I

Bank of France: Principal Accounts, 1928-1932 (end month)
(millions of 1928 francs)

	ASSETS			LIABILITIES			
				Note			
		Foreign	Discounts	Circula-	Deposits	Deposits	% Gold
	Gold	Exchange	Loans	tion	Public	Private	Cover
June '28	28,936	26,529	4,856	58,772	7,013	5,744	40%
Dec. '28	31,977	32,641	8,074	63,916	12,214	7,018	38%
June '29	36,625	25,732	10,615	64,921	7,075	11,041	
Dec. '29	41,688	25,914	12,274	68,571	7,850	11,737	47%
June '30	44,052	25,601	9,015	72,954	4,937	10,420	
Dec. '30	53,578	26,147	11,371	76,436	12,624	11,698	53%
June '31	56,426	26,187	8,376	76,927	8,513	15,187	
Dec. '31	68,868	21,211	12,285	85,725	5,898	22,183	61%
June '32	82,100	6,068	8,352	80,667	2,879	24,621	
Dec. '32	83,017	4,222	7,682	85,028	2,311	20,072	77%

Source: Figures compiled from *Principal Accounts of the Bank of France* (monthly record).

Publicly and privately, British officials attempted to set out what they believed to be appropriate monetary policy for the French to follow. In talks between British Treasury and French officials throughout 1929 and 1931, Britain's Frederick Leith-Ross insisted that insufficient note circulation in France (accentuated by the large frozen balances at the Bank of France by government bodies) was the major reason for continued high levels of gold imports.[15] A further factor, in his view, was the reduction of foreign lending by French nationals. The proper remedies, he maintained, were legislation allowing the Bank of France to acquire assets other than gold as a counterpart to liabilities, the promotion of cheap money in the Paris market, and a reduction of the government balances. Although Leith-Ross believed foreign lending would automatically revive once the need for additional currency had been satisfied, he urged the French government to ease the admission requirements for foreign securities on the French Bourse and encourage the flotation of foreign loans on the French market. Other measures which Leith-Ross believed might reduce the pressure on London included "artificial arrangements" for strengthening the pound through Bank of France purchases of sterling or discounting sterling bills for French commercial banks, the creation of a more active acceptance and discount market in Paris (although this might "seriously interfere" with the loan operations of the London market), and raising of loans in France by the British government or of credits by the Bank of England—which would encounter stiff opposition on political grounds. France had suggested that Britain could reduce the gold loss by keeping the discount rate higher in London than in foreign financial centers. For Leith-Ross, however, "to propose dearer money in London is to suggest decapitation as a cure for a toothache." [16]

During this same period, in public debate under the aegis of the Royal Institute of International Affairs of Britain and in the deliberations of the League of Nations Gold Delegation,

---

[15] The record of these talks is contained in British Treasury file T160 F12317/1-3, "Conversations with France on Financial Relations."

[16] "Gold Movements: Points for Discussion with the French Treasury," Leith-Ross Memorandum of February 12, 1931, BT, T160 F12317-2.

British economists put forward the same criticisms of French monetary policy and urged French officials to take the same corrective measures. By willfully accumulating gold beyond their needs, they argued, France and America were increasing deflationary pressures in general and Britain's difficulties in particular. With more cooperative policies and a more equitable distribution of gold, the British insisted, world liquidity would have been adequate to sustain a growing volume of production and a higher stable price level. Few persons, however, were as candid in public as Leith-Ross in private, who admitted: "It is easy for the French to regard us as seeking to interfere in their internal policy for selfish ends, while unwilling to make any contributions by altering our own policy." [17]

French treasury officials and economists alike rejected Britain's appraisal of conditions in France and the world economy. France did not suffer from an insufficiency of credit, its Treasury officials argued, but if domestic banks needed further discounts, the Bank of France could accommodate them with its sizable unused discount margin. They also maintained that France could not inflate its economy, as the British requested, without imperiling internal and external equilibrium. The government had removed technical impediments to foreign lending, but it could hardly encourage French nationals, scared by massive defaults earlier, to undertake substantial new foreign investment in the troubled climate of the late twenties. French investors might be willing to take more Brit-

[17] All, however, joined in proclaiming that British efforts to redesign French monetary policy came not from a desire to bolster the British economy but from a concern for international well-being. "In reply to any suggestion of this kind," Leith-Ross instructed, "we should emphasize that our interest in this question is not to defend the interests of the London market or to bolster up artificially an unsound economic position here. It is just as much in the interests of France to avoid further importations of gold with the consequent effects on international credit." See ibid.

ish securities, they argued, but could not be expected to invest in the dubious assets of less credit-worthy countries.

The views of the Bank of France and private French economists were expressed most succinctly by Charles Rist during the closing session of the Royal Institute's debates in February 1931. As he saw it, the true monetary problem was not too little but too much credit. Expansionary credit policies during the past six years, coupled with the increasing efficiency of production, had led to a serious disequilibrium between production and consumption. Excess production and insufficient demand were the true factors accounting for the continued fall in world prices. Hence, the British were confusing cause with effect in asking France to undertake an expansionary monetary policy. The Bank of France, or any other central bank, could not expand credit without prior demand—the key factor in economic recovery. Nor did French analysts feel Britain could rightly complain of a credit shortage; successive lowering of the Bank of England's discount rate and substantial foreign lending were hardly convincing evidence of capital shortage. Indeed, French officials felt Britain was investing abroad beyond its means—a luxury afforded only by capital on loan from abroad.

Although many in France admitted the redistribution of gold advocated by the British might be helpful to nations who felt constrained in their credit policies, they did not see it as a promising solution to Britain's troubles. Historically, Rist pointed out candidly, Britain had found no use for more gold than was absolutely necessary; consequently, it reloaned to other countries the majority of that gold as it came in. The traditional British penchant for lending would probably be repeated, and the gold would flow out as rapidly as it came in. Nor did the Bank of France look with favor on British suggestions for a change in French banking policy. In response to R. G. Hawtrey's repeated insistence that increasing the range of eligible reserve assets (i.e., including sterling) would enable the Bank of France to meet the liquidity needs of French banks without prior conversions to gold, Rist retorted: "That would mean a change in the whole conception we have had for over 100 years, which I think has been brought to us by Great Britain and by British example." Hawtrey's riposte at least added a bit of humor to the icy exchange: "I do not want to interrupt M. Rist but he is not allowing adequately for British hypocrisy, which always preaches one thing and does the exact contrary."[18]

Behind the Franco-British disputes lay a more fundamental set of issues which centered on the requirements for a sound and equitable monetary order. British experts suggested changes in French policy which they believed essential for the restoration of a viable international monetary system. But French authorities saw in the British proposals only artificial devices to serve Britain's particular interests—as Leith-Ross himself recognized. By urging French authorities to assist in the maintenance of French balances in London or to inflate the French economy, the British were, in effect, asking the French to underwrite the reserve role of the pound and the international investment position of the City—both of which the French viewed as dangerously unsound. Although the Bank of France did support sterling intermittently from 1928 through 1931, the Bank did not believe it wise or its duty to support an overextended Britain by massive sterling purchases. French authorities who had struggled mightily to reestablish domestic balance were understandably reluctant to inflate the economy deliberately at the request of outsiders. Yet the statistical evidence for their concerns is mixed. The balance of payments was tending toward equilibrium, but prices in France were falling, not rising. According to the *Statistique Générale*, the index of wholesale prices fell from 623 in 1929 to 543 in 1930 and 462 in 1931. Part of the dispute

---

[18] Charles Rist, "The International Consequences of the Present Distribution of Gold Holdings," in *The International Gold Problem*, op cit., p. 220.

may have been grounded in differing concepts of inflation. For British and American economists the concept generally means a price rise, while the French tend to define inflation as an increase in the money supply, which had indeed increased from FF63.9 billion in December 1928 to FF85.7 billion in December 1931 or by 34 percent (see Table 1). In any event, the stance taken by the French derived from their own unfortunate experience in the twenties and their desire to return the world to a more stable and equitable monetary system.

Financial Crisis, 1931

During the troubled summer of 1931, the political and economic issues which had divided France from Germany, Britain, and America reached their climax. French financial diplomacy, although highly criticized, was consistent with the views and policies France had expressed throughout the twenties. For France the dangers of German revisionism were too powerful to ignore. French leaders could not aid a Germany or an Austria bent on demolishing the European order. The records of the Bank of France and the British Treasury indicate a continuity in French monetary policy. Although French political and monetary authorities viewed Britain's position as dangerously unsound, they tried to aid Britain in every reasonable way they could to avert a worldwide financial collapse.

A brief review of the major events of the crisis-ridden summer of 1931 reveals the consistency of the French position —and the increasing isolation of France. Despite the conciliatory language in which it was framed, the Austro-German customs union accord of March 1931 was clearly the most audacious German initiative since the war to revive the ancient German dream of *Mitteleuropa* and the first step toward Anschluss with Austria forbidden by the Treaties of Versailles and St. Germain and the Geneva Protocol of 1922. France had taken the lead in excusing Austria from reparations payments and in extending generous loans so that Austria might be freed of the economic difficulties which increased its natural proclivity to union with its sister state to the north. The collapse of the Kreditanstalt, Austria's largest commercial bank, in May 1931, and the consequent Austrian request for foreign aid, provided France with an opportunity to seek the renunciation of the customs union project. Although the British criticized the French for introducing political considerations into a "purely economic" issue, the French insisted that the two could not be separated; economics had to be subordinated to politics and to plain morality. The financial needs of Austria —and soon of Germany—provided France with an opportunity to use its financial resources to further its own security as well as the general good.

Although French political leaders recognized the increasing seriousness of the German financial crisis and the repercussions on Britain and America, who both had heavy investments in Germany, they felt that the German government could not justifiably ask for a reparations moratorium or for foreign aid as long as it was spending heavily on revisionist propaganda, credits to the Soviet Union, or rearmament—all in violation of the Versailles Treaty. Thus, President Hoover's sudden and unilateral proclamation of a payments moratorium on June 21 was a particularly bitter pill to swallow. America, who fashioned the peace and then refused to ratify the Versailles Treaty, who denied any interest in reparations but continued to collect war debts, was now intervening in a matter of vital importance to France on behalf of the former enemy in order to protect (or so it was argued) the $600 million of American investments in Germany. French insistence on guarding the principle of Germany's obligation to pay during the moratorium year should hardly have been surprising or subject to bitter Anglo-American criticism. Having fought to secure the incontrovertible character of Germany's obligation to pay reparations, French leaders could not let yet another of Germany's obligations be swept away by the

American pen. When Germany sought financial aid in July, it is understandable that France would demand a renunciation of the German policies which threatened to alter the European status quo—rearmament (particularly the construction of "pocket" battleships), the customs union accord, and German revisionist agitation. At the London Conference of July 1931, the U.S. attempt to rescue Germany from the severe French demands dismayed and disheartened the French. By proposing the freezing of short-term foreign credits in Germany and rigid exchange control, the Americans, in effect, were instigating the stringent financial controls and autarkic policies later perfected by the Nazis.

While foreign attention was riveted on Austria and Germany in June and July, the British financial crisis deepened. France's role in this crisis has also been misinterpreted. During the previous year, it should be recalled, the Bank of France had not only refrained from converting its sterling holdings but, along with the U.S. Federal Reserve, had deliberately reduced its discount rate to a level below that prevailing in Britain. The Bank had also offered credits to British monetary authorities in the interest of supporting sterling. Now the actions of French private bankers in the face of the Austrian and German crises brought renewed pressure on the pound. When the first serious runs on sterling began in July 1931, the Bank of France renewed its offer of credits to the Bank of England. As initial British Cabinet objections to foreign credits gave way under the pressure of mounting crisis, the Bank of France joined the New York Fed in extending a credit of $125 million each.[19]

---

[19] Astonishingly, the credit was not announced until August 1, the day of the publication of the gloomy May Report which predicted a budgetary deficit of £120 million for the following year. The announcement of the credit at the same time as the pessimistic forecast was interpreted widely as a sign of weakness, and the Bank of England lost £4.5 million that same day.

Less well known, perhaps, was the Bank of France's voluntary offer to support sterling on the exchange markets. The Bank of France could hardly conceal its astonishment and dismay when the Bank of England instructed it to cease support operations. Despite repeated phone calls to the Bank of England, in which Governor Clément Moret insisted that leaving the market would result in a depreciation of the pound and further export of gold that the central bank credit was designed to check, the Bank of England insisted on abstention. The crisis was too severe, Bank of England director Sieppman informed the French, to resort to mere "palliatives" (which evidently meant actually using the credit). The public had to realize the gravity of the situation and the Bank of England would not hesitate to raise the discount rate or let gold flow out freely despite the suffering it would cause. Only after repeated calls and pleas was Moret able to persuade the British to use the French credit in support of sterling.

By August 13 the British were again seeking aid, but this time a longer-term loan for the British government. As the British learned firsthand, negotiating a government loan inevitably involves political conditions. The American house of J. P. Morgan, which was expected to head the private financial consortium, as well as the central banks of France and America, made it clear that further aid would not be forthcoming without an austerity program supported by the Cabinet, the Parliament, and the nation. The MacDonald Cabinet split over the reductions in unemployment insurance the economy proposals clearly implied. As the British press fumed in protest over the reactionary bankers' principles imposed on British domestic policy, MacDonald formed a National Government to ride out the storm. A further loan of £80 million ($400 million), this time drawing upon the resources of the private markets, was hastily arranged in Paris and New York, but the drain could not be stopped. Foreigners rightly suspected that neither the political nor the financial crisis had been solved. The Parliamentary Labour Party and the Trades Union

Council issued a manifesto pledging to oppose the National Government in the Parliament and in the country—which hardly reassured Britain's creditors. With the reports of the "mutiny" of the British Navy at Invergordon, Scotland, on September 15, the final onslaught began. It mattered little that reports of the strikes had been greatly exaggerated; convinced that the Rock of Gibralter was crumbling, foreigners hastened to withdraw their remaining funds.

After losses of £5 million on September 16, £10 million on September 16 and £18 million on September 18, the Bank of England informed the Fed and the Bank of France on September 19 of its intention to suspend convertibility. Both institutions were shocked and dismayed. French Finance Minister Flandin proposed a declaration of the solidarity of the pound, the dollar, and the franc as well as massive, unlimited aid. Both countries pointed out that over $74 million of the French credit remained to be used in the defense of sterling, but the Bank of England's Acting Director Harvey insisted the sums left in Paris were but a drop in the bucket. As Moret had feared and predicted, the Bank of England seemed to prefer the easiest solution, depreciation. On September 20, the Bank of England was relieved of its obligation to sell gold at the fixed price under the provisions of the Gold Standard Act of 1925; Parliament passed the necessary legislation the following day. As they had done throughout the crisis, the British government insisted that the collapse of sterling was not due to domestic financial policy or capital flight but to excessive foreign withdrawals.[20] It was one thing to go off with an unbalanced budget and uncontrolled inflation, the government continued, and quite another to relinquish convertibility only because of successive foreign withdrawals. In a

---

[20] For the text of the announcement of His Majesty's Government, see Marquess of Reading to HM Representatives in Washington, Paris, Berlin, and so forth, September 20, 1931, *Documents on British Foreign Policy, 1931*, vol. 2, Second Series, No. 247.

ringing expression of confidence in the pound and the nation, the British government affirmed that England's resources were enormous and its difficulties only temporary.

At the time the British suspended convertibility, the Bank of France still held about £62 million. The Bank's directors immediately expressed the hope—more in the nature of a directive—that British authorities would take energetic measures to restore confidence in the pound, renew investments in sterling, and prepare the way for a return to convertibility. Determined that the Bank of France would not have to assume the exchange loss on sterling in any case, Moret launched into a new controversy with the British government and the Bank of England. In a long letter to the Bank and the Treasury, and in subsequent discussions with Leith-Ross, Moret retraced Britain's financial difficulties since the return to parity in 1925 and French efforts, despite the profound risk involved, to ease Britain's troubles. The Bank of France had deliberately moderated its gold purchases in 1927 to avoid subjecting Britain to harsh deflationary pressures and to allow the Bank of England to introduce credit restrictions gradually. The Bank, however, had chosen not to reduce its external liabilities, but to attract new foreign capital through a high interest-rate policy. Anxious to avoid an exchange crisis, the Bank of France had refrained from converting its remaining sterling balances, reduced its discount rate in tandem with the Federal Reserve and, during the crisis summer of 1931, had given its own resources and those of the French market. When these arguments proved ineffective, Moret turned to threats, reminding the British that Britain owed all its gold reserves to the United States and France to repay the loans of £130 million. Future cooperation or financial aid would depend on the Bank of England's action in regard to France's sterling holdings. The arguments fell on unsympathetic ears. Leith-Ross insisted that Britain had been forced off gold "by circumstances much against her will" and obviously "could not discriminate between the various holders of sterling reserves." [21] When Moret warned that no country would hold sterling again if France were not compensated, Leith-Ross shrugged off the implied threat. Credit-worthiness resumed quickly even with depreciations much more serious than that envisaged for the pound. Besides, many observers in England believed there˙should be no return to the gold standard—at which point Moret threw up his hands in shock and dismay.

French attempts to secure a gold guarantee from the New York Fed on its remaining dollar holdings proved no more fruitful. Each country "must decide for itself if it wants to be on the gold-exchange standard or the gold standard, rather than seeking in disloyal fashion to receive all the benefits of the first plus the protection of the second," Governor Harrison admonished.[22]

In December, the Bank of France finally persuaded the French government to assume the loss of some 2,400 million francs. The French never forgot the experience; they were now convinced that the gold-exchange standard only opened the door to unsound enterprise and collapse. In their view, the British had committed an immoral act in suspending convertibility. In its year-end report, the Bank of France reminded the world that convertibility into gold was not an antiquated form of slavery but a necessary social discipline. By 1932, the Bank had liquidated all but FF1.3 billion of its foreign-exchange holdings and would devote much of the following year to liquidating the remainder.

[21] "Notes of an interview with Moret at the Bank of France, October 7, 1931," BT, T/60, F12666 (Bank of France Sterling Reserves).

[22] Banque de France, *Déliberations du Conseil Général*, séance of October 6, 1931, p. 526.

France and the Gold Bloc

The London Conference

At the London Economic and Monetary Conference, which convened in June 1933, French leaders again tried to convince the British and the Americans of the virtues of a return to fixed parities and the gold standard. Participants in that conference were divided into two schools. The internationalists, such as Cordell Hull and Ramsay MacDonald, argued that the only way out of the depression lay in a collective return to liberal practices and institutions, although they gave differing degrees of priority to a return to free trade and payments as well as stable exchange rates and unfettered markets. The nationalists were much less sanguine that restoring the old regime would bring recovery. For them, the free flow of international trade seemed less important than the promotion of industry and employment at home. Under existing conditions of recession and unemployment, there would be no unfettered gold standard, no free markets, and no free international lending. Loans or tariff concessions once extended were just as easily withdrawn, which made reliance on the outside world a risky enterprise. As John Maynard Keyes had advised just before the conference convened:

> Ideas, knowledge, science, hospitality, travel—these are the things which should of their nature be international. But let goods be homespun whenever it is reasonably and conveniently possible, and above all, let finance be primarily national.[23]

The dividing line between the nationalists and internationalists, however, is not so easily drawn. The French delega-

[23] J. M. Keynes, "National Self-Sufficiency," in *Yale Review*, vol. 22, no. 4, June 1933, p. 758.

tion, like the others, espoused contradictory principles. Prime Minister Daladier of France, for example, upheld the sanctity of free trade and the gold standard, yet championed national economic planning and the conclusion of marketing agreements:

> The French delegation believes that the first step is to put an end to the currency war and to restore to trade the essential guarantee of monetary security; the second step is to organize controlled agreements between producers in order that their work might be closely adjusted to the real possibilities of consumption.[24]

A more cynical view would cast each country's position as essentially nationalist, that is, as an attempt to work out the world's salvation along lines suited to its own particular interests. In any event, the unbridgeable gulf which separated France from the Anglo-Saxons can be seen most clearly by comparing their respective positions on national and international monetary policy.

Competing Monetary Objectives

For domestic and international reasons, Daladier and his Finance Minister Bonnet accorded first priority to a restoration of stable exchange rates. They argued that large fluctuations of the exchanges might not merely imperil national currencies and economies, but "might shake to its foundations the whole system of modern society"—a view which grew out of France's experience in the 1920s. The gold standard had fostered stable currencies and abundant international trade. Leaving it had led to inflation, insecurity, and hoarding; saving

[24] Quoted in Robert J. Dixon, "The London Economic Conference: Its Place in Economic History," unpublished M.A. dissertation, Georgetown University, 1934.

and investment had declined, and hence discouraged the up-turn in consumption and production which might spur worldwide recovery. A return to a pure gold standard would be most likely to lay the basis for the stable domestic price levels sought everywhere, although they themselves believed exchange stability to be the more immediate and important goal. In short, for the French, a return to fixed rates was the essential prerequisite for economic recovery.

American priorities were the exact reverse of the French. The first and overriding objective of President Roosevelt and his advisers was a high and stable domestic price level—free from the accidents of international trade, the international policies of other nations, or political disturbances in other continents.[25] President Roosevelt had freed the dollar from its gold chains two months prior to the opening of the conference precisely to achieve this goal.[26] It mattered little that Roosevelt and his academic advisers confused rising prices as a symptom of recovery with rising prices as a cause of recovery. The depreciation of the dollar and the economic upturn that would "inevitably" follow were not to be sacrificed to the fetishes of so-called international bankers.

The British delegation found itself riding the fence. From the British point of view, monetary policy should not be directed toward external exchange stability, but to the pursuit of cheap and plentiful credit at home. Vast public works on an

[25] Herbert Feis, 1933: *Characters in Crisis* (Boston: Little, Brown and Company, 1966), p. 287.

[26] The President's action program was based upon the theories of Professor George Warren, who held that increasing the price of gold would raise price levels directly and restore the balance between the prices of raw materials and consumer goods—believed to be the key to recovery. In Warren's view, no effort to restore prices to predepression levels could succeed unless the price of gold were first increased. See John Morton Blum, *From the Morgenthau Diaries* (Boston: Houghton Mifflin, 1959), vol. 1, p. 61.

international scale were also deemed vital for worldwide recovery. As a result of Britain's unfortunate experience with an overvalued pound in the twenties, senior officials of the British Treasury and the Bank of England were as reluctant as the Americans to stabilize currencies prematurely. As president of the Conference, however, MacDonald was faced with the uninviting prospect that the conference would fail unless a stabilization accord was reached. Moreover, the British feared that competitive depreciation by others, or the erection of further barriers to trade, might prejudice their own nascent recovery. For these reasons, MacDonald tried to reconcile the opposing positions of the French and American delegations.

Although President Roosevelt had barred permanent currency stabilization from the official agenda of the Conference, he approved a resolution calling for the attainment of monetary stability "as quickly as practicable."[27] This concession, of course, was only intended as a statement of ultimate intent; the United States would take concrete steps only when conditions in the United States were sufficiently favorable. In contrast, the anxieties and desires of France and the other gold-standard countries—Switzerland, Belgium, the Netherlands, Italy, and Poland—were focused on the immediate and unsettled present. French financial experts (Rist, Monick, and Bizot) had also been led to believe during preconference discussions with Roosevelt in Washington that stabilization of the dollar in the near future was a genuine possibility—almost a probability. Finance Minister Bonnet of France was determined to settle the stabilization issue before this key French goal floated away to the realm of ethereal principles.

Prodded by alternate pleas and threats from the French delegation, central bankers and Treasury representatives tried to reach an acceptable stabilization accord outside the Conference proper. After difficult negotiations—continuously in-

[27] President Roosevelt to the Secretary of State, May 30, 1933, *Foreign Relations of the United States, 1933,* vol. 1, p. 626.

terrupted by admonitions from Roosevelt—the financial representatives agreed to stabilize the dollar at $4.00 to the pound (its rate on May 31, when the President initially agreed to the scheme) and $.047 to the franc in mutual support operations. A leak to the press proved most untimely. American stock and commodity prices declined from the levels they had reached in late May and early June as the dollar-pound rate depreciated and the exchange market quotation firmed from $4.19 to $4.02.[28] President Roosevelt, angered by the perceived setback to his recovery program, dispatched a series of telegrams to the American delegation ruling out stabilization until the pound had reached $4.25. The American delegation was not to let its judgment be clouded by the winds "which blew through the corridors of the Banque de France, the towers of Wall Street and the grimy roosts of the bankers along Lombard Street." [29]

Bonnet, however, stood firm. Insisting that the gold-standard countries would be driven off gold with a stabilization of the dollar, he continued to press for an agreement to halt the dollar's downward drift. The draft agreement, which called for central bank cooperation for stabilization on an interim basis but left parities and timing to each government, was cabled twice to Roosevelt and twice rejected. The United States would not accept fixed formulas or allow its freedom of action to be limited by other powers. "Parts of the declaration," Roosevelt charged, "relate primarily to functions of private [i.e., central] banks and not to governments" and those parts which related to broad government policies "go so far as to erect barriers against our own economic fiscal development." [30] On July 3, the President expressed his views more

[28] Feis, pp. 183-84.
[29] Ibid., p. 185.
[30] Roosevelt to Acting Secretary of State, July 1, 1933, *FRUS, 1933*, vol. 1, p. 669.

openly. In a thinly veiled reference to the stabilization efforts of the French, Roosevelt declared:

> I would regard it as a catastrophe, amounting to a world tragedy if the Great Conference of Nations, called to bring about a more real and permanent financial stability and greater prosperity to the masses of all nations, should, in advance of any serious effort to consider these broad problems, allow itself to be diverted by the proposal of a purely artificial and temporary experiment affecting the monetary exchange of a few nations only. . . .
>
> The world will not long be lulled by the specious fallacy of achieving a temporary and probably an artificial stability in foreign exchange on the part of a few large countries only.
>
> The sound internal economic situation of a nation is a greater factor in its well-being than the price of its currency in changing terms of the currencies of other nations. . . .[31]

The French saw no purpose in continuing the conference. Roosevelt's message had clearly closed the subject of exchange stabilization, their primary purpose in coming. Keynes proclaimed Mr. Roosevelt "magnificently right." In a ringing denunciation of the gold-standard countries, "which cling frantically to their gold perches," Keynes called for "something better than the miserable confusion and unutterable waste of opportunity in which an obstinate adherence to ancient rules of thumb has engulfed us." [32] In the House of Commons, Winston Churchill reproved the gold-standard

---

[31] Roosevelt to Acting Secretary of State, July 3, 1933, ibid., p. 673.

[32] "Mr. Roosevelt is Magnificently Right," *Daily Mail*, July 4, 1933.

countries as angrily as Roosevelt had, stating: "I am tired of hearing that superior virtue and integrity attaches to the Gold Standard countries which already, like France, devalued to the extent of four-fifths of its indebtedness. . . ." [33] FDR urged the American delegation to ignore the French request for adjournment, explaining: "The people and press here are united in praise of our stand and regard the French position as highly selfish and ignoring utterly the objectives of the Conference." [34] For the French, however, stabilization was more than a "minor matter." Stunned and resentful at Roosevelt's reversal of earlier pledges, France and other gold-standard countries pressed for adjournment.

Few positive results came out of the last major economic conclave of the interwar years. The French organized the faithful into a gold bloc, the British retreated to the sterling bloc, and President Roosevelt commenced his gold buying program in earnest. The rift became more bitter as the year progressed. John Morton Blum recounts that Roosevelt enjoyed the shock and discomfort of the gold-standard countries when they realized the full extent of America's gold purchases. The Bank of France took up the challenge by converting its remaining foreign-exchange holdings to gold. At the end of 1933, the Bank announced with satisfaction that the last traces of the gold-exchange standard had been erased from its balance sheet. Governor Moret and the Bank also took the occasion in the Bank's year-end report to strike out at the peculiar and disruptive policies of the Anglo-Saxons:

> However attractive may be the artificial expedients which history shows that nations have always been inclined to adopt in a period of crisis, they really bring

[33] *House of Commons Debates*, 5th series, July 10, 1933, vol. 280, p. 786.

[34] Acting Secretary of State to the Chairman of the American Delegation, July 4, 1933, *FRUS, 1933*, vol. 1, p. 688.

nothing but illusory feelings of doubtful improvements immediately followed by disappointment.[35]

In what would prove to be the Manifesto of the Gold Bloc, the Bank of France continued:

Monetary stability is not only the most effective means of preparing for the return of lasting prosperity. It alone, it seems to us, can with continuity promote the just and orderly development of human society. To this principle France will remain faithful. Our country instinctively repudiates the facile and adventurous experiences which are contrary to its deepest interests and to the genius of its character.[36]

The following year, the gold bloc countries met in Geneva to organize themselves more formally (or, more appropriately, to huddle together, for there was little formal organization and even less cohesion). There was, of course, a common doctrinal affinity, reaffirmed eloquently by the Bank of France, which bound the six nations together and some historical precedent in the Latin Monetary Union of 1870, when French, Belgian, and Swiss francs were equivalent and circulated freely throughout the Union. From 1928 on, and particularly after sterling's depreciation in 1931, France had been the natural leader of the group. Yet even the basic affinities of the constituent countries differed. In the 1920s the Netherlands and Switzerland had clung to the old prewar parity as an act of faith while France and Belgium devalued. During the short three-year reincarnation of the bloc, French leaders would resort to the deflation they had once rejected to maintain the parity of the Poincaré franc, while the Belgians

<hr>

[35] "Annual Report of the Bank of France for 1933," *Federal Reserve Bulletin*, March 1933, p. 164.

[36] Ibid.

devalued and the Italians sealed themselves off by trade and exchange controls.

French Behavior in the Thirties

France's stubborn adherence to the principles and policies of the gold standard raises puzzling questions. The French were not constrained in their actions by any sense of loyalty or solidarity with the gold bloc but by a failure of imagination and a retreat into obsolete dogma. Throughout the 1920s, the French had carefully observed the experiences of other countries and consciously rejected revaluation and deflation in favor of devaluation and, eventually, prosperity. In the 1930s, successive governments ignored the lessons learned from France's neighbors and clung resolutely to an overvalued currency. Their unfortunate policies derived partly from doctrinal prejudice, partly from political considerations, and partly from sheer ignorance. In the first place, most French economists and financial leaders truly believed that the gold standard and fixed parities provided the only stable and just basis for national and international prosperity. Experience had taught that departure from the discipline of fixed exchange rates inevitably led to inflation, unbalanced budgets, competitive financial and trade practices.[37]

Second, the French believed they were immune from the depression. Enormous gold reserves, monetary ease, and increasing capital inflows to France in the early 1930s were all taken as signs of France's favorable position. In other words, politicians and the public alike neglected the forces of production and trade and concentrated on the nation's comfortable monetary position. They failed to recognize that France would have to adjust to the general worldwide fall in the price level either by deflation or devaluation. Moreover,

[37] See especially Jacques Rueff, *Combats pour l'ordre financier* (Paris: Plon, 1972), Chap. 1.

concern for domestic political stability militated against the devaluation of the franc or even a dispassionate discussion of the costs and benefits. Most politicians and the citizenry at large confused inflation and devaluation. They did not realize that devaluation was the inevitable result of wartime and postwar inflation, but tended to believe that devaluation was responsible for the rise in prices, the decline in the standard of living, and the loss of income on once sacred *rentes*. The middle classes as well as the workers were staunchly opposed to what was perceived as a further reduction in their well-being.

Finally, in addition to a sense of complacency and virtue, there was an unfortunate ignorance or blindness. The brief and sporadic moments of growth in France during the 1930s, which occurred largely as a result of major policy changes, went largely unnoticed by even those politicians and their economic advisers who instituted them. The failure to observe even the rudimentary statistical indicators of the day, coupled with the inability to benefit from the experience of the 1920s and the painful lessons learned elsewhere in the 1930s, were largely responsible for the depth and length of the depression in France in the mid-1930s.

Economic slump, budgetary deficits, monetary crisis, social upheaval, and endless foreign policy dilemmas form the dismal chronicle of these years. This multifaceted assault and the sheer pace of events battered down the fragile political and financial edifice constructed in the first postwar decade. Most governments were incapable of inspiring the country or of carrying out a coherent policy. As André Gide observed: "Nous entrons dans une ère nouvelle, celle de la confusion."[38] Not one of the policies pursued during this period—the willy-nilly deflation of 1933 and 1934, the Laval deflationary assault of 1935, or the Blum experiment from 1936 to

---

[38] Quoted in François Goguel, *La Politique des partis sous la IIIe République*, 4th ed. (Paris: Seuil, 1957), p. 321.

1938—was adequately conceived or executed to restore economic and political health in France.

De facto Deflation

As France's single-minded pursuit of monetary stability at the London Conference suggests, the French economy initially escaped the debilitating effects of the world depression. With an economy less specialized and more balanced between industry and agriculture, with production oriented toward the domestic market, and agriculture protected by tariffs, the French viewed themselves as a prosperous island in a sea of troubles. By 1933, however, signs of depression in France were, or should have been, apparent. Profit margins and production had declined, unemployment had increased.[39]

Prices had declined sufficiently to reduce the purchasing power of both the agricultural and industrial sectors, but not enough to increase the competitiveness of French products abroad.[40] Despite the decline in domestic and foreign sales, few political leaders recognized the essential problem: the disparity between French and foreign prices and the need to realign them. Most leaders opted for increased protection

[39] The index of industrial production fell from 94 in 1931 (1928 = 100) to a low of 78 in 1932, then rose to 88 in 1933, before falling back to 82 in 1934, and 79 in 1935. Unemployment was modest compared with other countries—never rising above 500,000 on the basis of workers receiving assistance—but a politically charged issue exploited by the forces of the Left. Figures from Alfred Sauvy, *Histoire économique de la France entre les deux guerres: 1931-1939* (Paris: Fayard, 1967), vol. 2, annexes, p. 528.

[40] French wholesale prices fell from 462 in 1931 (1914 = 100) to 407 in 1932, 388 in 1933, 366 in 1934, and 347 in 1935. Yearly exports fell from 30.8 billion Poincaré francs in 1931 to 20.0 in 1932, and 18.1 billion francs by 1934. Imports for these same years declined from 42.6 billion francs to 30.2 billion and 23.4 billion. Ibid., pp. 494, 563.

through import surtaxes and quotas which, of course, only served to freeze prices at their disparate levels. Even those who perceived the price problem failed to give it systematic thought. Much like England in the 1920s, a balanced budget was widely held to be the solution to all economic ills.

The four governments of 1933—Paul-Boncour, Daladier, Sarraut, and Chautemps—practiced classical fiscal deflation in an effort to turn the budgetary deficit around. No one considered the size of the price gap to be eliminated or the cost of deflating the domestic economy to achieve this. Deflation was not so much a systematic or agreed-on policy, but a dose of necessary discipline. By reducing expenditures and increasing taxes, all four governments hoped rather vaguely that they could reduce wages, prices, and pensions which kept French costs of production up. None appraised the economic or political obstacles realistically. The economic crisis had already hurt business revenues and profits which made it difficult for the government to increase tax burdens. Government revenues had also fallen off with the recession, making it difficult to reduce services without seriously impairing their quality. Successive governments also neglected the psychological barriers to even a nominal reduction of wages. Workers, unlike

---

Foreigners, benefiting from the depreciation of their currencies, could outsell the French in the French market and in other foreign markets. Sauvy, although acknowledging the theoretical and practical difficulties, illustrates the overvaluation of the franc by comparing retail prices in France and Britain, adjusted for a 22 percent overvaluation in February 1935, as follows:

Relationship between French and British prices, 1931-1939

	1931	1932	1933	1934	1935	1936	1937	1938	1939
Yearly average	.93	1.13	1.16	1.22	1.15	1.07	.85	.70	.73

For monthly figures, see ibid., pp. 508-09.

technicians, did not understand that the real cost of living would be reduced and felt their well-being and dignity were once again under attack. Moreover, a reduction in prices, even if successful, would not necessarily contribute to an upswing in demand because consumers, awaiting a further fall, would hold their purchases in abeyance. In any event, the attack on wages proved to be a political powder keg. Three of the four governments were thrown out on these issues, while the fourth, that of Camille Chautemps, was thrown out in the wake of the Stavisky scandal.[41]

On February 7, 1934, a shaken and weary Chamber welcomed the accession of the strong-armed, former President, Doumergue, to the premiership, flanked by Tardieu's moderates and Herriot's Radicals. Although Doumergue's government was quickly granted decree powers, parliamentary parties and the public were nearly unanimous in stipulating that the Poincaré franc should not be devalued. Few could see the difference between forced devaluation after the inflation of 1919-26 and a limited action to realign price levels in the interest of stimulating production and trade to reduce the deficits in the budget and the balance of payments. Even the Socialists, fearful of another attack on the standard of living of the workers, rallied to Finance Minister Germain-Martin's superstitious respect for monetary orthodoxy. Utterly confus-

[41] Stavisky was a small-time crook who sold millions of francs of false public bonds with the aid of powerful friends in the Chamber, government ministries, and the courts, which had dismissed his trial for previous violations eighteen times. Eager to get rid of Chautemps's left-leaning government, right-wing groups led by Action Française and the Croix de Feu organized a mass demonstration in front of the Chamber on February 6, 1934, to protest the alleged cover-up of the Stavisky affair. After violent clashes between the police and the demonstrators in which at least a dozen persons were killed and several dozen wounded, retired President Gaston Doumergue was called back, in the tradition of Poincaré, to restore order.

ing devaluation and inflation, the Finance Minister insisted:

> Certain people are advising devaluation. It cannot
> procure an adjustment between internal and external
> prices. In a country where the currency has already been
> amputated by four-fifths, to devalue, or inflate, would for
> certain provoke an increase in prices.[42]

By the spring of 1934, Léon Blum addressed the issue in print.
Although reluctant to draw a cause and effect relationship
between the depreciation of the pound sterling and England's
recovery, he pointed to the "coexistence" of the two:

> Since when has one noticed in England a recovery of
> economic activity? Since the pound sterling has de-
> preciated. I do not pretend that the monetary devalua-
> tion has been the direct cause of the economic upturn,
> but it was the point of departure of this upturn . . . .
> [T]he crucial fact in the English evolution has been the
> coexistence of monetary devaluation and an almost per-
> fect stability of prices.[43]

Even this hesitant recognition went too far for the conservative Prime Minister. An irritated Doumergue pronounced
decisively that his government would not countenance devaluation:

> As for the servants of the State, certain among them have
> lent a too compliant ear to those who have vaunted the
> merits of inflation, that is to say the devaluation of the
> franc. . . . Our little franc at four sous is worth gold. We
> must do everything to assure that it guards its value.[44]

[42] Quoted in Sauvy, p. 86.
[43] Le Populaire, April 4, 1934.
[44] Quoted in Sauvy, p. 87.

Only Paul Reynaud, a lone wolf of French public life during these years, argued from 1934 on that French leaders would only perpetuate the crisis if they continued to refuse to peg the franc to the dollar and the pound. In June 1934, before the French Chamber, he contrasted the economic recovery in those countries which had devalued to the situation in the gold bloc where "exports are falling, factories are closing, unemployment is increasing, commerce is being bankrupted and fiscal revenue is diminishing." [45] Calling for devaluation, Reynaud predicted accurately that if French authorities did "not carry out this monetary manipulation in cold blood, they shall have to do it in hot and, consequently, twice as drastically."[46] Germain-Martin rose to express the tired arguments which would be defended for the next two years:

> To devalue the franc would be to break the most sacred contract. What the State promises . . . is a certain weight of gold. . . . Devaluation means bankruptcy, systematic ruin. . . . An hour will come when, thanks to her policy, France will play a great role.[47]

Germain-Martin coasted at the helm of France's finances through the rest of 1934. The government's deflationary decrees initially increased public confidence and the Bank of France gained gold, while production and employment continued on their downward slide. The French deflationists were not even shaken out of their complacency by the success of the Socialists and the Communists in the spring elections, by the resumption of conscription in Germany, or the devaluation of the Belgian franc in 1935. In March of that year, Professor Baudhuin, long a proponent of devaluation and a member of

[45] Paul Reynaud, *In the Thick of the Fight, 1930-1945*, tr. James D. Lambert (London: Cassell and Co., 1955), p. 15.

[46] Ibid., pp. 1-2.

[47] Quoted in Sauvy, p. 89.

the University of Louvain's prestigious economic institute, publicly advised devaluation. His speech prompted a massive outflow of capital, a government crisis, and a new Cabinet under his university colleague, Paul van Zealand. At the beginning of April, van Zealand devalued the Belgian franc by 28 percent. The defection from the gold bloc had begun in earnest. Belgian prices rose; production, exports, and the gold reserves of the National Bank also bounded up, but the French were not moved from their deflationary mold.

The Laval Assault

Indeed, the Chamber granted Pierre Laval decree powers in June 1935 with the express stipulation that the franc would not be devalued. The law of June 8 stated:

> In order to avoid the devaluation of the currency, the Senate and the Chamber authorize the Government to take by decree until 31 October, 1935, all measures, with the force of law, to fight against speculation and defend the franc.[48]

To carry out the Chamber's mandate, Laval appointed an Experts' Committee grouping Rueff, Dautry, and Gignoux. The Committee was instructed to draw up decrees to reduce "excessive expenditure," remove "manifest abuses," and reestablish budgetary balance. Rueff recounts that, at that time, he believed that the franc was overvalued, that defense of the parity implied "the sacrifice of the French economy," and that the French did not realize the implications of the gold bloc's policies.[49] He also realized that the Chamber's dictum, by excluding devaluation, meant that French prices could only be realigned by "savage deflation." Although he thought deval-

[48] Text of law in Rueff, *Combats*, p. 45.
[49] Ibid.

uation was "indispensable," he cast his vote for the first of the Laval decrees, an immediate 10 percent reduction of all government expenditures, including salaries, public works programs, government services, and the interest on government bonds. "The program was rational, but absurd," Rueff recalls:

> It violated the principle which I established in the choice of the exchange rate of 1928 and whose validity was confirmed by unemployment in Britain, provoked by a parity that was too high. Unfortunately, the condition imposed by the Parliament—'restore without devaluation'—left absolutely no choice. It was necessary to act, even though one was certain to provoke grave difficulties.[50]

Moreover, by breaking the state's solemn engagements, the government weakened its arguments against devaluation juridically and morally.

These first July measures designed to restoring budgetary balance were supplemented with a second series of decrees later in the month designed to reduce the cost of living, defend savings, and promote economic recovery. The last two goals proved overly ambitious. Laval and his experts succeeded somewhat in reducing consumption, but at the cost of increasing unemployment. Furthermore, the government could not afford to reduce taxes and still increase its outlays for rearmament: Without fiscal relief, business production costs remained far too high. Worse yet, the government made no attempt to measure the gap between French and foreign prices but proceeded blindly in its deflationary assault. A third set of decrees in October—317 in total—contained a hodgepodge of measures aimed at reducing political discontent on the one hand (through social security reforms, programs to reeducate the unemployed, and the construction of workers'

[50] Ibid., p. 46.

housing) and protecting key markets through producer agreements on the other. As a result of this conflictual mix of expenditure reductions and increases, total government spending remained at the level of preceding years with diminished revenues, which increased the budget deficit to a record ten billion francs.

The balance sheet of Laval's 549 decrees appears mixed. There was a slight upturn in production but also a sharp rise in prices, which analysts later attributed to demand creation via borrowing from the Bank of France.[51] At the time, left-wing and moderate forces charged him with economic, financial, and monetary failure. The political and psychological legacy was particularly damaging. After three years of recession, Laval's brutal attack on wages flamed smoldering resentment and insecurity. The technicians' reasoning was lost on the workers who felt their precarious position was once again being undermined. Savage deflation at home, provocation by rightist leagues, and a far too indulgent attitude toward the Fascist dictators abroad, served to unite the formerly disparate forces of the moderate and radical left.

The Blum Experiment: Reflation and Devaluation

The elections of 1936 brought the triumph of the Popular Front which grouped together the Radicals, Radical Socialists, and Socialists with the support of the Communists. Each party kept its own autonomy, which meant that the common program could only be a ragbag of compromises. Aside from violent opposition to Laval's decrees and a desire to repeal

[51] See Sauvy, p. 164. According to his calculations, from July 1935 to May 1936, wholesale prices lost 19 percent, retail prices 8 percent, while industrial production increased 11.5 percent. In his view, the failure to perceive this "paradoxical recovery" was a signal example of the lack of attention given to economic indicators in the interwar period.

them immediately, there were few concrete measures. The heart of the Popular Front's program lay in a commitment to reflation—that is, an increase in purchasing power through an increase in wages and industrial expansion through increased provision of credit. The policy grew out of the belief that the depth of the economic crisis owed to insufficient demand. Increasing workers' purchasing power would increase demand and encourage higher production. Despite a threatened outpouring of capital, the Radicals refused to institute exchange control. Many Socialists joined them in believing it smacked of unsavory Fascist practices and would divide France from the Anglo-Saxons. Not even a hint of devaluation was allowed into the common program. Léon Blum, presenting his government to the Chamber on June 6, assured the deputies there would be no *coup d'état monétaire:*

> We do not intend to cover the expenses of our program by a monetary manipulation. The country has neither to expect or fear that one fine morning we will cover the walls with the white billboards of devaluation, the white billboards of a monetary coup d'état. It is not our thought, it is not our intention.[52]

The slogan "Ni dévaluation, ni déflation" was seductive. Everyone would benefit, no one would be hurt. Workers would be reabsorbed into productive life and their wages would go up, but the increased availability of credit would enable industry to absorb these extra burdens until profits rose again. Eventually production costs and prices would go down as fixed costs were spread over a growing volume of output. Agricultural prices would be allowed to rise, but the increased purchasing power of the urban sector would still allow an improvement in the standard of living. In short, the Popular

[52] Quoted in Pose, vol. 2, p. 705.

Front program was far more appealing than the deflation which had led to unemployment, growing deficits, and a low ebb in public confidence. Unfortunately, France's problem was not low wages but high prices, especially as these translated into foreign penetration of the domestic market and the loss of export markets abroad. The wage increases targeted by the Popular Front would only increase industrial costs and widen the gap between French and foreign prices—the major cause of *marasme* in France.

The victory of the left-wing cartel brought waves of demonstrations and widescale sympathy strikes in support of the Popular Front's objectives. Across the country, jubilant but insistent workers staged factory sit-ins. On June 8, Blum called together representatives of the labor unions and the *patronat* to try to end the crippling strikes and the social crisis. The Matignon Accords, agreed to after only a few hours of negotiations, promised the institution of collective bargaining, the readjustment of lowest wages by 15 percent and the highest wages by 7 percent with an average increase of 12 percent and an immediate increase in abnormally low wages. Legislative sanction of these provisions was soon followed by decrees which made paid vacations obligatory and called for a forty-hour work week as of October 1, 1936. The Blum government also took numerous steps to ease the crisis in the agricultural sector, most notably the establishment of a minimum price for wheat.

The French economy did not follow the path Blum and his advisers had foreseen. The strikes could only serve to dampen production—a downturn exacerbated by the new July and August vacations. The slowdown and delivery delays deprived many industries of key inputs and so brought near-stoppages in key industrial sectors. By September 1936, industrial production was 7 percent below the May level; gaps between French and foreign prices, instead of narrowing, continued to widen. In the four months to September, wholesale prices rose 12 percent and consumer prices about 5.5 percent.[53] Unemployment was not reduced but extended; France's external commerce underwent an unfavorable structural transition. Finding more secure markets abroad than in strike-ridden France, many Frenchmen began exporting raw materials rather than seeking to process them at home. Finally the Blum government could not reduce expenditures and maintain its social commitments, and hence fell back on the expedient of borrowing from the Bank of France to meet its payments . Accelerating capital exports reduced the Bank of France's gold reserve from FF62.8 billion in April to FF52.6 billion by September.

At last the government was forced to take the course it had solemnly rejected—devaluation. Rueff gives the credit for persuading Blum to take this politically charged step to his successor as financial attaché in London, Emmanuel Monick. As early as June 1936, Monick is said to have convinced the Prime Minister that France had only two choices: to maintain the parity of the franc and follow the German example of autarchy with the full panoply of exchange controls or to realign the franc with the dollar and the pound in full accord with the Anglo-Saxons.[54] The negotiations which culminated in the Tripartite Accord of September 25, 1936, were entrusted to Monick's able hands.

On September 25, the Bank of France ritually raised the discount rate from 3 percent to 5 percent and on September 26, Blum announced the realignment of the franc. Despite his own former declarations, Blum presented the devaluation as a systematic plan undertaken in cooperation with the Anglo-Saxons to realign price levels. The French people were shocked and disheartened by the disparity between the government's electoral pledges and its actions after four months. Instead of recovery with monetary stability, the nation was

[53] Sauvy, pp. 217, 223.
[54] Rueff, *Combats*, p. 98.

presented with devaluation amidst stagnation. Nor was the international aspect of the accord impressive. Although committed to mutual currency support operations, the three consenting governments could terminate the agreement on twenty-four hours' notice.

By the law of October 1, 1936, the franc was allowed to float between 43-49 milligrams of gold 9/10 fine—a devaluation of 25 percent to 34 percent—and an exchange stabilization fund was created and armed with about FF10 billion of the FF17 billion revaluation profits. French holders of gold were required to surrender their revaluation profits to the state but, as usual, the Bank of France had no record of gold purchases. The gold bloc had disintegrated. Several hours after passage of the French legislation, Swiss authorities announced a 30 percent devaluation of the franc. The following day, the Dutch government abandoned the gold standard and allowed the florin to float downward to reach a new equilibrium level about 22 percent below the previous parity.

The monetary operation did serve to realign price levels but left a host of other problems unsolved. For devaluation to spur recovery, France needed a favorable conjuncture of high world demand and increased domestic production to satisfy this demand. The risk, as in any devaluation, was that it would only lead to increased import costs and diminished export revenues. In these two respects, the forty-hour week was to prove fatal.

Even before the formal commencement of the forty-hour week there were serious troubles. First, production did not and could not increase as fast as expected. Strikes, factory troubles, and wage demands led at first to price, not production increases. Delivery delays and uncertainty as to future price levels also took their toll. Nor was the climate of struggle conducive to raising output. Second, the analysis of the unemployment problem in France had been much too simple. Unemployment was concentrated among agricultural and low-skilled workers, with few opportunities to absorb them, while there was an unfilled need for skilled workers and special professional categories. Finally, the most serious limitations of all were imposed by the shortened work week. While the government had hoped to ease unemployment by bringing more workers into the labor force, it exacerbated it by requiring employers to pay the same wages for a forty-hour week as for a forty-eight-hour week—an increase of 20 percent.

The public, as usual, blamed France's troubles almost wholly on devaluation and quickened the pace of capital export. For Rueff and the other two advisers charged with managing the Exchange Stabilization Fund, the fundamental problem was the government's budgetary deficit. Until the government's finances were brought back into balance and inflationary finance checked, there would be no public confidence. The franc would not find an equilibrium level in the exchange markets and the debilitating loss of capital and gold would continue.[55] Largely because of the Committee of Experts' pressure, Blum announced a pause in his reform program in February 1937. This brought on the inevitable political backlash. The Right, which viewed his program as a catastrophe and resented his attack on their cherished doctrines, refused to cooperate. Left-wing circles, convinced that the wealthy financiers had deliberately aggravated the regime's financial difficulties by exporting capital, were even more bitter and resentful. They had believed the Popular Front would bring a new economic and social order, not capitulation to the disgruntled capitalists.

Alongside the growing political discontentment, the government's financial difficulties increased. By the end of 1936, the Exchange Stabilization Fund had depleted its funds in a futile defense of the franc, and the government could not find

[55] For the series of letters Rueff dispatched to the Prime Ministers and the Finance Ministers of the period, which set out the complexity of economic and financial problems and offered detailed solutions, see ibid., pp. 50-122.

the monies it needed for either its ordinary expenditures or exchange support on the French money market. In mid-June 1937, the experts resigned, indicating their total lack of confidence in the government's financial management. In desperation, Blum demanded decree powers, including capital controls, for a period of six weeks. Although he edged by the Chamber, the Senate refused to entertain capital controls, insisting that artificial barriers would only mask the real problems prompting the outflows. Without exchange controls, the Blum program would only have increased the hemorrhage of capital, and Blum resigned after posing the question of confidence in the Senate. After one year Blum's experiment had fallen victim to the contradiction between freedom of capital movements and the government's attack on the possessors of capital.

From June 1937 through April 1938 paralysis reigned. Camille Chautemps's Radical government, supported by the other Popular Front parties, was successful in obtaining decree powers but less so in achieving a more fundamental reversal of France's economic and financial fortunes. Under the guidance of Finance Minister Bonnet, the franc was allowed to float to its lower limits (a depreciation of 34 percent), and the revaluation profits were used to pay back some of the state's debt to the Bank of France. Several public works programs were annulled and taxes stepped up sharply. The Socialists, however, refused to sacrifice the forty-hour week, which limited a budding recovery in industrial production, profits, and the state's revenues. By the spring of 1938, the Popular Front was deeply divided by external political events—especially the Spanish Civil War; its economic program set back by renewed world recession. Industrial production fell below the 1936 level, while unemployment soared. Blum returned to office when the Anschluss occurred in March 1938, but this time he supplemented his request for capital controls with a classical program which included sizable expenditure reductions, energetic fiscal measures (such as the capital levy), and interim short-term inflationary measures (such as increased advances from the Bank of France or further devaluation) to meet the immediate crisis in the state's finances. To succeed, Blum would have needed the faith and support of warring classes which was not forthcoming. No class or group was willing to sacrifice its perceived interests or well-being. In a reciprocal denial of responsibility, the Right and the Left called on each other to shoulder the new burdens. After the same legislative shuffle between the Chamber and Senate, Blum resigned on the question of confidence on April 8, 1938. In many ways the Popular Front was one of the great casualties of the Maginot Line, which had created this mortal indifference, this smugness, this denial of responsibility in all quarters. It was not so much the Blum program which was placed into question, but France's very preparation for the war which was now certain.

The Czech crisis increased public awareness of the dangers France faced and the need to prepare more seriously for war, but the nation was still not prepared politically, psychologically, or economically for the effort. On May 4, 1938, Prime Minister Daladier devalued the franc for the fourth time—without reference to the Tripartite Accord. By simple legislative fiat, the currency would not be allowed to fall below FF179 to the pound. Along with the monetary operation, designed primarily to ease the state's short-term financing difficulties, the Prime Minister attempted to instill a new sense of realism. A series of decrees gave incentives for production and supplier credits to vital industries and increased taxes to cover expenditures for national defense. A second train of decrees three weeks later set out to expand vital public works programs (ports, canals, schools, and hospitals) and to extend the work week, which Daladier believed was the key to recovery.[56] The Prime Minister's proposals for a lengthening of the work week prompted the resignation of two key minis-

[56] See his August 21, 1938, speech, "The Forty Hour Week," in his *In Defense of France* (New York: Doubleday, 1939), p. 54.

ters and the bitter protests of the Left, but was implemented by the more courageous industries. The Maginot Line mentality seemed to reign in all quarters. In the military as well as the economic sphere, Paul Reynaud was one of the few to call attention to the conflicts in the French posture. France could either abandon its offensive alliances with Poland and Czechoslovakia and try to live behind the Maginot Line or keep the nation's commitments and create the offensive army which would allow it to honor them. Reynaud summarized: "Ayons la politique de notre armée ou l'armée de notre politique." The same line of thinking should have directed French economic policy but, still traumatized by the war of 1914-18, the French people were not prepared for economic or military battle.

Reynaud took over the Finance Ministry in November 1938. His reputation allowed him to win decree power easily. Eager to implement the programs he had so long advocated, Reynaud moved quickly to increase rearmament expenditure and to build up government revenues. Between November 12 and November 15, Reynaud promulgated fifty-eight decrees, which aimed at restoring budgetary equilibrium through stiff increases in taxes and the price of public services, as well as draconian economies. The French nation, which had counted on this clever statesman to find "le truc pour tout arranger," resented his tough and classical increase in fiscal levies. Once again warring political groupings refused to sacrifice their particular interests or favorite programs for the required efforts. Each group held its particular well-being to be vital for the health of the nation. The Left complained that modifications in the public works programs and employment schemes would reduce the purchasing power of the workers and so bring a slide back into depression. As Léon Jouhaux, president of the Confédération Générale du Travail, charged at Nantes:

The intended program of recovery is supposed to be based on an increase in production, but the financial reforms and the fiscal measures can only result in an increase in the cost of living and a reduction in purchasing power.[57]

The Right, in turn, insisted that it was the new fiscal burdens which would cause a downturn in economic activity. A young Giscard d'Estaing reproved:

> The decrees will probably serve to aggravate the situation in that they throw another portion of the weak reserves of French wealth into the furnace and because they allow the Government to raid the French Treasury once again. M. Reynaud has set forth this hypothesis himself in sentences which threaten to become the most somber of prophecies.[58]

The Reynaud program did generate an increase in military spending, and with it an increase in production and income. Production rose about 15 percent between November and June—an annual rate of 22.5 percent—and unemployment fell below June 1932 levels. Price disparities decreased and the trade balance improved. In contrast to the international tension, the internal political climate improved. Savings remained in the country this time and the Bank of France gradually gained gold. The increase in purchasing power did not keep pace with the rise of industrial production, but there was an acknowledged upturn in the standard of living. Without rearmament, the economic upturn might have been even more pronounced, for production increased sharply in response to the lengthening of the work week. Yet there were limiting psychological factors to full recovery. Levels of confidence and initiative were abysmally low. The Left, for example, resented a work week extended to fifty hours. Many

[57] Quoted in Sauvy, p. 332.
[58] *Revue de Paris*, December 1, 1938.

industrialists, in turn, were hesitant to lengthen the work week in their factories. Fearful of workers' reprisal or of oversupply and reduced profits, they preferred to let orders pile up in more secure fashion. The recovery, although respectable, went little noticed at the time.

On the eve of World War II, the French nation was not, as Daladier insisted, "more united, more resolute, stronger" than ever before.[59] Yet, the disastrous perspectives of bankruptcy and inflation had been put aside; production and trade were on the rebound; and the franc, although worth only 10 percent of its prewar value, held steady in the exchange markets. The need for a greater effort had been recognized but not adequately met. Despite the new realism and a promising start down the road to recovery, France was still far too weak, divided, and bewildered to withstand the onslaught of the second great holocaust.

[59] "France and Her Will," broadcast of March 29, 1939, in *In Defense of France*, p. 204-05.

CHAPTER 4

Retreat from Leadership:
The Evolution of
British Economic Foreign Policy, 1870-1939

ROBERT J. A. SKIDELSKY

To understand what Britain's monetary authorities believed they were doing in the interwar years, Robert Skidelsky argues that one must first comprehend the prevailing view of how the prewar gold standard operated; for it was the restoration of this system. or, more accurately, a mythical retrospective version of it, which animated British monetary policy after World War I. Numerous tactical errors characterized Britain's policies in this period and seriously weakened its prospects for a sustained recovery. But the greatest weakness of all was that the foundation of power and influence upon which Britain's monetary supremacy had been built was simply no longer there. The following subtly argued essay goes well beyond a monetary history of the period in question to venture an explanation for the decline of the British Empire itself.

Introduction [1]

It is usually only after the collapse of a system that people seriously start trying to find out how it really worked. Thus, in the late 1960s, the postwar economic order could still be, and usually was, described in terms of Bretton Woods, its institutions (IMF, World Bank, etc.) and its rules of conduct.[2] Indeed, the main feature of the post-1945 system has been seen as the development of "international economic institutions."[3] Even though economists talked about dollar

[1] This paper was first presented to a meeting of the Monetary Seminar of the Lehrman Institute on November 2, 1973. It has benefited greatly from discussions on that occasion and subsequently.

[2] See, for example, Eric Roll, *The World After Keynes: An Examination of the Economic Order* (1968).

[3] A. G. Kenwood and A. L. Lougheed, *The Growth of the International Economy, 1820-1960* (1971), p. 310.

149

scarcities and dollar gluts, the preponderant military and economic power of the United States was rarely given its proper weight in formal explanations of how the system worked. In particular, the idea of hegemony as a condition for international order was rarely discussed, at least in the economic field.

The collapse of the dollar standard in 1971 has naturally stimulated interest in the conditions of international economic order. Two conflicting views dominate the field. There are those who believe that an international economic system requires a leader, manager, or underwriter—all three terms are used synonymously. There are those who believe that what is required is an objective, impersonal mechanism for adjusting national interests to each other, such as is afforded by a gold standard. The first view finds favor among Anglo-American economists; the second with French economists, particularly Jacques Rueff. Translated into more familiar terms, they may be called the imperial and balance-of-power theories of international relations. Both seek support in the functioning of the world economy before 1914. For the pluralists it worked well because of the existence of an international gold standard, whose principles were abandoned after World War I. For the imperialists, by contrast, the gold standard worked well because Britain managed or underwrote it. It was Britain's position, not the gold standard, that was primary to the well-being of the nineteenth-century world economy. Indeed, without British management, the gold standard could not function—a supposition which is held established by its collapse in the interwar years when Britain was no longer able to provide the requisite leadership.

My own conclusion, which I shall attempt to establish in the next few pages, is that the imperial position is nearer the truth than the balance-of-power one, though there are difficulties about the concept "imperial" as implied to Britain's role. The pluralists, however, seem to be right in one very important sense, which is their perception that the imperialist *tour de force* cannot be sustained and that therefore a system which depends on the exertions of a preponderant power is inherently unstable in the long run. The reason is that imperial functions weaken the power performing them, so that a system "managed" by a single power is always tending to revert to a plural system. Indeed, a more plural system was clearly taking shape before 1914. But, on the record of events between 1900 and 1945, it cannot seriously be claimed that pluralism provided a basis for international economic order. Compared to the last years of the ninteenth century, there was no international economy left by 1939 but simply half a dozen or so major economic units, each with its circle of clients, and with a very low degree of mutual interdependence. The answer to the imperial problem, it would seem, is not to abolish international authority or claim that there is no need for it, but to find a different basis for it. This, after all, has been, as it remains, one of the primary quests of our epoch.

The Nineteenth-Century System: Theory and Practice

The first requirement is to form an accurate view of how the nineteenth-century economic system actually worked. The rather abstract observations that follow are intended to provide a framework for the subsequent discussion.

In a command economy, the importance of power is obvious to all. The system is based on the presumption that B will not do what is necessary unless A compels him or her to do it, A usually being the government or the state. The role of power is much less obvious in a market system, where it is assumed that individuals act in economically beneficial ways not because they are compelled but because it is in their individual self-interest to do so. It is not a question of B's interests being subordinated to A's, but rather of the self-interest of all being secured by the market. Indeed, it is precisely the market's supposed ability to insure everyone's self-interest, rightly conceived, that makes unnecessary the "power" and "intervention" of the government in the economic sphere.

The government's role is purely facilitative: to make private enterprise possible, not to run the economy.

The first basic difficulty in the textbook account of how markets work is historical. There is no known case of market economies being created by consent, that is, of people voluntarily submitting to marketplace decisions. Market economies were created by state power, then turned against feudal barriers in the interests of entrepreneurial minorities. Far from being welcomed, they were, in fact, fiercely resisted by majorities unrepresented in the political process. Indeed, it was the existence of political, social, and economic "asymmetry" which enabled market economies to be established in the first place. Creating the conditions needed by the market system required a much more positive state than classical theory usually implies. Moreover, this role was continuous.

Although the market claims to maximize the real income of all parties to the market bargain, this is a rather abstract notion when set against the vast inequalities of reward that actually result to the various factors of production—notably capital and labor—and the fact that some groups are always losing ground in a dynamic situation. Markets are thus seen to have both beneficial and adverse effects. Thus, the need for two types of government intervention is created. The first is to secure consent for their adverse effects; the second is to compensate for them by transferring resources from one group to another, by passing protective legislation, and so forth. Government intervention has to maintain the political and economic asymmetry of the market economy as well as offset the worst evils resulting from it. Both types of intervention have been continuous since market economies were established. The way in which they involve governments in ever-deepening policy contradictions does not directly concern us now. The important point is that market systems have never possessed the independent legitimacy that textbooks claim for them. Far from abolishing power, markets can only be sustained by power.

These conclusions apply equally to a system of international exchange. A command economy embracing many countries, such as the Soviet bloc, is clearly seen to depend on power exercised from the center. On the other hand, an international market economy is more usually conceived of as a system into which member-states freely enter for their mutual benefit and agree to sustain in their mutual interest—viz., the nineteenth-century free trade/gold standard system. But historically this is not so. The "world economy" was initiated by forcible conquest; and historically most multinational economic systems have been imperial ones.[4] Further, as in a domestic market system, the inequalities of power and reward built into the system—indeed, responsible for its creation—have to be both maintained and compensated for. Power and intervention are as much required in the international "free market" as in the international command economy.

In a domestic market economy, power functions and economic functions are performed by government. In an international market economy, they are generally performed by a governing nation, the strongest power militarily and economically. The adjective "imperial" may give a misleading idea of the role of such a power, since it implies overlordship (formal or informal). It has rightly been pointed out that Britain's nineteenth-century empire, large though it was, was very far from being coextensive with the international economic system as a whole. However, a nation is not required to govern every unit of an international system to perform governing functions for the system as a whole. By a governing nation, I mean simply one whose weight in the system is so great that the system could not exist without its constant exertions. This is precisely the role being claimed for Britain in the nine-

[4] For example, the Mediterranean economy of classical times was coextensive with Roman power and did not survive its collapse. The main historical debate on this point concerns the date of that collapse. According to Henri Pirenne, the Mediterranean economy was sustained by Byzantine power into the eighth century A.D.

teenth-century world economy. Without Britain (or its equivalent) there would have been no international economic system, merely a collection of national economies enjoying marginal trade relations.

In order to make clear what is being claimed, it is first necessary to know what is meant by an economic *system*. At what point does the exchange of goods and services between nations—economic relations—become an economic "system," an "international" economy? Surely, at the point, however difficult that is to define, when output starts to depend significantly on commerce; in other words, when the production and sale of goods comes to depend significantly on foreign supplies and foreign markets. This is in fact what happened in the nineteenth century. Foreign trade grew at a much higher rate than world output, signifying the increasing dependence of the latter on the former: the world proportion of foreign trade to world product increased from 3 percent to 33 percent between 1800 and 1913.[5] This is what one means by the development of an international economic system, and it is the degree of interdependence suggested by such a figure that is inconceivable in the absence of something approximating international government. Marginal relations, of course, do not require any such supranational authority, but they do not constitute an economic system. For the nineteenth-century world economy, Britain constituted such an authority.

Britain's "weight" rested on three pillars: power—chiefly naval, but also military; economic supremacy—commercial, industrial, and financial; and prestige, based on British achievements, but supported by the spread of British populations and British ideas. From this weight flowed British functions in the system. Indeed, it is a key argument of this essay that the asymmetry, without which no international system can be established, obliges the leading power to intervene from time to time if the system is to be sustained. Every

5 Kenwood and Lougheed, op. cit., p. 91.

"responsibility" follows logically and inescapably from the initial inequalities of power and reward.

The first governing function which flowed from Britain's "weight" was that of maintaining world order. The need for politically maintained order as a condition for the growth and maintenance of an international economic system has been denied by the free traders. According to textbook descriptions, such a system develops in a seemingly spontaneous manner out of the disparity between countries' demand for goods and services and their ability to supply them. Marginal trade, for example, in luxuries, is undoubtedly of this kind. But no country will voluntarily risk the high degree of dependence of output on commerce entailed by an international system unless assured of a favorable and predictable international environment. The most obvious type of such environment is one which it directly controls and manipulates to its own advantage. Trade relations in the seventeenth and eighteenth centuries were largely conducted in privileged trading blocs—the old mercantile empires of Britain, France, Holland, and Spain—all established by forcible conquest. Victorious in turn in the mercantile and Napoleonic wars, Britain, in effect, took over this mercantile world and refashioned it to serve the needs of its industrial monopoly. The world market of the free traders was thus brought into being by British military and naval power to serve the needs of the world's workshop and carrier. And, of course, Britain inherited thereby primary responsibility for international order.

Britain's nineteenth-century functions in this respect have been generally recognized by the phrase *Pax Britannica*. The British *Pax* rested first and foremost on the British Empire which by 1914 encompassed one-quarter of the globe. The second prop was British naval supremacy which guaranteed the freedom of the seas to the commerce of all nations. Naval power, allied to economic leverage, was also exerted to insure domestic institutions, political and financial, compatible with a high level of economic exchange. China and Japan were opened up, Greece and Egypt brought back to economic "good sense" by naval bombardment, and Britain exerted strong influence on the political and financial development of Argentina and Brazil. Finally, even in the European balance-of-power system, Britain occupied a key role based on its position as balancer, a role which it filled, as Cobden acidly remarked, with a "Cyclopean eye to her own aggrandizement" elsewhere. Britain's importance in establishing and sustaining the order and political and social uniformities without which a high level of economic interdependence would have been unattainable can scarcely be disputed.

Britain's role as economic guarantor was in fact twofold—commercial and financial. Like its power political functions, they flowed directly from the unequal development between Britain and other countries. The single most important economic cause of the development of an international economy was the British industrial revolution which created the need for foreign supplies and foreign markets. The growth of nineteenth-century international trade is essentially the growth of British exports and imports. By 1860 the international economy consisted of a collection of disconnected trading blocs. The chief ones centered on Britain: Britain, India, China; Britain, Latin America, the Southern United States; Britain, Western Europe, and the Baltic states. For each of these groupings, Britain was the largest market and the largest supplier of manufactured goods (for example, Britain took 46 percent of United States' exports in the 1850s). After 1860 "the earlier pattern of largely disconnected trading arrangements centered mainly on Britain gave way to a new multilateral trading system based on a worldwide pattern of economic specialization." [6] But world trade continued to flow in the channels set by Britain's industrial development (exchange of manufactured goods for raw materials and foodstuffs), and Britain's role in this trade remained outstand-

[6] Ibid., pp. 103-04.

ing. Thus Britain's share of total world imports of primary products was 30 percent in 1876-80, dropping to 20 percent in 1913. Its share of world export trade in manufactured goods fell from just under 40 percent in 1876-80 to 25 percent in 1913. However, it was not just the size of the British market that was critical to the nineteenth-century world trading system, but the access to that market guaranteed by free trade policy. This was of great importance to the preservation of the international economic system in the late nineteenth century when tariffs were going up in all other industrialized or industrializing countries.

Britain's gradual conversion to free trade, as opposed to just freedom for its own trade (the mercantilist position), is a good illustration of how functions and responsibilities flow inevitably from initial superiority. It has often been argued that without the availability of monopoly profits in overseas markets there would have been no British industrial "takeoff." [7] There would also have been no international economic system. The union of commercial and technological supremacy produced as its first fruit a British export economy greatly inflated from previous "norms" by new possibilities. But by the same token it produced a need for greatly expanded imports, not just or even mainly because supplies were located abroad, but because an expanding British market was needed if foreign customers were to earn the sterling with which to buy British goods. In part, the growth of the British import market was a natural consequence of increased incomes brought about by industrialization; but it was also the result of conscious policy, pursued at the behest of the manufacturing interests. The size and guaranteed freedom of the British market provided that assured market without which major export industries could not have been developed overseas. After 1870 Britain's willingness to "import primary products

[7] See, for example, E. J. Hobsbawm, *Industry and Empire* (1968), Chap. 2.

regardless of the consequences for British agriculture" [8] was critical in sustaining incomes in developing countries. Of great importance was the fact that the British market was kept open during depression. This enabled debtor countries to make their interest payments without deflating their economies at a time when British capital exports tended to fall off, thus keeping international trade at a high level and sustaining the second pillar of the nineteenth-century economic system, its monetary structure.

As with free trade theory, textbook accounts of the international monetary system miss the nineteenth-century reality. We are presented with a supposedly self-equilibrating system—the gold standard—where no key currency either exists or is needed, and no managerial functions need to be performed.

Under the gold-standard theory it was impossible for countries' current accounts to remain permanently unbalanced, that is, either in surplus or deficit. A surplus country would gain gold; a deficit country would lose it. According to Hume's "price specie flow" mechanism, any flow of gold in or out of a country automatically induces price changes (via changes in the quantity of money) leading to a restoration of equilibrium in the current account. For example, the loss of gold occasioned by an import surplus would bring about lower export prices, thus enabling more exports to be sold abroad and hence restoring the current account to balance. (Refinements were later added, but this remained the basic theory.) Hume's argument was designed to prove that the mercantilist obsession with a favorable trade balance (in order to accumulate precious metals and stimulate domestic activity) was bound to be self-defeating. Monetary hegemony was no more possible than imperial hegemony because both produced automatic reactions tending to restore a natural balance. The

[8] Derek H. Aldcroft and Harry W. Richardson, *The British Economy, 1870-1939* (1969), pp. 81-82.

existence of metallic standards, in other words, guaranteed an even distribution of economic power.

The first obvious comment on this argument is that it does not square with what actually happened in the nineteenth century. Britain ran an almost continuous and usually enormous current account surplus from 1815 to 1914. And the reason for this is that for most of the nineteenth century Britain was economically *sui generis*—qualitatively in a quite different position from any other country in the world. Britain's commercial and industrial supremacy initially gave its goods a monopoly or quasimonopoly position in world markets. Its growing current account surplus consisted of the monopoly or quasimonopoly profits of those who provided those goods and services. An increasingly important component of Britain's current account surplus derived from profits received by the City of London for specialized financial services, particularly insurance and sterling bills of exchange. The latter mark the start of sterling's career as international money. The classic balance-of-power theorists, writing at a time when all European powers were roughly at the same stage of economic development, could not conceive of the immense disparity of economic power which made possible such developments. On this immense disparity, not on the supposed balance of power, was built the nineteenth-century monetary system.

For the obverse of Britain's surpluses were others' deficits. Since it was impossible to adjust surpluses to deficits by price changes, given the built-in inequality in the price of British goods and services and those of primary producers, the only way for economic exchange to continue and grow was for Britain to finance its trading partners' deficits—to lend them sufficient sterling to cover their import surpluses from Britain. In other words, overall balance in payments between countries was achieved not through gold movements leading to relative price changes, but through transfers of capital, on both long and short term, from surplus (mainly manufacturing) to deficit (chiefly primary producing) regions. The returns from these loans (investment income) in turn helped swell the "invisible" component of current account surpluses. In this process, Britain played a leading part.

London was the chief source of the world's nineteenth-century capital requirements. With £4,000m. invested abroad by 1913, Britain owned 43 percent of the total stock of overseas investments. The real value of British-owned capital abroad in that year probably exceeded the total American capital invested abroad today.[9] These economic functions were not unique. France, with £1,900m., owned 20 percent of the total stock of foreign investments in 1913. Herbert Feis has reminded us that "out of the small purse of the French bourgeoisie, the Russian monarchy could draw the substance for its monumental plans, the Austro-Hungarian Empire equip itself with railroads, banks, and factories, the Turkish sultan spend without accounts, Italy endure the anxieties of the first years of unification, and the small Balkan states establish their national existence." [10] By 1913, Germany had 13 percent of the total stock, and the United States 7 percent. Nevertheless, Britain remained by far the most important single source of foreign funds after 1870.

London was also the main conduit of short-term finance before 1914, the "lender of last resort." According to David Williams:

When her own funds were fully stretched she was able to draw on—through the mechanism of interest rates—the liquid resources of other countries—outstandingly European—not normally engaged in extensive international short-term lending. This continuous outflow of funds

[9] See Andrew Glynn and Bob Sutcliffe, *British Capitalism, Workers and the Profits Squeeze* (1973), p. 19.

[10] H. Feis, *Europe the World's Banker, 1870-1914* (1930), p. 37.

from London had special significance in helping to avoid damaging dislocations of international trade. . . . The ability to borrow short-term in London was also a significant factor in mitigating a fall in commodity prices. This was instrumental in maintaining incomes in many overseas countries.[11]

From the world point of view, then, London's money market was "an international credit mechanism under expert British control." [12]

Two factors explain London's rise as the center of long- and short-term finance. The first was the international acceptability of sterling as a means of payment, which derived from Britain's importance in world trade, the extreme stability of the pound between 1821 and 1914 (based in turn on Britain's massive current account surplus), and the high standard of British acceptance houses. The fact that so many pounds were held in private and official banking systems gave the Bank of England its leverage over short-term money flows.

The second factor was the ease of "real" transfer. It was crucial to the nineteenth-century economic system that a foreign loan result in an equivalent export of goods, thus avoiding a loss of gold, deflation, and unemployment. Among the factors which insured that export of goods would follow export of capital were the strong bilateral ties between capital exporting countries and their clients (for example, colonial governments invariably placed their orders for railways and other utilities with the mother country), and the fact that the provision of capital was often accompanied by insistence on control and management of the foreign enterprise.[13] This not

[11] David Williams, "London and the 1931 Financial Crisis," *Economic History Review*, April 1963, p. 517.

[12] W. A. Brown, *The International Gold Standard Reinterpreted* (1940), i, xv.

[13] Feis notes that railways were built in China, Mexico, Argentina,

only helped insure sinking fund and dividend payments, but also facilitated purchases from the home country. What, then, happened to the money lent abroad? Part of it never went abroad at all, but was spent directly in the lending country on buying capital goods (railways, etc.). Part of it was spent in the borrowing countries, raising their incomes and hence their purchases of goods from the lending countries. A. G. Ford writes: "It was very important for her operation of the gold standard pre-1914 that *ex-ante* British foreign lending ... generally increased British exports relative to imports ... and so facilitated its transfer without balance of payments disruption and prolonged gold loss." [14] The critical point is that real transfer was made possible, or at the very least facilitated, by politically maintained (i.e., imperial or quasi-imperial) economic relations between lenders and borrowers.

To go further, not only did Britain "manage" the prewar international economic system, but it is unimaginable that such an international economic system could have developed in the nineteenth century without such management. The reason is simple. The very harshness of the adjustment procedure between nations envisaged by "pure" free-trade and gold-standard theories would have destroyed the international system (as in fact it did between the wars) had there not been different mechanisms for securing such adjustment. The ameliorating mechanisms were based on Britain's preeminent position in the world economy. On the one side there was the size of the British market, guaranteed by free trade policy even during the depression; on the other, the capital flows from

---

Brazil, Rhodesia, India, and Turkey under British management and/or control. Almost all the mine properties were under British control and management, as well as oil and rubber concerns. (See op. cit., p. 25.)

[14] A. G. Ford, "Notes on the Working of the Gold Standard Before 1914," *Oxford Economic Papers* (1960).

London, which normally enabled debtors to finance their import surpluses and which formed the core of an increasingly complex and roundabout system of multilateral payments. If keeping a free market for imports, maintaining a flow of investment capital, and acting as lender of last resort are the marks of an "underwriter" of an international system,[15] then Britain certainly fulfilled this role in the nineteenth-century international economy.

This fact suggests a general observation, which is that situations of mutual dependence are far more likely to develop out of radical inequality than out of mutual balance, for it is only under conditions of radical inequality that a unit becomes sufficiently powerful economically to see firm advantages in constructing an economic system outside its own frontiers. From this initial advantage, which then has to be compensated, develops the whole structure of mutual dependence sketched above.

The Fragility of the Prewar System

The nineteenth-century system rested on a set of unequal, but complementary, relations between industrial nations and primary producers, with Britain playing a key role, through its imports and capital exports, in linking the two sides together. The stability of these arrangements in turn enabled the establishment and maintenance of stable currencies. Already before the war this system was starting to disintegrate.

The critical new factor was the emergence of an increasingly plural international system. Paradoxically, the new pluralism was promoted by the hegemonic power itself. Foreign lending on the British scale had the inevitable consequence of diffusing industrialization and shifting the capacity to innovate from Britain to other countries—particularly the United

[15] Charles P. Kindleberger, *The World in Depression, 1929-1939* (1973), p. 28.

States, Germany, and Japan. In this sense the pluralists were right in their view that no country could *permanently* maintain a current account surplus and that economic hegemony, through the burdens it assumed, would ultimately become self-destructive. The crucial point for the international economy, however, was that competition and rivalry were built into the new pluralism. One obvious consequence of the spread of industrialization was that the competitive aspects of international trade increased relative to the complementary aspects. But more fundamentally, economic pluralism spilled over into a struggle for a new political pluralism. The new economic equality was incompatible with the exercise of key economic and power functions by a single power. This was the really non-negotiable factor in the prewar international system, and the issue that led to two world wars.

The spread of industrialization immediately created a paradox. It greatly increased global interdependence, since the enlarged industrial metropole became even more dependent on foreign supplies and markets. But increased interdependence came at the precise moment when new democratic and nationalist forces were showing a heightened intolerance for the *Pax Britannica*. In other words, interdependence was growing, but in the face of an increasingly unpredictable international environment. In theory, either of two adjustments might have staved off disaster. The first was to raise international authority and/or cooperation to the level of the new interdependence. The other was to reduce interdependence to the level of existing international authority and/or cooperation. The first pointed to new international institutions, economic strategies on a world scale, even "world government." The second led to a revival of empire—that classic attempt to square interdependence with national interest in a world of jostling great powers.

In the last years of the old order, what Polanyi calls "half conscious preparations for autarchy" were more in evidence than attempts to find a new basis for an international economic system. The history of tariffs is instructive. Tariffs are common instruments for two entirely conflicting economic purposes. On the one hand, they can be used as instruments of exclusion to protect national economic interests from foreign competition. As permanent elements in a national economic system they point toward diminished international trade and greater self-sufficiency. On the other hand, tariffs may be used as bargaining instruments for a negotiated pluralism. In the last quarter of the nineteenth century creators and advocates of tariffs oscillated between viewing them as bargaining counters to secure freer trade and as permanent elements in economic systems. Whatever their views, however, the average level of tariffs rose almost continuously up to 1914. In other words, tariffs, though still moderate by later standards, were starting to become permanent obstacles to international trade and their growth pointed toward a retreat from the very high level of interdependence reached by the end of the nineteenth century. Thus, the emergence of competitive pluralism coincided with the growth of autarchic tendencies even as London perfected its technical skills in managing the prewar gold standard.

As we have seen, the emergence of a more plural world automatically diminished the legitimacy of Britain's role and its power to fulfill it. The chief threat to Britain's role as economic underwriter came from the narrowing of its current account surplus. From 1870 to 1913 Britain's trade gap increased threefold in value, reflecting its weakening competitive position vis-à-vis Germany and the United States. In 1877 Robert Giffen, head of the statistical department of the Board of Trade, wrote: "There has not since the free trade period been such a decline in our foreign trade. . . ." The rate of growth of exports (5 percent between 1841 and 1870) dropped to 2.7 percent between 1881 and 1913, despite the boom years 1906-13.

To survive Britain adopted two basic strategies which complemented each other up to a point. The first was the intensified exploitation of its empire and satellite markets. Increasingly excluded by tariffs from European and North American markets, British exports fled to Asia and Latin America. The role of India, where Britain was able to insure a "politically established and maintained" trade surplus, became increasingly important. The second strategy was to expand receipts from "invisible" earnings, both by stepping up the rate of capital exports to the developing world (which also helped merchandise exports) and by specializing in providing financial and shipping services. Thus, depending on which component of the balance of payments one treats as significant, one can either say with S. B. Saul that "the key to Britain's whole payments pattern lay in India," [16] or with W. A. Lewis that "having ceased to command an abnormal share of world trade in manufactures, Britain temporarily maintained her balance of payments by achieving an abnormal share of the world's shipping, insurance, and other commercial services." [17] It only required the deterioration of one or both of these components for the whole external position to crumble—and with it the nineteenth-century gold standard system.

The decay in Britain's situation produced a somewhat confused debate on Britain's future. Three lines of thought may be discerned.

Britain, as we have seen, had started off as the workshop of the world. As its industrial efficiency declined, it seemed plausible to suppose that it should concentrate increasingly on its banking and other services. The important distinction between industrial and finance capitalism was made by Halford Mackinder in 1900. British commerce, he argued, might be faced with contraction, but the need for finance would continue to grow. "It appears, therefore, quite possible," he declared, "that the financial importance of the City of Lon-

[16] Quoted in Hobsbawm, op. cit., p. 123.
[17] W. A. Lewis, *Economic Survey, 1919-1939* (1949), p. 77.

don may continue to increase, while the industry . . . of Britain becomes relatively less." [18] The view that Britain should specialize in finance pointed to a rationalized internationalism with London as the "brain" of the world system. It is far from dead in the European context today.

For those interested in industry and employment, however, this solution was not just unacceptable but totally destructive. Joseph Chamberlain and leaders of the Tariff Reform Campaign (1903) argued that promiscuous foreign lending was the last thing Britain ought to be doing, for far from creating new markets for British manufactures, it promoted the industrialization of the world behind tariff barriers: a process destined to knock Britain's traditional exports out of business. Chamberlain wanted Britain to abandon free imports, as its main competitors already had, and construct a self-contained imperial system based on complementary exchange—a proposal which reflected the ongoing shift of Britain's trade and investment to the primary producing empire countries.[19] The imperialists, in short, wanted Britain to abandon its claim to "manage" a world system, and concentrate on developing its Empire.

A far more drastic retreat yet was envisaged on the Left of British politics. According to J. A. Hobson, bloated internationalism, including foreign investment, stemmed from the lack of internal markets. He argued that if national income

[18] See R. Skidelsky, "The Grand Alternatives," in Derwent May, ed., *Good Talk* (1968), p. 144.

[19] The Empire's share of British exports rose from 26 percent in 1870 to 34 percent in 1910; Latin America's share rose from 8.8 percent to 12.2 percent in the same period. Before 1870 the main areas of investment had been Europe and America. "After 1870 more than two-thirds of British overseas investment went to regions of recent settlement. . . ." By 1913, 47 percent of British investments had been made in the Empire. (Aldcroft and Richardson, op. cit., Chap. 3 and p. 86.)

were more evenly and justly distributed, the need for international trade and finance would largely disappear. In Chapter 6 of his classic *Imperialism* (1902), Hobson denied the "necessity to open up new foreign markets; the home markets are capable of indefinite expansion. . . . Whatever is produced in England can be consumed in England." In other words, Hobson was advocating a "Little England" program of national self-sufficiency.

These different solutions to the world's economic problems were widely canvassed in all the major countries before World War I, but hostilities broke out before the debate could reach any resolution. The problem, however, had already been starkly posed. How was it possible to preserve economic order in a world where, as the German historian Erich Marcks observed, "everything interacts and affects everything else, but in which also everything collides and clashes"?

The Restoration of the Gold Standard: 1918-25

During World War I, gold exports were suspended. Britain was on a "managed" paper standard, with the official dollar-sterling exchange pegged at $4.76. British deficits incurred by the purchases of necessary foodstuffs, raw materials, and munitions were financed by selling off American assets and borrowing from the United States and the Dominions to the net amount of £1,290 million.[20] At the same time, inflationary war finance raised the British price level threefold between 1914 and 1920. To start peace with a depression was politically

---

[20] E. V. Morgan, *Studies in British Financial Policy, 1914-1925,* pp. 323-26. Britain's payments deficit with America and the Dominions was in fact much larger, but it was compensated to some extent by its surplus with its allies—France, Russia, and Italy. Britain's difficulty in financing World War I accurately pinpoints its relative decline. In the Napoleonic wars, Britain had financed its allies; in World War I, it ended up being financed by the United States.

impossible. Rather than attempt to restore the prewar parity by deflation, as the so-called gold standard rules required, Britain freed the exchanges in March 1919. The value of the pound rapidly dropped, reaching $3.40 in February 1920. From the end of 1922 to 1925 it fluctuated around $4.50, until the prewar parity of $4.86 was restored in April 1925.[21]

Despite the dislocations of the war, the logic of Britain's position seemed to dictate a restoration of the nineteenth-century economic order. Logic was heavily overlaid with nostalgia. In a world of dissolving standards, return to stability became a psychological obsession. The prewar gold standard, symbol of a liberal capitalist order which had just hurled back the challenge of Prussian imperialism and was menaced by the specter of working-class revolution, provided that stability. The old bankers' internationalism now comingled with the transatlantic current of Wilsonian idealism, as embodied in the League of Nations. The reluctance of the United States to step into the leading position to which its economic and moral weight entitled it, once more thrust the managerial role on Britain, whose own interests and traditions were in any case well-adapted to it.

It thus became the fixed object of British policy to restore the prewar gold standard as quickly as possible. Moggridge notes the "unanimity of informed business, financial and political opinion" in favor of restoration, though there were some differences on timing: its endorsement by the Labour Party testifies to the continued hold of "globalism" on British political life.[22]

The return to the gold standard, in fact, comprised a

[21] The early postwar appreciation of sterling was apparently less the result of policies designed to restore the pound to its prewar parity, than it was a reflection of "hot-money" inflows from the European continent.

[22] D. E. Moggridge, *The Return to Gold, 1925: The Formulation of Economic Policy and Its Critics* (1969), p. 67.

number of separate operations, justified by different arguments. In general terms, the restoration of the gold standard was justified in terms of its effect in insuring that nations lived "within their means" (with an eye here to growing trade union power), securing general monetary order, and promoting trade liberalization and increased employment in Britain's languishing export industries.[23] That Britain should "take the lead" was justified by reference to Britain's traditional responsibilities in world finance. The choice of the prewar parity reflected the special interests of the City of London. To devalue would be to write down sterling assets and suggest to foreigners that London was not a good place to hold their money. The prewar parity was also the only parity at which it was felt the gold standard could be reanointed, as it were. Stabilization at a reduced parity would be an act of political management and would open the way for future governments to choose currency depreciation as an alternative to balancing accounts.

Most of these arguments were beside the point. The nineteenth-century gold standard was not a substitute government, as many supposed, but a facility for certain types of transactions. The so-called disciplines of the gold standard were either not required or were performed by other institutions. To expect a restored gold standard to act as a government was to give it a role it never had in the nineteenth century and could not be expected to play in the twentieth.

A related mistake was to imagine that there existed some generally accepted rules of the game above and beyond national interests. This is a good example of British ethnocentrism. The British had generalized their own national practices—or what they imagined their national practices to

[23] For the employment argument for returning to the gold standard, see R. S. Sayers, "The Return to Gold, 1925," in S. T. Pollard, ed., *The Gold Standard and Employment Policies Between the Wars* (1970), pp. 89-90.

have been—into an objective code of good behavior which other nations would follow more or less automatically. It was Keynes who observed, reasonably enough, that other nations might define their interests in terms other than a British code of behavior, and that Britain was therefore foolhardy to try to restore a system which it could no longer control or influence.[24] But Keynes was ignored.

The precariousness of Britain's postwar position was reflected in its inability to discharge effectively its traditional managerial functions. First, the surplus for capital exports had been cut down by the growing import surplus and a fall in income from overseas investments—indeed, there is some doubt about whether it existed at all. As a result, new overseas issues amounted to £115m. per annum between 1920 and 1929, compared with £200m. per annum in the years leading up to the war: their real value had fallen even more than their nominal value.[25] For a number of years Britain's declining propensity to invest abroad was compensated by heavy American foreign lending, particularly to Europe and Latin America, "but the United States was less suited to the role of creditor in the sense that she was unwilling to receive all her interest payments in the form of commodity imports."[26] Between 1928 and 1930, America cut down simultaneously on lending and imports. The consequence was a steady accumulation of gold by the United States at the precise moment when the world desperately needed capital to offset the deflationary spiral. By 1930 America held 50 percent of the world's gold reserves, France another 20 percent. In addition, France had become the world's largest short-term creditor. The British accused both, but especially the French, of "not playing

[24] See J. M. Keynes, A Tract on Monetary Reform (1923), Pt. 3.

[25] Net capital exports were probably less. The prewar stock of overseas assets—£4,000m.—had been reduced to £3,700m. by 1929, largely owing to sales during the war.

[26] Aldcroft and Richardson, op. cit., p. 92.

the game"—in other words, of not taking their international responsibilities seriously, or more to the point, of not managing their internal policies so as to enable Britain to export more and thus carry out *its* managerial functions. But this ignored not only the nature of capitalist competition, but also the fact that both nations, being largely self-sufficient, were much less dependent on world trade than Britain. National interests were differently defined. In the British view, there was a world economy, with London as its apex. To the French, there were simply national economies which entered into relations of mutual and limited convenience. This issue now came to the forefront for the first time since the early nineteenth century with the collapse of the British hegemony.

The second weakness in Britain's postwar role was the radical deterioration in its short-term economic position. Its implications and consequences will be discussed in the next section. Here it is only necessary to make two points. First, in the absence of modern fiscal techniques, persistent domestic unemployment ruled out the prewar practice of frequent changes in discount rates. In fact, at precisely the moment (1918) when the Cunliffe Report enunciated the doctrine of an "automatic" monetary system, the state was being forced to take account of the domestic repercussions of monetary policy. Second, the general atmosphere of insecurity after the war transformed the cosmopolitan loan fund into a mass of "hot money," beyond the control of London or any center, seeking not employment at a reasonable rate of interest, but security against domestic disturbances, and capable in its panic flights of bringing about the collapse of currencies. The immediate cause of the downfall of the gold standard in 1931 was the movement of this "refugee" money.

The third factor, on which the other two ultimately hinged, was the further decline in Britain's own economic position. British exports had regained only 81 percent of their prewar volume by 1929, despite the fact that the volume of world trade grew in this period by 27 percent. Britain's share of world exports declined from 13.9 percent in 1913 to 10.8 percent in 1929, its share in the export of manufactured goods from 29.9 percent to 23.6 percent.[27] At the same time, the volume of imports was 15 percent above prewar by 1929, though the increasing trade deficit implied by these figures was partly offset by an improvement in the barter terms of trade. The results were not only a lessened capacity for foreign lending, but a growth in domestic unemployment, which averaged 10 percent during the decade. The argument that it was necessary to restore the gold standard in order to restore the British economy to health is a classic case of confusing cause and effect: It was the British economy that had to be restored to health in order to enable London to influence the working of the gold standard. "The City suffered from the foolish ego-centricity of the fly on the rim that thought it made the wheel go round." [28]

The Economic Consequences of Mr. Churchill?

Ever since Keynes's famous essay of that title was published in 1925 it has been generally accepted that, in returning to the gold standard at the prewar parity, Britain "overvalued" its currency. The argument is that, with internal prices as they were, the cost to foreigners of buying British goods was fixed too high to enable the sale of sufficient exports to keep the domestic economy at full employment. At the same time, the relatively high interest rates needed to protect convertibility at the restored parity made borrowing for domestic purposes unattractive. With a lower parity (Keynes's own suggestion) Britain, it is claimed, would have been able to increase its exports enough to restore full employment. By implication, a lower parity would have given Britain a better economic base

[27] Derek H. Aldcroft, *The Interwar Economy: Britain, 1919-1939* (1970), p. 253.

[28] Pollard, op. cit., p. 16.

from which to manage the restored gold standard system.

There are several doubtful points about this argument. First, the phenomenon of Britain's postwar mass unemployment had preceded stabilization by at least five years. Indeed, it appeared for the first time when the pound was floating downward and remained at a high level throughout the period of the "float." [29] Second, the argument that stabilization at a lower parity would have helped British exports assumes that Britain's competitors would have refrained from "competitive devaluations." But as R. S. Sayers remarks: "To anyone who reads the diary of Moreau, Governor of the Bank of France at the time, it is crystal clear that the French deliberately stabilized at a rate perpetuating the artificial advantage recently enjoyed by French export industries. . . . Hence, a lower level of the pound would have meant an even lower level for the French and Belgian francs." [30] But the fundamental mistake of the "monetary" arguments is surely the assumption that Britain's exporting difficulties dated only from the 1920s. In fact, Britain's exporting position had been weakening steadily since the 1870s, and but for mass emigration—there was a *net* emigration from Britain of almost six million between 1870 and 1914—a substantial unemployment problem would have developed in the prewar British economy. As Henry Clay remarks, Britain had "too many eggs in too few baskets." Before the war, cotton accounted for one-third, coal and steel for one-fifth of total exports. Britain was supplying 70 percent of the world's export of cotton manufactures, 80 percent of the world's coal exports, and practically the whole of the world's exports of ships. The spread of protection was already

[29] This is one reason why it is difficult to accept N. Kaldor's argument that a floating exchange rate would have increased exports sufficiently to have absorbed heavy unemployment in Britain's traditional export industries. (N. Kaldor, "Conflicts in National Economic Objectives," *The Economic Journal*, March 1971.)

[30] Sayers, op. cit., p. 93.

threatening this trade (except in ships) before 1914; after the war this process was accelerated.

> It was not so much the raising of existing tariffs that constituted the decisive changes; it was the narrowing of the gaps in the wall of tariffs through which or over which exports had to make their way. Before 1914 the gaps were numerous and wide, and British exports could always spread in new directions when defeated by a new tariff from one country; after 1920 the gaps were fewer . . . and the task of finding equivalent outlets for industries which held already such a predominant position in export markets . . . became an impossible one.[31]

The expectation of "recapturing our lost export markets" after the war rested mainly on the optical illusion of Germany's temporary removal as a competitor. From the mid-1920s, however, Germany regained and even improved on its old position. No doubt Britain's coal exports—despite the switch from coal to oil—would have benefited somewhat from a lower parity, but no "purposively managed currency" would have saved Lancashire from the double effect of the grant of fiscal autonomy to India in 1917 and the rise of Japanese competition, the new mills in both countries being largely equipped by British capital and know-how. It was the destruction of the privileged British market in India—the rise of Asia, not the overvalued pound, which destroyed the basis of the nineteenth-century British economy. If a lower parity "would have provided a better basis on which to solve those problems which centered around the transition of the industrial structure from the nineteenth to the twentieth century," [32] it nevertheless "remains difficult to conceive of a

---

[31] Henry Clay, "The Place of Exports in British Industry after the War," *Economic Journal*, June-September 1942, p. 147.

[32] Moggridge, op. cit., p. 79.

realistic full employment rate [of exchange] in the circumstances of the time." [33]

In view of Britain's deteriorating external position, the question arises: To what extent was Britain trying to manage the world economy on borrowed money? The evidence, admittedly unsatisfactory, is presented in the appendix. From this we can see that an annual current account surplus of over £200m. between 1911 and 1913 had been reduced to £111m. a year in the 1920s. Since over the period 1921-29 as a whole Britain was earning just about enough to balance its flow of long-term foreign lending, one might conclude that it had indeed scaled down its pretensions to the level of its capacity, though at a price in unemployment. But this assumption ignores the radical change in the short-term position. Even before the war London may have been moving into deficit on its short-term account.[34] As a result of the war, the short-term position grew unequivocally weaker. Although it is impossible to calculate the size of these balances precisely, London's net liability to foreigners must have been in the order of £500-£600 m. by 1928. Here was the basic crack in the British financial structure in the 1920s. Britain's current account surplus was simply not sufficient to balance both its long-term lending and its short-term debts. Instead of appropriating part of the surplus to liquidate those debts, Britain in fact increased them in the years 1924-27 by using short-term inflows to finance a rate of long-term lending far in excess of the current account surplus of those years. This deteriorating short-term position did not matter much as long as foreigners were content to hold sterling. But once the international li-

[33] Aldcroft, op. cit., p. 252 (note).

[34] See A. Bloomfield, *Monetary Policy under the International Gold Standard* (1959), p. 42. "For despite a widespread stereotype to the contrary, I am not at all convinced that from 1880-1914 Britain's short-term foreign assets did consistently exceed its short-term foreign liabilities."

quidity crisis developed in 1931, the balancing item itself became the item that had to be balanced. And this could not be done. The only method of liquidating London's liabilities was to devalue the pound.

According to David Williams, "it was this inability to either retain previously invested funds in London or to attract further investment by foreigners that was the root cause of London's short-term difficulties." [35] But in view of London's huge net liability this is rather like the plea of the insolvent tycoon who cries "bad luck" when his paper empire collapses. The truth of the matter is that the London bankers were determined to go on lending as lavishly as possible—for their own profit, but not without a sense of responsibility for the international system as a whole—and hoped that no one would notice that they were insolvent. And no one did until the Macmillan Report gave the world a glimpse of the true position in June 1931. More importantly, purely technical analysis of the composition of London's assets and liabilities ignores the political implications of the situation. London was not a financial Vatican City; it was the seat of a British political hegemony which its own financial activities helped to sustain. A surplus position gives a country important political leverage. Through foreign lending it can gain control of other countries' resources and to some degree dictate the terms of their participation in the international system. A surplus enables it to finance the foreign-exchange costs of empire and "peace keeping." All of this may be irksome enough to others, but when this imperial role, and the privileges which go with it, is based on borrowed money, it becomes doubly intolerable. French financial diplomacy directed against London in the dying days of the gold standard system cannot be understood except as a revolt against Britain's imperial claims which had lost their basis in economic reality. The French played the classic role of the spoilers of a spoilt system.

[35] Williams, op. cit., p. 522.

Toward an Empire Bloc?

At the heart of the nineteenth-century international economic system lay Britain's relations with its clients of the formal and informal empire. The centrality of this relationship to international trade and money flows gave Britain its role as manager or underwriter of the international system. With the disintegration of the wider system in the interwar years, there was an increasing tendency to see the economic future in terms of blocs. Imperial, regional, or continental self-sufficiency was raised as an explicit alternative to an "integrated" world economy, particularly by the fascist powers, but also by many in the United States and Great Britain. Russia, of course, had become largely autarchic by the late 1920s. The questions to be asked in this final section are: To what extent did Britain consciously try to develop an "empire option" in the 1930s? And to what extent was such an option available?

The view that the British elites came to see their future in imperial rather than international terms finds its support in a number of intellectual, political, and practical developments. What Professor Drummond has called the "imperial vision," comprising economics, defense, and social engineering, dates from the last quarter of the nineteenth century.[36] Its three critical ingredients have been well described as money, men, and markets. For Britain, the export of men and money would not only immediately reduce unemployment and employ excess savings, but also create sheltered export markets, based on common sentiment reinforced by tariff preferences. Defense would be helped by the retention of British subjects under the British flag, and social ills would be cured by increasing farmers

[36] See Ian H. Drummond's two books: *British Economic Policy and the Empire, 1919-1939* (1972) and *Imperial Economic Policy, 1917-1939* (1974).

rather than city dwellers. The Dominions needed capital and claimed they needed immigrants. Except for Canada, they certainly needed the British Navy. There was assumed to be a "natural" division of trade between British manufactures and empire primary products. British and empire interests in imperial development were thus assumed to be complementary. Essentially the empire visionaries wanted to reestablish nineteenth-century British supremacy on the narrower basis of formal empire "by means of preferential tariffs, state-aided Empire settlement, and subsidized capital export...." [37] Hobsbawm sees this as a conscious British strategy for survival.[38]

For the first time since the mercantile period, the idea of economic blocs was openly discussed in the interwar years. According to their chief British theorist, Leo Amery: "Once political issues, whether of defensive security, or of social reform, or of standard of living or of stability of employment, began to dominate the field, [the] system ... of economic individualism, and of its corollary, economic internationalism ... was doomed." The theoretical basis of Amery's rejection of the international division of labor was his view, also echoed by Keynes,[39] that most modern mass-production processes could be performed equally efficiently in most countries and climates. At the same time, Amery recognized that "the technical developments of modern production all demand so wide a range of varied natural products, so large a market to secure the maximum efficiency of mass production, so powerful a financial basis, that few of the existing countries into which the world is divided constitute economic units adequate to modern conditions." The solution to the paradox was neither national self-sufficiency nor nineteenth-century international-

[37] Drummond, *Imperial Economic Policy*, p. 35.
[38] Hobsbawm, op. cit., pp. 124-25.
[39] In his article, "National Self-Sufficiency," in *New Statesman*, July 8, 1933, p. 37.

ism, but rather the bringing together of nations "in groups large enough to satisfy the technical requirements of modern production, and yet also sufficiently held together by some common ideal, some permanent co-operative purpose, to enlist the forces of economic nationalism on their behalf." For Britain, that "wider basis, political and economic" was the British Empire.[40] The creation of the Ottawa Preference System in 1932, and the evolution of the sterling area can thus be viewed as attempts to translate into practice elements in the imperial vision. The fact that Neville Chamberlain, the son of the greatest imperial visionary of them all, was in effective charge of Britain's economic policy during this period strengthens the supposition.

In fact, the link between the imperial vision and what happened in the 1930s, either in intention or result, is extremely tenuous. Simplifying, we can say that the dominant trend during the decade was toward national, not imperial, self-sufficiency. Insofar as British leaders came to see an alternative to this, it lay in the conception of a reorchestrated world economy under American leadership.

It is not possible to see in the various arrangements Britain made with its Dominions in the 1930s much evidence of the "imperial vision." If the British delegation to Ottawa had any philosophic position, it was to restore world trade as rapidly as possible. Lowering interimperial tariff barriers was seen as a step toward this eventual aim. But there was not much philosophy of any kind at Ottawa. Delegates to Ottawa acted as representatives for their national industrial or agricultural interests, not as imperial politicians planning a glorious common future. At Ottawa divergent national interests were temporarily linked together by a set of fragile arrangements which had no real prospect of creative evolution.

The basic flaw in the imperial vision, which Ottawa ex-

[40] Leo Amery, *The Forward View* (1935), esp. pp. 111, 115.

posed, lay in the notion of a "natural" division between British manufactures and Dominion primary products. In reality, Canada, Australia, South Africa, and India were all interested in developing their manufactures, while Britain, for many different reasons, wanted to protect its agriculture. A further barrier to the construction of an imperial system lay in the extensive relationships still extant between Britain and other countries. For example, Argentina could only service its sterling debts by exporting to the British market, thus creating a triangular clash between British, Dominion, and Argentine livestock interests. The insufficiency of common interests gave Ottawa all the agonies of an EEC negotiation and few of the benefits.

The story of the Agreements themselves can soon be told. Britain wanted to expand its sales of manufactured goods to the Dominions and India. Therefore, it wanted them to lower their tariffs against British goods while maintaining their existing tariffs against foreign goods. The result, which would have been a net reduction in trade barriers, could then have been sold in England as a step toward freer trade, thus keeping the Cabinet united. Unfortunately, the Dominions were not prepared to give British imports an improved position against their home manufactures. In the end the only way this difficulty could be resolved was by agreeing on a set of principles (verbal formulas would perhaps be more accurate) to be applied to particular cases by tariff boards. These principles were that the Dominions would protect only those of their industries "which are reasonably assured of sound opportunities of success," and that protective duties should only be high enough to offset the lower British cost, not to give home producers an advantage against British ones. Thus, instead of the immediate concessions they had hoped for, the British merely won promises of better behavior in the future.[41] In

---

[41] See Drummond, *Imperial Economic Policy,* op. cit., pp. 238-39.

return, the Dominions wanted guaranteed free and unrestricted entry for their products—wheat, timber (Canada), frozen beef (Australia), frozen lamb, butter (New Zealand), and a wide variety of canned and other fruit—plus higher duties on foreign foods.[42] But, as Drummond has pointed out, British agriculture "needed protection from the Dominions as much as from foreign countries." [43] Britain made more tangible concessions than the Dominions. It promised to impose no duties on empire meat until mid-1936 and no quotas until July 1, 1934, and pledged strict control of nonempire foreign imports of chilled beef, frozen beef, veal, mutton, and lamb for five years. (This hit Argentina especially hard.) It allowed Dominions free entry for their dairy products and fruits for three years while imposing higher duties on foreign products also for a specified period. (This situation hurt third countries like the United States and the Scandinavians.) Only on wheat did the British manage to avoid any concession of substance by retaining the right to lower the duty on foreign wheat if empire wheat prices rose above world prices, or if empire production could not supply British needs. As Drummond concludes: "There was little Imperial warmth in the conference bargaining." [44]

The chief result of Ottawa was to divert trade toward Empire countries without, however, "clearing the channels of trade between them" as Stanley Baldwin had hoped. Interimperial trade rose as a proportion of the trade of all Empire countries, but the trade of none of them regained its 1929

[42] Under the Import Duties Act of 1932, Britain had adopted a protectionist system, thereby abandoning almost a century of free trade. However, it had exempted Dominion products from the new duties. At Ottawa the British used this free list as a bargaining counter to extract concessions from the Dominions.

[43] Drummond, *Imperial Economic Policy*, op. cit., p. 253.

[44] Ibid., p. 252.

levels. The Dominions benefited more from the preference system than did Britain. Britain promised to continue to exempt empire products from duties imposed under the Import Duties Act in return for vague promises. The results of this bargain were reflected in the trade flows. British exports to Empire countries increased by £13m. in 1933 and £28m. in 1937 over their projected increase from the 1922-30 levels, but empire exports to Britain rose by £46m. in 1933 and £98m. in 1937 over the levels projected from the same period. At the same time, the agreements probably hurt Britain's exports to third countries, by depriving Britain of bargaining flexibility and deflecting foreign competition into other markets. The British had been outnegotiated. With a century of free trade behind them, they had no experience in this type of bargaining. "Surely it is extraordinary that such neophytes should attempt to construct seven major trade agreements in thirty-one days."[45]

But it is important to stress that the results, adverse or otherwise, were relatively unimportant. The fundamental fact is that Ottawa did not help Britain to recover, in a smaller area, its previous trade dominance. This meant that prosperity could no longer be based on export industries even if the export market were conceived as an imperial one. In this sense, the Ottawa Agreements increased, not diminished, the trend to national self-sufficiency.[46]

The failure to clear the channels of trade also resulted in the blocking of empire finance. Britain no longer had a current account surplus. It restricted imports so that borrowers could not pay their debts in exports. In any case, the "home-market-led growth" made home investment more attractive than foreign investment. The sterling area (Empire countries plus Scandinavia and Argentina) thus differs from the old gold

[45] Ibid., pp. 286-87.
[46] Ibid., p. 284.

standard system in the crucial respect that London was no longer a source of finance, long-term or short-term, which of course reinforced restrictive commercial policies. As far as long-term capital movements go, there was a net inflow of capital into Britain during the 1930s representing repayment and realization of foreign assets. This, together with defaults and refundings, at a lower rate of interest, reduced the income from invisibles, from £362m. in 1929 to £230m. in 1938. Following the disastrous experience of 1931, the short-term money market was heavily controlled. What the Bank of England did essentially, through the Exchange Equalization Account, was to sterilize short-term inflows by converting them into gold, thus preventing them either from appreciating the pound or upsetting domestic economic activity. Since France was the only major country remaining on the gold standard between 1933 and 1936, it was the chief victim of these policies. The British adoption in the 1930s of the French technique of the 1920s of sterilizing short-term money shows how far the conception of British national interests had changed since 1931.[47] The inflow of gold and short-term funds was much larger in the 1930s than the deficit on basic balance, but some part of it—the "sterling balances," which amounted to £500m. in 1939—may have paid for some of Britain's import surpluses with Empire countries. The change in Britain's external position may be illustrated by the simple fact that whereas in the 1920s it was borrowing money to increase its foreign investments, in the 1930s it was selling off those investments and borrowing money to pay for its vital imports.

By the mid-1930s, it was becoming increasingly evident that the imperial option was failing to provide a satisfactory basis for Britain's economic development. Britain was growing

[47] For a summary of the operations of the EEA, see L. Waight, *The History and Mechanism of the Exchange Equalisation Account* (1939).

more self-sufficient, willy-nilly, as exports failed to recover. By 1938, with the home market expanding far faster than the export market, exports accounted for 11 percent, and imports for 18 percent, of the GNP, compared with 28 percent and 31 percent respectively in 1913. But as these figures show, the trend toward self-sufficiency was stronger on the export than on the import side. In 1938, British exports were only about 70 percent of their 1929 volume; imports, on the other hand, were about the same as in 1929. "The problem," as Aldcroft explains, "was not the unusually high level of imports but rather the failure of exports to expand to meet the importing propensity of a growing economy." [48] The growing gap between the volume of exports and imports was compensated to some extent by an improvement in the terms of trade. But the fact remains that exports and "invisible" items together could no longer pay for imports. As W. A. Lewis remarks: "Britain was living on her capital." [49]

The obvious strategy, which the British government pursued as late as November 1936, was to try to adjust the balance of the Ottawa Agreements in Britain's favor. Whether this would have succeeded is doubtful. Failure would probably have increased the already strong pressure for further protection. From the end of 1936, however, political considerations began to draw Britain, France, and the United States together in face of the growing fascist threat, thus opening out economic possibilities of a quite different nature.

Although the British had experimented in national and imperial economics, they had never fully abandoned their internationalist past, which remained an integral part of the political culture. As we have seen, the Ottawa negotiations were expected to lead to freer trade; at the World Economic Conference of 1933, the British government hoped to engi-

[48] Aldcroft, op. cit., p. 256.
[49] Lewis, op. cit., p. 85.

neer the restoration of the gold standard with a suitably devalued pound. Again, the sterling area was never seen as an
exclusive monetary unit. "Stability within the sterling area is
not incompatible with the general restoration of greater stability with the dollar and gold; indeed it makes an important
contribution towards the restoration of a common standard." [50] Politically, most British public figures continued to
believe that autarchy led to, and was a preparation for, war.
Moreover, it was increasingly felt that the attempt to
maintain exclusive possession over empire markets and resources furnished the "have-not" powers with a plausible argument for expansion.[51] "To restore the open door in the
dependent colonies seems to the naked eye the first main
contribution that the British empire could make to world
appeasement."[52] These intellectual considerations would not
themselves have been decisive; but when the British discovered that the price they would have to pay for a greater
measure of security against Germany was substantial concessions to America's growing economic internationalism, their
own intellectual traditions did not stand in the way.

The first steps toward reorchestrating the world economy

[50] J. H. Richardson, *British Economic Foreign Policy* (1936), p. 55.

[51] The argument of Germany, Italy, and Japan was that since
Britain had an empire why shouldn't they. The fallacy in this was
that Britain did not "have" an empire in the way in which these
powers hoped to "have" theirs. The Dominions were independent
nation states. India had achieved fiscal autonomy in 1917, and the
Government of India, though nominally subject to Westminster,
ran the country in what it considered to be India's interest. The fact
that the British empire was no longer an empire in the mercantilist
sense was an important reason why the British were unwilling to do a
deal with Hitler on the basis of the empire for the British and Europe
for the Germans.

[52] H. V. Hodson, in E. Thomas Cook, ed., *The Empire in the
World* (1937), p. 56.

came with the Tripartite Monetary Agreement of 1936 and the Anglo-American Trade Agreement of 1938. The first, as Kindleberger observes, "constituted a significant step in rebuilding the international economic system." [53] The United States, Britain, and France agreed to hold their exchanges steady with each other for twenty-four hours and not to indulge in competitive currency devaluations. It was contemptuously described as a "gold standard on a twenty-four hour basis," but for the first time since 1933 "exchange rates were discussed, technical arrangements made and international cooperation built in the monetary area."[54] The most significant fact, however, was that only one signatory—the United States—felt strong enough to peg its currency to gold, that is, to pay gold on demand for dollars. This was the real start of the dollar's career as "underwriter" of the international economic system. The Anglo-American Trade Agreement of November 17, 1938, according to its most fervent advocate, Cordell Hull, "reversed the protectionist trend that had developed [in Britain] in the previous eight years, and made major breaches in the preferential tariff wall erected around the British Empire in 1932." [55] Britain's acceptance of it was dictated by the need to gain American support in the looming conflict with Germany. By these measures, Britain took its first tentative steps back to globalism, but this time as follower rather than leader.

The argument of this section has been that the empire option was no longer viable in the 1930s, if it ever had been. The competitive and plural aspects were starting to outweigh the complementary and unequal ones; and because this was so,

[53] Kindleberger, op. cit., p. 257.

[54] Ibid., p. 260.

[55] As Hull remarked: "The agreement was of marked benefit to American agriculture, removing duties entirely on wheat, lard, and flour and reducing them materially on rice, apples, pears, and some canned fruits." Cordell Hull, *Memoirs* (1948) vol. I, p. 530.

Britain could no longer provide the leadership needed to create and sustain an imperial system. Hence, the increasing British tendency of the decade was not toward imperial, but toward national, self-sufficiency. However, this did not seem a satisfactory solution to Britain's long-run economic problem. Politically, neither imperial nor national self-sufficiency could any longer protect Britain from its more dynamic American and German challengers. Britain rejected both the national and imperial options to take up the German challenge, in order to secure for itself a privileged place in an American-run system which was more congenial to British traditions than the privileged place in the Greater German system which Hitler offered. In other words, the imperialist program was at least partially realized on an Atlantic basis under American, not British, leadership.

Conclusion

The importance of Britain's formal and informal imperial relationships for world trade and finance gave Britain a key role in sustaining the international economic order before 1914. Even before 1914, however, its weakened position within its own system, as well as the decreasing significance of the imperial system to the international economy as a whole, had begun to destroy its ability to function as underwriter. Helped by the war, the process of disintegration culminated in the interregnum of the interwar years when there was no international system at all. Contrary to what has been argued, the dominant trend in the 1930s was not toward empire, but toward national self-sufficiency: What was true of Britain was true also of Germany, Italy, the United States, and Japan.

The major conclusion of this survey is that there is no easy road to a negotiated pluralism. Indeed, the historic alternative to an international economic system managed by a single power—the only type of system we have had so far—seems to be national self-sufficiency, since empires are out of date unless they are communist. History may suggest, therefore, that prospects for reestablishing an international monetary system or even building regional systems on the basis of a negotiated pluralism are not very bright. But, of course, history is no infallible guide to the future.

APPENDIX
U.K. Balance of Payments, 1880-1939
(millions of pounds)

	Trade Balance	Net Income from Invisibles	Current Account Balance	Net Long-Term Investments	Basic Balance	Net Gold Movements	Short-Term Capital Movements	Residual or Balancing Item
1880	-121	154	33	-36	-3	+3		
1890	-86	194	108	-99	9	-9		
1900	-167	213	46	-38	8	-8		
1910	-143	317	174	-167	7	-7		
1911	-122	324	202	-197	5	-6		1
1912	-144	346	202	-197	5	-5		
1913	-132	367	236	-224	8	-12		4
1921	-165	284	119	-116	3	11		-14
1922	-77	250	173	-135	38	13		-51
1923	-98	267	169	-136	33	16		-49
1924	-211	282	71	-134	-63	12		51

Year								
1925	−259	306	47	−88	−41	10		31
1926	−339	324	−15	−85	−100	−12		112
1927	−265	347	82	−105	−23	−3		26
1928	−233	356	123	−108	15	−7	23	−31
1929	−259	362	103	−47	56	16	−27	−45
1930	−282	310	28	−19	9	−5	17	−21
1931	−323	218	−105	1	−104	23	−99	170
1932	−217	166	−51	21	−30	−17	−100	147
1933	−196	196	0	−6	−6	−201	179	28
1934	−221	214	−7	−36	−43	−142	26	159
1935	−185	217	32	−40	−8	−56	−54	118
1936	−260	243	−17	26	9	−227	129	69
1937	−339	283	−56	11	−45	−99	−12	156
1938	−284	230	−54	40	−14	74	−137	77

Sources (1) 1880-1913: B. R. Mitchell and Phyllis Deane, *Abstract of British Historical Statistics*, p. 334. This series is not strictly comparable with the interwar years; for long-term movements, see Matthew Simon "The Pattern of New British Portfolio Foreign Investment, 1865-1914," in J. H. Adler, ed., *Capital Movements and Economic Development* (1967), pp. 52-53.

(2) 1921-38: Aldcroft, op. cit., pp. 261-63.

London's Foreign Liabilities, 1927-1931 *
(millions of pounds)

Date	Assets †	Liabilities ‡	Net Short-term Foreign Liabilities
June 30 1927	122.9	376.0	253.1
December 31 1927	139.7	419.2	279.5
June 30 1928	165.4	443.3	277.9
December 31 1928	200.5	502.9	302.4
June 30 1929	202.5	453.8	251.3
December 31 1929	175.7	451.1	275.4
June 30 1930	175.3	456.6	281.3
December 31 1930	161.0	434.5	273.5
March 31 1931	152.9	407.1	254.2

* Data taken from table in Walter A. Morton, *British Finance*, 1930-1940 (1943), p. 36. Reprinted there from the Macmillan Report, pp. 42-43.

†Total sterling bills accepted on foreign account.

‡Aggregate of deposits, bills, and so forth held in London on foreign account.

Note: The Macmillan Report's estimates of London's liabilities are generally reckoned to be far too low. David Williams writes (op. cit., p. 528): "Foreign liabilities in June 1930 would thus seem to have been of the order of £750m. –£760m.," compared with the Macmillan Report's total of £456.6m. These are, of course, gross liabilities. Aldcroft (p. 273) estimates a net liability of £430m. in June 1930. As liabilities had been run down since 1928, the assumption of a net short-term liability of £500m. –£600m. in that year does not seem unreasonable.

CHAPTER 5

Preparing the American Ascendancy: the Transfer of Economic Power from Britain to the United States, 1933-1944

BENJAMIN M. ROWLAND

The task I set myself in the following essay was to explore some of the forces underlying the transfer of economic leadership from Britain to the United States and to set this series of events in the framework of the book's common inquiry, that is, whether an economic system needs a leader at all. Although slow to intervene in the world of international politics, post-New Deal America moved quickly to assert several cherished economic principles, arguing that if the world adopted them, a durable peace would follow.

Britain and France did not especially want (nor in my view did they need) an American-determined economic system, but an American alliance. Out of distress they took the former and hoped it would lead to the latter. My essay and Robert Skidelsky's differ over whether Britain had a viable economic alternative to the American-led system. To Skidelsky the economic empire to which Britain turned in 1932 only made further decline inevitable. My own view is that the failure of the economic empire flowed more from United States' opposition than from its own inherent structural weaknesses. Moreover, there was little in American self-interest to justify the degree of opposition to Britain which materialized.

In the dozen years from the "First New Deal" to the conference at Bretton Woods, the United States joined in three efforts to restore stability to the world's major currencies. The first attempt, at the London Economic Conference (1933), ended in failure and the second, the Tripartite Agreement (1936), in low-level compromise.[1] Bretton Woods, however, saw the dollar installed as the key currency, and the United States as the single stabilizer of a system which would endure for more than two decades beyond the end of hostilities.

Until very recently few would have seriously disputed the West's collective good fortune in the outcome, for the dollar provided the foundation for a period of growth with stability unprecedented in modern history. Those remaining skeptical about the prime importance of a stabilizer in the international economy could be invited to ponder the lessons of interwar

[1] For a more detailed discussion of these negotiations, see the essays by Cleveland and Kooker in this volume.

history where, it is said, a festering economic crisis gave birth to a system of political-economic blocs which, in turn, led to war.

As happens not infrequently, however, the changing present obliges a reconsideration of the past. And today, although there are many persons who would hope to see the dollar restored to its recent preeminence, there are many others who believe that it is the dollar's preeminence itself which has been the monetary system's most serious flaw.

The difficulties in reaching common agreement over a monetary system are, of course, broadly political as well as economic. Though the state of the monetary system at a given moment may reflect a host of technical difficulties, it also frequently expresses the conflict in political aims and ambitions among its principal members.

This essay explores the political dimension of the interwar stabilization attempts in Anglo-American relations and the pattern of events which allowed them ultimately to be resolved in America's favor. While not denying that formidable technical obstacles stood in the way of improved economic relations, it is primarily the story of how Anglo-American rivalries in their broadest sense become entangled with, and hence complicated further, ongoing plans for monetary and economic reform.

Prologue: The View from Britain

In a widely held British view stabilization and monetary reform in the interwar period were special instances of a far broader question in Anglo-American relations; namely, should Britain yield to America's growing power or attempt to pit herself against it? Political and economic wisdom seemed to counsel opposite strategies.

In the logic of politics one did not join with, but confronted, the most powerful actor in the international system by combining with other lesser actors to create a rough balance of power. Economic logic, at least of the prevailing liberal sort, counseled a different strategy. Since the best economic system was the one which was largest and most open, one did not oppose the most powerful actor in the system, but joined with him to reap the advantages of stability which he alone could provide. The two views confronted each other as a paradox; pluralism, the political safeguard of one system, was the economic impediment of the other. How did these conflicting perspectives operate in practice?

By the 1930s, there was nothing original in the notion that America would challenge and probably supplant Britain as the world's foremost power. Indeed, fifty years before the Great Depression, William E. Gladstone saw America replacing Britain as the "head servant in the great household of the world." In the manner of one who views events from afar, Gladstone felt "no inclination to murmur at the prospect. . . . We have no more title against her than Venice, or Genoa, or Holland has had against us." [2]

Not everyone, to be sure, held Gladstone's views, especially as the moment of transfer loomed nearer. Following World War I, a growing neomercantilist group in Britain argued that not only was state power essential to undergird an economic order, but that leadership of the system itself was the source of substantial seigneurage benefits. In this view, the Gladstonian vision was little more than a polite capitulation. Liberalism was a strategy suited to a stronger Britain with fewer rivals. If Britain's failing strength no longer permitted that domination of the world at large which made the liberal solution attractive, her strength could at least be turned to winning a privileged position in a substantial part of the world. In the neomercantilist view, British weakness and economic self-interest were two powerful arguments for a British-led economic bloc. For some, Britain's best alternative to gradual decline

[2] William E. Gladstone, "Kin Beyond Sea," *North American Review*, vol. 127, 1878.

within a liberal system seemed to lie precisely in an imperial economic bloc with its own currency and preferential system of tariffs. In the interwar years, this viewpoint found its leading spokesman in Leo S. Amery, a former Colonial Secretary and longtime activist in empire affairs. Unlike Gladstone, with his vision of a peaceful and legitimate devolution of power from Britain to the United States, Amery viewed America as the wrecker of economic order generally and of Britain's place within it in particular. America's vast size and parochialism made that country ill-suited to succeed Britain as world economic leader. "The international gold standard has broken down," Amery observed in 1931, "because it has proved incapable of coping with economic nationalism, more particularly when that nationalism has developed on the American scale. To restore it requires a measure of international agreement . . . which is today unattainable." The easier alternative, "because it is within our control," was to reduce American export balances and increase sterling area trade, a move which would, "by definition" strengthen the sterling standard.[3]

Amery's solution was a rival economic nationalism centered on Britain, her dependent colonies, and the Dominions. It found its justification not only as a way of recovering from the depression, or as a counterpoise to American power, but as a political-economic imperative in its own right. If Britain returned to the old liberal system of open trading and stable exchanges, Amery believed, she would dissipate her economic resources and ultimately lose her standing as a world power. A prudent policy—combining retrenchment and empire development—might allow Britain to mend and retain something of her former stature. Otherwise, Britain's decline would be swift and inevitable.

With the collapse of sterling in September 1931, events appeared to move Britain's economic policies in Amery's direction. But tempting as these separatist solutions were for

[3] Leo S. Amery, *My Political Life*, vol. 3, pp. 417 ff.

many, several key issues in Anglo-American relations constrained Britain's scope for independent action. The war debts question was one. Put simply, although Britain viewed war debts as morally untenable and economically ruinous, she feared the consequences of default, with its implication of an end to sterling's international role, even more. With good behavior, Britain might win a further moratorium, rescheduling, or even forgiveness. Another factor was the price of sterling itself. With sterling well below the dollar—sterling parity which prevailed before September 1931—Britain was willing to pay a great deal to keep the dollar from following sterling down and so retain the presumed advantages for British exports. For these and other reasons, until the London Economic Conference in June 1933, Britain, if not exactly on her best behavior, took great care to avoid alienating the United States irreparably. But to no avail.

Far from stabilizing as Britain hoped, Roosevelt pushed the dollar down to a point even below the old dollar-sterling rate. The war debts question lingered for nearly another year, until Britain allowed herself to be declared in default in April 1934. Roosevelt's lack of cooperation allowed critics like Arnold Toynbee to task the United States for a "spirit of national solipsism," rivaling Hitler's withdrawal from the League of Nations' disarmament talks.[4] But it also gave Britain a rare if shortlived freedom to follow economic policies akin to those favored by Amery and others.

To the Tripartite Agreement:
The View from the United States

Over the course of the 1930s, America's political-economic policies moved from a self-absorbed nationalism to economic internationalism coupled with political neutrality. To those

[4] Arnold Toynbee, ed., *Survey of International Affairs*, *1933* (London: Oxford, 1934), p. 27.

who would become America's allies, the latter was small improvement over the former. In this regard, the "real" lesson of the 1930s was perhaps not that economic internationalism was essential to the world's well-being, but that success in enlarging the sphere of economic activity (which might or might not have been critical to recovery) would require comparably increased political guarantees.

With the American decision to revalue gold, the world split into three principal currency blocs—each corresponding roughly to the political-economic sphere of influence of its leading member. On the European continent, France led a gold bloc made up of countries determined to maintain the gold values of their respective currencies. Britain's sterling bloc was a hodgepodge of countries, based on but not limited to the empire, tied to the mother country in diverse ways for reasons of sentiment and economic expediency.[5] Finally, a dollar bloc comprehending much of the Western Hemisphere grew up around the United States.

Whether the blocs were a good in themselves, an unqualified "bad," or only a useful expedient on the way to recovery were questions on which there was little agreement either within the leading countries or among them. As noted above, Britain had developed the case for her own imperial bloc to a high level of sophistication. The British were less than eager, however, to accord the same rights of preferential association to other nations and, in 1933, effectively vetoed a regional arrangement among Belgium, Luxembourg, and the Netherlands.[6]

[5] Some in the sterling bloc tied the value of their currencies to the pound, while others simply held the pound as a reserve asset. Others used the pound as only one among several reserve assets. See Imrie de Vegh, *The Pound Sterling: A Study of the Balance of Payments of the Sterling Area* (New York: Scudder, Stevens and Clark, 1939).

[6] Neville Chamberlain explained that his government could not countenance exceptions to most-favored-nation trade, other than full-fledged customs unions, "except those based on historical as-

France and the gold-bloc countries with their overvalued currencies could make perhaps the best logical case for a trading bloc—protection having long been understood to be the chief alternative to devaluation, but France feared alienating her two powerful neighbors, Britain and Germany, and so did not press the scheme.[7]

From time to time, even Roosevelt toyed with the notion of a world organized around blocs of countries "capable of being grouped into more or less logical and self-contained economic units. . . . [He] thought that the British Empire might be one; that Belgium, France, and Spain with its colonies might be another; that Germany, Holland, etc. might be another. . . . There would, of course, be a natural unit in the Far East."[8] A tolerance for the economic blocs of others, however, was the exception rather than the rule in American politics. Indeed, even during the so-called First New Deal, when American economic policies were at their most nationalistic, America's case against her bloc rivals in general and against Britain in particular was developing apace. Pronouncements against Britain's foreign economic practices soon became a staple of United States policy.

To justify his own gold and silver revaluation policies, Roosevelt pointed accusingly to the "beggar-thy-neighbor" devaluation of the British. America's exports had declined, he argued in October 1933:

sociation such as are already generally recognized," that is, except for the British Empire. See *Survey of International Affairs, 1933,* op. cit., p. 50.

[7] See Gilbert to Hull, October 27, 1934, *Foreign Relations of the United States,* 1934, vol. 1, p. 611.

[8] *FRUS, 1935,* vol. 1, pp. 375-76. Thomas Hewes, to whom Roosevelt revealed his thoughts, "suggested that such a plan would seem to require a very material rearrangement of the internal economy of particular countries. He [FDR] said this was true and they ought to do it anyway."

Not because our own prices, in terms of dollars, had risen, nor because our products were of inferior quality, not because we did not have sufficient products to export. But because, in terms of foreign currencies, our products had become so much more expensive, we were not able to maintain our fair share of the world's trade. It was, therefore, necessary to take measures which would result in bringing the dollar back to the position where a fair amount of foreign currency could again buy our products.[9]

Britain's Exchange Equalization Fund was another early target for Roosevelt's displeasure. Although the Fund was designed in theory merely to smooth day-to-day fluctuations in sterling, Roosevelt and his Secretary of the Treasury, Henry Morgenthau, tended to see in it a plot to keep sterling undervalued against the dollar. Be that as it may, the British Fund was no match for the President's gold-purchase policy, which drove the dollar price of sterling briefly as high as $5.50 before gradually allowing it to come to rest in the neighborhood of $5.00.

With Roosevelt's fitful blessing, Cordell Hull was also beginning to bring pressures to bear on Britain's economy from the side of commercial policy. Hull's particular nemesis was the Ottawa system of imperial preferential tariffs, which he considered to have been "the greatest injury, in a commercial way" to the United States during his long public career.[10]

Hull and Morgenthau shared many important economic assumptions, but as America's economic policies turned grad-

[9] Radio address by FDR, October 22, 1933. Quoted in Lester V. Chandler, *America's Greatest Depression* (New York: Harper & Row, 1970), pp. 164-65.

[10] Quoted in Arthur Schlesinger, Jr., *The Coming of the New Deal* (Boston, 1959), p. 253.

ually away from their absorption with domestic recovery to restoring international stability, the differences in outlook between the two Secretaries took on more and more importance.

At first glance, Morgenthau gave every appearance of being the more nationalistic of the two. He undertook the task of executing the President's gold revaluation policy with a levity which would have shocked foreign central bankers and finance ministers had they been present to witness it. In fact, his view of the international economy was not as cavalier as it appeared; in any event, it was less so than Roosevelt's. For example, when Roosevelt announced in 1935 that he wanted to "tinker" with the price of gold to gain a momentary tactical advantage over the Supreme Court, Morgenthau drew the line by threatening to resign.[11]

Hull, by contrast, appeared the dedicated internationalist. Having won his first major victory in the Trade Agreements Act of 1934, Hull pressed on until his two principal rivals for the direction of America's commercial policy—George Peek and Raymond Moley—were obliged to resign from government. Hull believed currency stabilization the essential precondition for restored trade and embraced it accordingly. On this question as on others, he collided with the lingering economic nationalism of Morgenthau and Roosevelt. To win Britain's acquiescence to a round of tariff negotiations, Hull was willing to allow the pound to regain some measure of its advantage before the dollar devaluation. Morgenthau was furious; he denounced Hull for poaching on Treasury territory, calling his proposal "one of the most anti-New Deal broadsides he had seen in a long time." Roosevelt agreed, noting: "J.P. Morgan has as much influence in the State Department as he ever did."[12]

[11] John Morton Blum, *Roosevelt and Morgenthau* (Boston, 1970), pp. 60-63.

[12] Ibid., pp. 64-65.

Hull's willingness to adjust the dollar-sterling exchange in Britain's favor, had he been able to overcome the objections of Roosevelt and Morgenthau, might well have neutralized many of Britain's fears regarding stabilization. But his plans, in their totality, raised potentially even graver problems for Britain, and indeed, touched on the question of Britain's very political survival. Hull's policies, masquerading as internationalism, were in fact predicated on nationalism of the very narrowest kind.

Hull was schooled in a kind of "economic utopianism," not unlike the Cobdenite doctrines which dominated political-economic thought in Britain during that country's heyday and also had ample precedent in American history. His views recalled Washington's "Farewell Address," in which the out-going President urged Americans to avoid "entangling alliances" and encouraged them to build a robust commercial nation. They embodied something of John Hay's "Open Door Notes"—a plan at the turn of the twentieth century for ending imperial rivalries in China by granting equal commerical access to all interested parties. Hull imagined a world order in which an economic system was abstracted from, and substituted for, the normal play of power politics among nation-states. If the world would only adopt his economic principles, he was fond of saying, "there will no longer be need for spheres of influence, for alliances, for balances of power, or any of the special arrangements through which, in the unhappy past, the nations strove to safeguard their security or to promote their interests." [13]

From the vantage point of domestic American politics, Hull's emphasis on the pacific mission of economic internationalism made tactical good sense. It gave him leverage not only against his bureaucratic rivals of the First New Deal but also against extreme isolationists like Senator Gerald Nye who

[13] As quoted in Richard N. Gardner, *Sterling-Dollar Diplomacy*, rev. ed. (Boston, 1969), p. 6.

appeared to fear any and all excursions into the international economy because they would draw the nation into war. Yet the very reasons which explained the growing popularity of Hull's doctrines in the United States—they could be undertaken without a corresponding political commitment—also went far in explaining Britain's extreme reluctance to embrace them.

Britain's response to America's nascent economic internationalism is fairly summed up in the position of her Chancellor of the Exchequer, Neville Chamberlain. Like most of his colleagues, Chamberlain's views were a compound of radical and traditional beliefs. The traditionalist in Neville Chamberlain insisted on a balanced national budget, regretted abandoning war debts payments to the United States (even though he had been among the most virulent critics of war debts in principle), and looked forward to restoring sterling to its former world primacy. On the other hand, in his radical incarnation, Chamberlain was among the principal advocates of a viable and largely self-sufficient imperial economy which he, like Leo Amery, viewed as Britain's last best hope for remaining a world power in an increasingly hostile world. He quite unambiguously saw the United States as Britain's major rival and was willing to promote Britain's goals at America's expense. In other circumstances Chamberlain might have adopted a less defiant attitude toward the United States. A commitment of political aid, for example, might have moved Chamberlain from his nationalistic course. But long experience had soured him to high-flown American rhetoric. By heeding the American will-o'-the-wisp, Britain had been thrust forward too often, to her own ultimate cost. Hull's economic idealism struck him as naive, self-serving and, unlinked as it was to any political commitment, positively injurious to Britain's international position. In self-interest, Chamberlain felt obliged to safeguard Britain's future in a world of economic blocs.

In the summer of 1935 conversations between William

Bullitt, then American Ambassador to Moscow, and Frank Ashton Gwatkin of the Foreign Office revealed the substantial gulfs existing between the British and American positions. Ashton Gwatkin indicated that the impasse might be broken by unilateral American trade concessions. Britain's monetary policy followed necessarily from a weak merchandise balance, due in no small measure to high American tariffs. Britain's negative trade balance was a constant drag on sterling. The pound regularly threatened to sink below the dollar—thereby leading to the loss of gold, rising interest rates, and continued deflation and unemployment. A reduction in the American tariff was the necessary corrective. But when Bullitt pointed out that Neville Chamberlain had "definitely stated that stabilization would not be acceptable to the British Government until war debts were settled," Gwatkin responded somewhat lamely saying that while he and Chamberlain both agreed that the war debts problem was "insoluble," he himself did not think that stabilization, "a declared goal of His Majesty's Government, was to be made forever dependent on the settlement of a problem which would never be solved." [14]

Chamberlain's linking of war debts to currency stabilization also served him well in keeping at arms' distance Cordell Hull and his Trade Agreements Program—a program regarded, not incorrectly, as a thinly disguised attempt by the Americans to pry open the imperial preferential trading system. Of course, Chamberlain's reluctance to engage the United States in a sweeping economic settlement reflected his preoccupation with Britain's strategic as well as economic position. Not trusting, indeed, almost thoroughly dismissing the possibility

[14] F0371 17880 A7471/3169/45, August 6, 1935. Bullitt, who could give as well as he got, informed Ashton Gwatkin that many observers in the United States regarded Britain's nonpayment of war debts as "an insurance against the United States ever again becoming involved in a foreign war. At the price of many thousand million dollars, the United States had acquired detachment."

of American support in a potential conflict, Chamberlain felt he could not further expose his country by dismantling the empire economy. In the abstract, the United States might be the preferable bulwark for Britain's faltering international position. But the empire, for all its problems, was the more reliable. Thus, in Chamberlain's mind, there could be no thought of appeasing America at the cost of the empire, especially since the course of appeasement held no certain prospect of American cooperation in time of crisis.[15]

Until the Tripartite Currency Agreement of September 1936, the stabilization question straddled a broad array of polemical issues within the United States and Britain and between them. In Britain, Chamberlain would not consent to a discussion of the issue without first receiving satisfaction for the accumulated political grievances between his country and the United States. Meanwhile, non-resolution acted as a forward line of defense against American incursions into empire preferences. In the United States, preoccupation with domestic recovery and widespread fear that foreign economic commitments must eventually lead to political commitments were sufficient to curb unilateral American initiatives. Mutual distrust and suspicion compounded the difficulties. It was not the most promising climate for concerting economic policies.

The Tripartite Agreement

A French currency crisis in March 1935 first alerted Morgenthau to the possibility of a stabilization agreement among

[15] The empire's strategic value to Britain during the 1930s has been vigorously contested by Corelli Barnett, *The Collapse of British Power* (1972). But even though there was a very serious prospect of Commonwealth neutrality in a European war, British officials believed that they could at least depend on the empire as a secure source of supply. The same was not true with the United States,

the dollar, the franc, and the pound. His reasoning, it seems, had little to do with the restoration of trade. The Treasury, as opposed to Hull's State Department, "did not think that such exchange fluctuations as were taking place really stopped any trade that would otherwise be undertaken." Instead, as Harry Dexter White explained to British officials later in the spring, American reasoning was twofold. Sooner or later, a collapse of the gold-bloc currencies—that is, France, Switzerland, and the Low Countries—was held to be inevitable. Better, then, that the bloc devalue together than to collapse one by one. Moreover, if Britain and the United States offered to cooperate with France and the others, they would be strongly placed to suggest acceptable limits to devaluation, thereby minimizing the damage to their own trade and reducing the danger of further competitive devaluations.[16]

Britain found the proposal singularly unappealing. As British officials saw it, the real problem was not the overvaluation of the gold-bloc currencies but the undervaluation of the dollar. Britain's Ambassador to Washington, Sir Ronald Lindsay, noted: "It was impossible to think of stabilization at current rates under such conditions. Our smaller gold resources would be swept away and we should be rapidly faced with the necessity for further deflation which is out of the question."[17] Lindsay disliked saying no to the United States on any issue, but in this matter he felt that "such communications as we have to make to America about stabilization ought to be couched in words of one syllable and written with insulting clarity." [18] In any event, France was no more eager to

---

doubly bound by the Johnson Act which prohibited lending to countries in default on war debts, and by the neutrality laws.

[16] PRO T188 116 X/K 1440, Sir Frederick Phillips - Harry Dexter White, memo of conversation, May 15, 1935.

[17] PRO T188 116 X/K 1440, March 13, 1935.

[18] Lindsay to Leith-Ross, March 29, 1935.

devalue than Britain was to stabilize. Morgenthau's initiative was thus brought up short.[19]

A further flight from the franc followed the German reoccupation of the Rhineland in March 1936 and rekindled Morgenthau's interest in stabilization. Eagerness to take a strong stand against the Germans and fear that an economic crisis might drive France to embrace fascism were two potent political reasons which now joined Morgenthau's economic calculations. After discussing the matter with Roosevelt, Morgenthau sent a message to Chamberlain through a British intermediary. To his surprise, Chamberlain expressed himself in complete agreement. In Britain, too, the overriding motive for stabilization was concern over the deteriorating political situation. But concern over the fate of France was joined by a general wariness at giving offense to the United States, since it was now clear that Britain would be dependent on the United States in the event of war. The decision to cooperate was not one that Britain reached with any great enthusiasm. It sprang, instead, from a failure of alternatives. Britain had explored and would continue to explore diplomatic options by which she might contain Germany and Japan without the aid of the United States, but the Stresa Front Strategy, which imagined a joint Anglo-French-Italian response to German aggression, grew less and less plausible after Italy joined the Spanish Civil War and pursued her own imperial ambitions in Abyssinia. Moreover, the imperial economic system, which was looked to by more than a few observers as Britain's ultimate haven, was itself increasingly faction-ridden. Quarrels over internal tariff levels and market shares for British, imperial, and foreign producers seemed to rule out forever a further concerting of imperial economic, to say nothing of political and strategic, policies. Thus, Britain dropped her objections to a measure of stabilization as she would later cease to resist a degree of trade

[19] French efforts to remain on gold are sketched in Paul Einzig, *World Finance, 1935-1937* (New York, 1937).

liberalization, less from the intrinsic economic merits of following such a policy than from a growing fear of alienating the United States.

The monetary order which followed upon the Tripartite Agreement was not, in fact, very orderly. In theory, the franc could devalue between 25.19 percent and 34.35 percent of its former parity; the dollar between 50 percent and 60 percent of its earlier gold parity; while the pound remained completely free. The facts, to be sure, suggested a somewhat more stable system. Since March 1935, the dollar-sterling rate had held steady in the neighborhood of $5.00. Trade recovery and increases in official gold stocks both seemed to augur well for continued stability. In the fall of 1936, even Neville Chamberlain was moved to express a note of optimism. With greater international cooperation, he declared in October 1936: "I do not see myself any insuperable difficulties in the way of our ultimately arriving again at a currency system based on the free exchange of gold." [20] As suggested above, however, Chamberlain's words probably flowed less from the heart than from the exigencies of an increasingly strained political and strategic situation. Significantly, it was Britain who attached the most stringent reservations to the Tripartite Agreement. British officials, for example, were responsible for the formula which would allow the Agreement to be abrogated on twenty-four hours' notice.

In the remaining years of peacetime, both Britain and France paid full lip service and more to the advantages of the Tripartite Agreement, although they found it in many respects quite cumbersome. Enjoined by the Agreement from imposing exchange controls or from making a further once-for-all devaluation, the franc drifted aimlessly downward for the next year and a half, from a rate of 75 to the pound before the Agreement to around 175 in the spring of 1938. The

[20] Bank for International Settlements, *Annual Report, 1936-37*, p. 27.

Agreement no doubt helped in preventing the downward pressure on one currency from becoming a competitive race to devalue among them all. On the other hand, the moral commitment not to resort to exchange controls and to maintain stability, enforced by the desire to stay in America's favor, was widely seen as the cause for delay in currency adjustments justified by fundamental economic conditions.[21] For technical reasons the pound had benefited disproportionately from the instability of the franc, as well as from the brief "dollar scare" in the summer and fall of 1937, but after March 1938 it also experienced downward pressures. The following nine months witnessed a marked decline in Britain's visible trade balance owing to the recession in the United States and Britain's own rearmament drive. Before the year was over, Britain had expended nearly a quarter of her official gold stocks (which peaked at 867 million pounds in March 1938) in the defense of sterling. Despite evidently sincere efforts to maintain parity, the dollar value of sterling fell by around 4 percent. Evidence suggests that only a fear of alienating the United States kept officials from allowing the pound to drop even further, for by 1938 Britain was fully committed to courting American public and official opinion through a major trade agreement, the terms of which, American officials insisted, would have to be renegotiated if the pound continued to fall.[22] Not economic logic but political necessity sustained the pound from

[21] Paul Einzig argues that French authorities resisted making a large, decisive, "once-for-all" devaluation, and instead allowed the franc to drift down slowly and in stages because of American (and some British) pressure to keep devaluation at a minimum. He also argues that since the franc's decline was essentially a reflection of domestic inflation and social turmoil, fears that France would obtain a competitive edge through devaluation were entirely unfounded. Einzig, *World Finance, 1937-1938*, (New York, 1938), pp. 69ff.

[22] See Department of State Archives, 611.4131/1776A, Feis to Morgenthau, September 9, 1938; and Foreign Office Archives, FO 371 21507 A8648/1/45, Treasury Memo, November 16, 1938.

mid-1938 to the beginning of the war in September 1939.[23]

By the end of 1938, the non-Axis powers were falling increasingly within the ambit of an American-led international economic system. To be sure, it was not yet the formal system to be called into being at Bretton Woods; but, for all practical purposes, the hierarchy of authority which would govern the postwar system had already been established.

What were the forces drawing Britain, France, and the United States together at the end of the decade which had been absent at the outset? To some extent, the nations had no doubt learned through hard experience that economic openness held out benefits unobtainable through policies of economic exclusivity. But, it strains credulity to argue that these were determining factors, for, in the eyes of many, the bloc policies which France and Britain were being pressed to abandon had more than sufficient compensating advantages to justify their perpetuation. The economic order of the late interwar period faithfully reflected a political order in which American found herself increasingly in a position to dictate, and Britain and France increasingly compelled to follow. However, despite America's favored position, conditions for a formal consolidation of economic power under American leadership remained absent because the United States was still unprepared to underwrite Britain's security. Britain could not bind herself to an unknown quantity; nor, indeed, could the United States demand many more concessions, for fear of driving Britain into a fundamental accommodation with Germany and the Axis powers.[24]

---

[23] For a similar conclusion see Lowell M. Pumphrey, "The Exchange Equalization Account of Great Britain, 1932-1939," *American Economic Review*, XXXII (1942), pp. 803-16.

[24] American fears of an Anglo-German accommodation might explain why Cordell Hull consented to the signing of the Anglo-American Trade Agreement in November 1938, despite British failure to meet many American demands. See my "Commercial Conflict

To the Bretton Woods Agreements

Entry into World War II provided America with leverage to reshape the world economy which her own earlier isolationism had ruled out. Consciousness of her swollen power and the unlikelihood of its continuation after the war also lent urgency to the project. Pierrepont Moffat, long active in America's British and Dominion policies, noted that "unless we availed ourselves of the present situation to obtain a commitment from the members of the British Empire to modify the Ottawa Agreements after the war, we would ultimately be virtually shut out of the Dominion markets." [25]

While the Treasury and the State Department fully shared the goal of a one-world economy under American leadership, each promoted somewhat different ways of attaining it. Hull's hopes for a world restored rested on Article VII of the British Lend-Lease Agreement signed in February 1942. In effect, Britain, for aid received during the war, would abide by nondiscriminatory trading practices in the postwar period.[26] Morgenthau approached the British problem from a different set of perspectives. In contradistinction to Hull, Morgenthau thought that foreigners would not agree to nondiscriminatory trade unless the United States lowered its own tariff walls. As this was unlikely to happen (because of growing anti-free trade sentiment in Congress), monetary policies increasingly appeared the better method. More importantly, perhaps, a premature commercial restoration boded ill for his own

---

and Foreign Policy: A Study in Anglo-American Relations, 1932-1938," unpublished Ph.D. dissertation, The John Hopkins School of Advanced International Studies, Washington, D.C., 1975, Chap. 8.

[25] Nancy Hooker, ed. *The Moffat Papers*, (Cambridge, Mass., 1956), pp. 352-53.

[26] See Gardner, op. cit., pp. 54-68.

stabilization plans. If Britain were obliged to trade freely after the war she would surely resist fixing the value of her currency in terms of gold.

Morgenthau's reservations about Article VII should thus not be mistaken for softness toward Britain. He simply saw a more direct route to the same goal. Given its control over Lend-Lease, it was a simple matter for the United States to mix grants of Lend-Lease aid with sales, and thereby control the level of Britain's reserves. In January 1943 Morgenthau recommended and Roosevelt approved that, for the duration of the war, British reserves would not fall below $600 million nor rise above $1 billion. Britain, thus weakened, would have no choice but to follow the American lead in a postwar monetary system.[27]

Hull, meanwhile, argued that Britain should be allowed more, not fewer, reserves; without them, she would never consent to commercial freedom after the war.

American plans for a new monetary order, which emerged in the Bretton Woods negotiations, complemented the other instruments of U.S. wartime economic policy, that is, they imagined American leadership over a clientele to some extent deliberately weakened by American policy.

The substance of the Bretton Woods Agreements is familiar and may be dealt with briefly. Testifying before the House Banking and Currency Committee, Dean Acheson summed up the agreement in the following four principles. Each country should: (1) define money in terms of gold; (2) keep money within 1 percent of its defined value; (3) not restrict current transactions in its currency; (4) consult the Fund before changing parity. These principles, said Acheson, were the rules of the game. Follow them, and the world would avoid the chaos of the interwar period.

---

[27] Morgenthau's efforts to curtail British reserves inspired Churchill to send the following to Roosevelt: "We have not shirked our duty or indulged in any easy way of living. We have already spent

It was no secret that America dictated the essential terms of the Bretton Woods Agreements. In his rival "Clearing Union" proposal, Keynes sought an initial commitment of $25 billion which might be supplemented later according to need. The commitment of a subscriber to the Clearing Union was "open-ended": it need not be limited to the size of his subscription: The object, Keynes argued, was to aim at "starting off every country after the war with a stock of reserves appropriate to its position in world commerce, so that without undue anxiety it can set its house in order during the transitional period." [28] In contrast, Harry Dexter White, author of the American proposal, held a much more restrictive view on these questions of liquidity. The assets for Keynes's Clearing Union were "bancor"—fiat money to be created by the common consent of the participants. In White's stabilization fund, subscriptions would be paid in gold and national currencies. Subscribers were protected by limited liability; they could lose no more than the total of their subscriptions. Moreover, White's Fund called for a substantially smaller volume of assets than Keynes's Clearing Union—$5 billion as opposed to $25 billion, and more rigorous rules concerning their use. Keynes would have the resources of the Clearing Union alleviate "undue anxiety" during the transition period. White, on the other hand, insisted that the fund use its re-

practically all our convertible foreign investments in the struggle. We alone of the Allies will emerge from the war with great overseas debts. I do not know what would happen if we were now asked to dispense our last liquid reserves required to meet pressing needs, or how I could put my case to Parliament without it affecting public sentiment in the most painful manner and that at a time when British and American blood will be flowing in broad and equal streams and when the shortening of the war even by a month would far exceed the sums under consideration." (*FRUS, 1944*, vol. 3, p. 46.) Over strong American objections, Britain succeeded in accumulating nearly $2 billion in reserves by the end of the war.

[28] Quoted in Gardner, op. cit., p. 85.

sources to rectify short-term imbalances—criteria which proved to be so strict that the Fund, as adopted, was unable to make any loans at all until 1947 and the emergence of the more generous American mentality associated with the Marshall Plan. The final figure for subscriptions to the Fund was $8.8 billion, a sum clearly more in keeping with the American than the British proposal.

On questions of adjustment—the manner in which a country would correct its imbalances—the British proposals enjoyed little more success. With an eye to Britain's likely future deficits, Keynes, in effect, had proposed that creditor nations bear the burden of adjustment.[29] Britain's single major victory in the Bretton Woods negotiations was to retain the "scarce currency clause"—a consolation prize, as Sir Roy Harrod saw it, for her wholesale concessions in other areas of substance. If the Americans persisted in running a surplus during the postwar period, that surplus would presumably be reflected in declining dollar balances within the Fund. When this occurred, dollars could be declared scarce and debtor countries allowed to discriminate against dollar goods until dollars became abundant again.

If the scarce-currency clause rendered Bretton Woods acceptable to the British, it hardly caused them to view the Agreements with enthusiasm. In Britain, as in the United States, certain groups found it impossible to reconcile Bretton Woods with their conception of national interest. The "die-hard" imperialists, eager not only to retain but also to consolidate the Ottawa system and sterling bloc, found able spokesmen in Leo Amery and Lord Beaverbrook, both

[29] An early version of White's plan contemplated a sharing of the adjustment burden between creditor and debtor nations, and gave the Fund powers to intervene directly in domestic economies to enforce its decisions. In later drafts, however, in deference to a conservative Congress, White deleted the Fund's powers of direct intervention.

members of Churchill's War Cabinet. The Bank of England, a quasi-official observer for interests in the City of London, also took strong exception to the Bretton Woods proposals on the erroneous assumption that Britain could manage by herself in the postwar period.

Keynes himself cherished no illusions about Britain's capacity for independent action. In the end, it was Britain's dependence (and not White's language, which he referred to contemptuously as "Cherokee") which persuaded him to support Bretton Woods. Sir Roy Harrod argues that Keynes, an economic nationalist during the 1930s, was converted to liberalism in the fall of 1941: "He, like the Americans, disliked reverting to the law of the jungle. His instincts were for international co-operation." [30] In the broadest sense, Harrod's interpretation is undoubtedly right. Keynes, like the Americans, preferred stability to chaos and multilateralism to bilateralism. But his search led him through regions of thought which were not immediately evident in American utterances on the subject. Conceptually, Keynes's Clearing Union proposal was the most grandiose of all his undertakings. It was a synthesis of his liberal thinking of the 1920s with his humanitarian nationalism of the 1930s. The Clearing Union proposal, properly executed, would marry a stable international system to the welfare state. Of America's commitment to international stability, there could be no doubt. But what of the other half of the equation? Keynes was disturbed by what he saw as intransigent dogmatism on the part of American officials. He regarded Article VII of the Lend-Lease agreement in its early form as "the lunatic proposals of Mr. Hull." [31] In the same spirit, he chided a colleague at the embassy in Washington for succumbing to America's point of view on commercial policy:

[30] Sir Roy Harrod, *The Life of John Maynard Keynes* (New York, 1951), p. 525.

[31] Ibid., p. 512.

As you know, I am, I am afraid, a hopeless sceptic about this return to nineteenth-century *laissez-faire* for which you and the State Department seem to have such a nostalgia. I believe the future lies with—(i) State trading for commodities; (ii) International cartels for necessary manufactures; and (iii) Quantitative import restrictions for non-essential manufactures.

Yet all these future instrumentalities for orderly economic life in the future you seek to óutlaw.[32]

Keynes's general suspicion of American motives spilled over into the Bretton Woods proposals as well. He was not cheered by the scarce-currency clause. It was, he declared, in 1943: "A half-baked suggestion, not fully thought through, which was certain to to be dropped as soon as its full consequences were appreciated. I cannot imagine that the State Department would put forward as its own solution the rationing of purchases from a scarce-currency country." [33]

Although the substance of the Bretton Woods proposals represented a major victory for the United States, the final document was a testament to the elusive nature of international agreements. What, in fact, would be the character of the final system? Keynes stoutly maintained that Bretton Woods was exactly the opposite of a gold standard. This was not, however, the view of the United States. Acheson applied his considerable skills in debate to bridge the apparent gap: "The British like to say that this is a departure from the gold standard. We like to say that this resembles the gold standard.

[32] Ibid., p. 568.

[33] Ibid., p. 547. His judgment was correct, for the scarce-currency clause referred only to a scarcity within the Fund and not the world at large.

Neither of us has any differences as to what the plan provides. We differ in the words we like to use about it." [34]

Ambiguous in its central points, the final document also contained enough safeguards to allow a member country to pursue virtually any course it wanted. There was, for example, Article IV, section 5 (f):

> The Fund shall concur in a proposed change (in parity) . . . if it is satisfied that the change is necessary to correct a fundamental disequilibrium. In particular, provided it is so satisfied, it shall not object to a proposed change because of the domestic, social, or political policies of the member proposing the change.

Taken at face value, the passage conceivably allowed a country deliberately to run up a large deficit, declare itself in fundamental disequilibrium, and be rightfully entitled to exchange adjustment. The difference between this and "competitive devaluation," as more than one critic pointed out, was difficult to discern.

Was There an Alternative?

The mutual exertions of the British and Americans at Bretton Woods, it might be argued, rendered the document void of any usefulness, especially for the critical transition period expected to last four or five years after the hostilities. The United States, by limiting the size and scope of the Fund, assured that it would not soon be a major source of dollars. By virtue of Articles IV and VII (the scarce-currency clause), the British could be reasonably confident that the Fund would not restrict their ability to devalue or discriminate in trade. In short, the Fund, in its final form, would not be particularly

[34] *Bretton Woods Agreement Act*, Senate Hearings, p. 23.

useful for either stabilization or recovery. To be sure, the architects of Bretton Woods were calling for not one, but two institutions—a fund and a bank. The fund would provide money for short-term stabilization, the bank for long-term recovery. But short-term stabilization implied a basically sound economic structure to begin with. Why then, have a fund at all? Why not, at least, defer its operations until recovery was a fact? Because, the United States argued, a durable peace must be based on sound economic principles. It was hard to break down the barrier of American rhetoric. In the end, the British, conscious of their dependence, did not try.

In the general circumstances prevailing some dominant economic role for the dollar was inevitable. At the war's end, the United States would hold $20 billion, nearly two-thirds of the world's $33 billion in gold reserves. It is difficult to imagine a system in 1945 in which the dollar did not play at least a correspondingly prominent role. But if American predominance was inevitable, the character and long-term pretensions of an American-led system seem more open to question.

Although to do so cuts against the grain of Hull and Morgenthau's most deeply held convictions, one cannot help but wonder what the postwar economic institutions might have resembled if the United States had not been so hell-bent on destroying the vestiges of Britain's interwar economic system. There was, in fact, an unofficial American proposal which opened with the premise that the United States should restore Britain's currency to at least a measure of its former eminence as rapidly as possible. This was the so-called key-currency plan of John H. Williams, a professor of economics at Harvard and a vice president at the Federal Reserve Bank of New York. Williams feared that in the intensity of debate, the real issues—the restoration of stability and multilateralism—had been lost to view. Bretton Woods, with its restrictive terms, would drive Britain to adopt the very measures the new monetary system was designed to prevent. Given the desirability of these goals, the main question, as

Williams saw it, was "whether we should approach this problem in terms of a general international monetary organization or whether we should begin with the major countries whose policies and circumstances will have a dominant effect on the character of postwar trade and currency relations and whose currencies are the chief means of international payments." [35] Other than a sort of specious internationalism, what was there to be gained by a fund "composed of a miscellany of 44 national currencies, most of which are not used as international means of payment," he wondered?[36] Williams did not imagine that his plan would lead to formal economic equality between Britain and the United States. On the contrary, America would be the senior and Britain the junior partner for some time to come. Moreover, because it was a contentious issue, Williams avoided rather studiously the political implications of his plan. "I have always intended to state my point in purely technical terms, without any implications about the Great Powers doctrine or anti-democratic processes that have sometimes been read into it," he insisted. As "a matter of logic as well as mechanics," it seemed to him inescapable that "in a world practically all of whose trading is done in one or another of these currencies [i.e., sterling or the dollar], the central fact must be the establishment between them of exchange stability around which other national currencies can be grouped."[37]

England would leave the war owing her creditors from $12 billion to $16 billion.[38] While these might be funded, there would be the further matter of large postwar deficits owing to

[35] Ibid., p. 326.

[36] Ibid., p. 320.

[37] John H. Williams, *Postwar Monetary Plans and Other Essays*, 3rd ed. (New York: Knopf, 1947), pp. xxxv-vi.

[38] "That England should have to bear it [the sterling balances] alone," Williams believed, "is just as questionable from the standpoint of equity as was the Inter-Allied debt." See ibid., p. lxxxvi.

the loss of foreign assets, foreign markets, shipping, and the need for large imports during the transition period. America's major task, as Williams saw it, was to create the conditions for Britain's speedy recovery, which implied bringing to an end the pernicious leveling instincts of Hull, White, and Morgenthau. "If this could be done, the task of general monetary and trade organization would not be difficult. If it is not done, I am becoming only more convinced . . . that the approach in terms of a general world monetary organization will fail."[39] Williams warned that the costs would be great: "The situation calls for heroic measures, going far beyond anything that the fund or the bank would legitimately undertake."[40] But he considered the results worth the undertaking.

Williams spoke not only for himself but for major New York banking interests as well. If the overt Anglophilia of his proposal did not rule out its serious consideration, the latter connection certainly did. For Morgenthau, at least, was waging a two-pronged war—to curb the power of England and the power of Wall Street in the international economy.[41]

Conclusions

Morgenthau's vision of international economic order did not long survive the ending of hostilities. Attacked first by the Wall Street interests, whose role he had hoped to supplant, it soon fell prey as well to the bleak realities of reconstruction

[39] Senate Hearings, p. 323.

[40] Senate Hearings, p. 324. Although Williams came closer than others to imagining the costs of reconstruction he, too, rather underestimated the final bill, placing it in the range of $5-6 billion. This may help to explain Keynes's rather abrupt dismissal of the key-currency scheme as one of "giving the United Kingdom $5 billion and telling the rest of the world to 'go hang.' " Williams, op. cit., p. xxi.

[41] Morgenthau stated publicly that his dominant objective as

and the Cold War.[42] Ironically, within three years of Bretton Woods, it was Williams's key-currency system and not the universalism of Hull and Morgenthau which best characterized the emerging economic order.

Poor judgment or lack of measure was not limited to the Americans alone. Curiously enough, criticism of the Williams plan came not just from those in America who saw it as a threat to dollar supremacy, but also from many in England who believed that it would rule out forever a restored international role for sterling. Thus, British policy resisted funding the overseas sterling debt, preferring instead to use the debt as the foundation for a closed monetary and trading unit not unlike the interwar imperial economy.

If America's interwar and wartime experience holds any lessons for post-Smithsonian monetary and economic order, they would seem to lie, not in making the case for a "single stabilizer" but in helping to recall how extraordinary were the circumstances which allowed such a structure to come into being in the first place, for in the final analysis, the preponderant stabilizing role which Morgenthau sought, and which others still hope to reattach to the dollar, would seem to depend on an accretion of power not likely to be repeated or sanctioned under conditions prevailing now or in the foreseeable future. As dollar hegemony was an accident of war, so its demise should perhaps best be understood as a by-product of recovery. In such circumstances, economic order is unlikely to be imposed from above. It must flow instead from a compact among various centers of power—centers which share

---

Secretary of the Treasury was "to move the financial center of the world from London and Wall Street to the United States Treasury," to found institutions which could be "instrumentalities of sovereign governments and not of private financial interests, to drive . . . the usurious money-lenders from the temple of international finance."

[42] The best discussion of the transition remains Gardner's *Sterling-Dollar Diplomacy*, op. cit., pp. 224 ff.

certain interests even as they compete vigorously in others. The system may be no more immune from abuse than any other system. But there is no reason why the normal restraints of prudent statecraft should not apply as well. Indeed, a system which recognized explicitly the intertwining of power and economic order may find in its own assumptions the best of all arguments for restraint.

CHAPTER 6

The Historiography of the Interwar Period: Reconsiderations

DAVID P. CALLEO

Rival versions of international monetary order find their corollaries in rival versions of international political order. The concluding essay explores the broad meanings of the pluralist and imperial variants of order in the world political economy as they affect our understanding of the past and influence our policies in the present.

225

International monetary issues often prove a particular expression, in economic metaphor, of general international political issues. The monetary system itself, moreover, has frequently been a principal arena in the struggle among states for preeminence and accommodation. Thus, our essays on international monetary policies during the interwar period not only demonstrate a close connection between money and politics, but provide major insights into the general history of the time. In this period, at least, monetary history shows itself a branch of general history. Moreover, the historiography of the monetary system reflects the same cleavage between imperial and balance-of-power interpretations which divides general historians on this period. These rival interpretations, based as they are on rival theories of the international state system, lead not only to different views of the past but to radically different prescriptions for the future.

The Imperial View

What will be described here as the imperial view has had wide currency, not only among British and American political and economic historians, but among American political and economic leaders, most notably those of a strong "Atlanticist" persuasion. The imperial view may be summarized thus: Without a hegemonial power dedicated to the status quo, or "world rule of law" or "structure of peace," and determined to uphold it, disorder and conflict are inevitable. Hence, although postwar American imperialists have often spoken of the balance of power, they give it a rather special definition: An overwhelming superiority of force held by the hegemonic power.[1] This imperial theory applied to the interwar period yields two dogmas of great service in orienting postwar American policy: First, appeasement of aggression is self-defeating; second, economic blocs lead to economic collapse followed by war. The general thrust of these principles, in effect, opposes international pluralism. As prescriptions proved by history, they are, of course, highly serviceable to rally support for America's postwar hegemony over the West.

Nowhere has this imperial perspective found purer expression than in the characteristic views of British and American historians about the international financial history of the interwar period.[2] In essence, the economic troubles of the in-

[1] For a straightforward and well-argued statement of the view and its consequences for the United States, see Eugene V. Rostow, *Law, Power and the Pursuit of Peace* (Lincoln, Neb., 1968), p. 124.

[2] See William A. Brown, *The International Gold Standard Reinterpreted* (New York, 1940), especially Book 3, Parts III and IV; Arthur I. Bloomfield, *Monetary Policy Under the Gold Standard* (New York, 1959); Charles P. Kindleberger, *The World In Depression, 1929-39* (Los Angeles and Berkeley, 1973); Derek H. Aldcroft and Harry W. Richardson, *The British Economy, 1870-1939* (London, 1969), p. 96; also Peter H. Lindert's more nuanced view, "Key

terwar era are traced to the decline of that financial hegemony which Britain is supposed to have exercised before World War I, and which no one, in particular the United States, successfully assumed afterwards. Upon what historical evidence is this imperial view based?

Before World War I, London was incontestably the world's biggest capital market, and sterling the most widely used currency for international transactions.[3] London's and sterling's preeminence have inclined imperialist scholars to describe the prewar gold standard as, in reality, a Sterling Exchange Standard. Britain exercised, it is said, world financial hegemony.[4] By setting London's Bank Rate, Britain is said to have set the money supply, not only for the empire and the economic dependencies in Latin America, but also for the continent and the United States.[5] British loans went to deficit countries,

---

Currencies and Gold, 1900-13," *Princeton Studies in International Finance* (Princeton, 1969), no. 24.

[3] World sterling holdings at the end of 1913 amounted to $455.5 million, of holdings of German currency to $152.3 million, and French franc holdings to $275.1 million—of which the Russian state bank held $221.8 million. See Lindert, op. cit., pp. 18-19.

[4] Brown's thesis is "that the relatively successful functioning of that [gold] standard before the war was due to the attainment by London of a central clearing position in the world's international financial system." Postwar "adjustments entailed the sacrifice of the positive contributions of a single dominating center to the successful operation of the international gold standard." Brown, op. cit., x, xi. Kindleberger's view is succinctly stated: "The world economic system was unstable unless some country stabilized it, as Britain had done in the nineteenth century and up to 1913. In 1929, the British couldn't and the United States wouldn't." Kindleberger, op. cit., p. 292. The same view is reflected somewhat by Skidelsky and Cleveland.

[5] The U.S. Federal Reserve system was not founded until 1914. The United States was, at that time, faithful to the international gold standard. Active American monetary management developed

thus financing development and avoiding those disastrous contractions in credit which would otherwise have occurred from the loss of gold. Britain's financial power, of course, rested upon a solid economic foundation. Its reciprocal trade relationship with the world's primary producers, vast industrial strength, and huge foreign investment earnings all reinforced its world financial preeminence.

Britain's economic power, in turn, went together with military and political power. While America and Russia were still preoccupied with filling their own empty spaces, and Europe's competing states canceled each other's strength, Britain's huge world empire and impregnable fleet provided the political power and prestige to sustain her financial role. Thus, it is said, sterling was the world's reserve currency—no one worried that sterling was not good as gold.

This view of the prewar system leads to a corollary analysis of the interwar system, which may be summarized roughly as follows: The British imperial structure was showing signs of strain by the turn of the century. Meeting the German challenge in World War I fatally weakened the foundation of Britain's position. In order to defeat Germany, Britain had to sell her foreign holdings and borrow heavily from the United States.

After the war, the British sought to reestablish the prewar system and regain their own position within it. By 1926 the pound was pegged to its prewar parity; a massive program of investments flowed out from Britain to restore the old overseas position. But British finance no longer rested on a sound base. Nineteenth-century savings had been lost. Industry was in decline. The City's capital now came increasingly from foreign short-term funds—borrowed short and loaned long.

---

only with the breakdown of the international system by the end of World War I. See Lester V. Chandler, *The Economics of Money and Banking* (New York, 1973), pp. 184-85.

Policies to protect the pound at its prewar level, after the French and Germans had devalued, further depressed the British domestic economy and blighted its industrial rejuvenation. Meanwhile, the French and the Americans refused, as the British saw it, to accept their responsibilities as creditor nations. The massive American and French gold inflows were not rerouted to London to provide liquidity for the essential financial services needed by the world system.

In the standard imperialist histories of this period, the French and American stereotypes both appear. The French are dogmatic, obstinate, selfish, and jealous. Their passion for impractical logic combines with their envy of the British, short-sighted greed, and general bloody-mindedness. They gloated over Britain's discomfort until the system collapsed. In any international system, the French, it is suspected, can be counted on to play the dog in the manger. The Americans, in contrast, are steeped in isolationism—loftily unconcerned with maintaining a system as such, but active to the point of brutality in serving their own greedy special interests. The Hawley-Smoot tariff stands as a landmark of this irresponsibility. This is the bad American-isolationist, run by special interests and irresponsible in the use of its great power—the America always lurking behind the populists.

To carry this imperial thesis to its conclusion: As the pound collapsed 1931, the world system broke down completely. International economic life dried up as nations turned to mercantilist blocs. Economic nationalism—reflected in the uncooperative attitudes earlier—now turned to beggar-thy-neighbor devaluations, high tariffs, controls, and planning. The depression deepened. In the end, recovery came through rearmament. The economic blocs, especially that of the Nazis, reflated their economies by preparing for war and intensified the state's power over domestic life. Economic conflict among these armed nationalist blocs was inevitable, and war followed inexorably from this conflict.

After World War II, with America overwhelmingly dominant, hegemony was restored and hence a new world economy came into being. The United States, it is said, accepted its historic responsibility. The Bretton Woods system, like the gold standard, masked the reality of hegemony under the forms of pluralism. Credit flowed from American overseas aid, military spending, and investments; postwar prosperity has been the result. Now, as American hegemony has begun to falter, the time of troubles returns. The French have been playing their customary role, renewing the continental challenge to a faltering Anglo-Saxon world system.

Such, in brief, is the imperial view. How correct is it?

The essays in this volume offer the foundation for a critique and an alternate view. In particular, Judith Kooker's essay presents the views of a French school which blames the liberal system's interwar collapse on Britain's pretensions to hegemony, an hegemony which it had neither claimed nor enjoyed in the classic gold standard. And Bruce Brittain's essay, by seeing the blocs of 1930s forming a relatively stable, successful, and internationally integrated economic system, challenges the second part of the imperialist view, namely, that economic blocs lead to conflict among nations.

The Historical Record:
The Gold Standard and Its Demise

Assessing the imperial view in its financial dimension requires confronting three historical issues: First, how did the gold standard actually function before World War I? Did Britain exercise financial "hegemony"? The second question flows from the first: Was there a qualitative change in the gold standard after World War I? Did Britain lose an hegemony which it had held before? Can Britain's inability to sustain financial hegemony in the 1920s thus be considered the cause of the international financial collapse of 1931? And third, was the bloc system which followed the collapse in the 1930s as unintegrated and conflicted as most historians have claimed?

Contrasting Theories of the Gold Standard

That imperial view of the gold standard which sees England exercising financial hegemony appears to rest upon a number of specialized studies of the pre-1914 banking systems. Many scholarly specialists, reacting against their student textbooks, deny that the gold standard before World War I was automatic and unconscious and stress instead the managing role played by central banks and the Bank of England in particular. In the classic view of the gold standard, a country in payments deficit lost gold because foreign creditors demanded rapid settlement. Losing gold reduced a country's monetary base, and thus the national money supply, a development which deflated the economy, lowered prices, and improved the trade balance. By a similar process, external surplus was meant to lead to an inflow of gold, which gradually expanded a country's money supply, raised prices, and returned its foreign accounts to equilibrium.[6]

[6] The textbook view originates from David Hume's price-specie-flow mechanism, the concept which informed the official British inquiry on the financial system, the Cunliffe Report of 1918, which sought to explain how the gold standard should again function in the postwar world. The "rules" were meant to show how central banks had and should automatically respond to changes in their external accounts. Bloomfield and others, on the other hand, stress discretionary management by central banks before 1914, often to prevent gold flows or counteract their supposedly automatic effects. "Clearly, the pre-1914 gold standard system was a managed and not a quasi-automatic one from the viewpoint of the leading individual countries." Bloomfield, op. cit., p. 60. But a recent dissertation, statistically analyzing "lagged relationships" in rules of the game procedures, argues that the Bank of England did follow the "rules." See Kelly Matthews, "Rules of the Game: A Spectral Analysis of the Gold Standard in Great Britain and the United States, 1879-1914," doctoral dissertation, University of Colorado, 1973.

Research, however, shows national gold reserves less responsive to basic balance-of-payments disequilibria than the classic model suggests. Except in political crisis, little gold flowed from one major center to another. Instead, central banks, and especially private individuals, often did not convert their foreign currency into gold but instead held substantial reserves in certain "key" foreign currencies, specifically the pound, the franc, and the mark. That such large foreign-held balances existed in these "key currencies" suggests that the major centers were not adjusting rapidly and automatically to equilibrium, but instead were running substantial external deficits.[7] How then did they husband their gold reserves? In many instances, whenever a major center began losing gold, its central bank raised the discount rate. The consequent higher interest rates, it is thought, served to restore payments to equilibrium—both immediately by attracting short-term capital from abroad and ultimately by deflating the domestic economy to improve the trade balance. For a variety of reasons, the major centers are thought to have had power to attract funds from abroad with ease.[8] Thus, according to this view, the peripheral countries financed the deficits of the major centers and the gold reserves of the main centers re-

[7] See, for example, Lindert, op. cit., pp. 25-30. Gold-point manipulation was sometimes used to control gold flows. See Bloomfield, op. cit., pp. 52-53.

[8] London's preeminent capacity to attract funds came from the large size of Britain's economy, and especially from sterling's role as the world's vehicle currency. Since sterling was commonly used in international transactions, foreigners held sizable sterling deposits. If the Bank rate rose, London's foreign lending would be cut down to make funds available at home; the increased domestic demand for money would also repatriate sterling assets from abroad, and even foreign funds and gold. This movement of funds into London would cause a demand for alternative funds in foreign countries and result in higher interest rates there. For a description of this process see Cleveland's essay. See also Lindert, op. cit., pp. 42, 67.

mained stable, despite persistent payments deficits. Peripheral countries, however, also guarded their gold. When in deficit, they financed themselves with those balances which they had built up in the key currencies, until a decline in their money supplies or other factors prompted adjustment. When necessary, they borrowed from the main centers. A significant part of these loans was generally kept on deposit in the lending country, thus further encouraging the use of reserve currencies.

This view of the prewar gold standard belies any sharp break between prewar and postwar practice. Scholars like Jacques Rueff, however, see the Genoa Conference of 1922 marking a fundamental change in the international monetary system.[9] According to Rueff, in place of the prewar gold standard, the major countries turned to a gold-exchange standard. Under this new system, instead of adjusting immediately to payments imbalances by gold inflows and outflows, central banks were permitted to hold surplus foreign currencies, most particularly sterling and the dollar, as part of their own national reserves in place of gold. Britain was thus permitted to run regular deficits; the surplus sterling accumulated as monetary reserves in other central banks.[10] The device, unknown, according to Rueff, before World War I, allowed London to be a major financial market in the 1920s, although Britain no longer generated a sufficient current account surplus to be the world's principal foreign lender. For reasons later developed by Rob-

[9] See Jacques Rueff, *The Monetary Sin of the West* (New York, 1972), pp. 52-53: "The extension throughout Europe of the gold-exchange standard between 1922 and 1928 . . . was a turning point in history."

[10] The United States, still wary of entangling international involvements, did not encourage the dollar's use as a reserve currency, especially after 1927 when Britain's vulnerability to French pressure was apparent. See Stephen V. O. Clarke, *Central Bank Cooperation, 1924-1931* (New York, 1967).

ert Triffin in relation to the dollar, sterling's position gradually deteriorated.[11] Increasing sterling balances were held by foreigners who did not want them, and who thus began demanding gold. Throughout the later 1920s, the British, still lending a huge amount abroad, complained of a shortage of world liquidity and feverishly sought to borrow more and more to cover an evergrowing sterling debt. Both private and official holders grew more and more apprehensive about their holdings in sterling. Inevitably, the gold-exchange system crashed in 1931, only to be restored after World War II, and, Rueff argues, with strikingly similar results.

If we accept the imperial view of the prewar gold standard, however, the postwar Genoa system seems not so drastic a break with prewar practice. Both before as well as after World War I, the major financial centers, including Paris, would appear to have operated reserve currencies and thus induced foreign holders to finance their balance-of-payments deficits. When under pressure, the major central banks could attract foreign funds by raising interest rates. They thus controlled, indirectly, the money supplies in other countries. Why, then, did the system break down after World War I and not before? Here, the imperial view steps forward with a general historical and geopolitical theory based on the decline of Britain.

After World War I, it is said, Britain's military and political power was greatly weakened, along with her economic and financial strength. London, supported by Paris and New York, was unable to sustain its old hegemonic position. Sterling no longer commanded its old prestige. Hence, the international system, lacking its necessary hegemonic power, ultimately collapsed, not to be restored until after World War II.

Thus, it is said, history proves hegemony to be the economically best arrangement for the global system, even if these optimum political preconditions are admittedly not al-

[11] Robert Triffin, *Gold and the Dollar Crisis* (New Haven, Conn., 1961) and *The World Money Maze* (New Haven, Conn., 1966).

ways attainable. Those persons holding such views are wont to observe how the world's economic system has long been more integrated than its political system. Whereas the world economy grows highly interdependent, they say, the nation-state continues to prevail as the formula for organizing political power; hence, the ideal economic order remains elusive, except in those happy eras when one nation's predominance establishes a stable and open world order.[12]

Hegemony Before 1914?

Whatever the value of this hegemonic principle as a general prescription for the present, the history of the gold standard does not, in my view, give it much support. For a start, the financial system before World War I was not imperial. Even if formerly exaggerated, the differences between the 1870-1914 period and the interwar and postwar periods remain critical.[13] While central banks, and the Bank of England in particular, played a larger discretionary role in managing the system than a simple-minded view of the gold standard might suggest, those who call Britain's early role hegemonic, and thereby mean to stress the continuity of British and American positions and pretensions, confuse two distinct situations.

It is useful to sort out the attributes which might be said to

[12] The whole view finds a striking early expression in Clarence Streit's *Union Now* (New York, 1939), p. 70. Streit believed world monetary stability before World War I to be based on British hegemony and saw "no hope of restoring the enduringly stable money the world enjoyed in Britain's prime without restoring first its essential basis, namely, a single overwhelmingly powerful government that is responsible for it." Streit saw the "overwhelmingly powerful government" as an Atlantic Union which the United States, in close partnership with Britain, would lead.

[13] See Marcello de Cecco, *Money and Empire: The International Gold Standard, 1890-1914* (Totowa, N.J.: Roman and Littlefield, 1975).

constitute monetary hegemony.[14] Presumably, the hegemon must be a major dispenser of funds abroad—as lender, investor, tourist, conqueror, or protector. The essence of its monetary hegemony would seem to lie in its capacity to force other countries to finance its balance-of-payments deficits. A reserve currency is said to provide the means. Foreigners—individuals or governments—hold the deficits as monetary reserves in place of gold. Thus, the United States, for example, has been able to finance its postwar basic balance-of-payments deficit since World War II—an outflow corresponding closely to American arms and investments abroad.[15]

Closely related to its hegemonic function of issuing the reserve currency is the hegemon's capacity to draw funds from the periphery. Because the hegemonic center is the largest and most efficient market for money, it draws both capital and borrowers from the peripheral countries.[16] Not only may bankers at the center thus determine where capital will go in the periphery, but conditions in the central capital market determine, in effect, the money supplies for the whole system. The central bank of the center country, when it undertakes such measures as changing the discount rates or reserve requirements, or open market operations, manages to control not only the money supply at home but also in the other countries throughout the system. Thus, it is commonly observed, actions taken by the Federal Reserve Bank of New

[14] Susan Strange allows for a more sophisticated and subtle interpretation of international monetary relationships. See her *Sterling and British Policy: A Political Study of an International Currency in Decline* (London, 1971).

[15] See David P. Calleo and Benjamin M. Rowland, *America and the World Political Economy* (Bloomington, Ind., 1973), pp. 95-99.

[16] The center's attraction of savings from the periphery is even likely to exceed its investments into the periphery. See Hans O. Schmitt, "The National Boundary in Politics and Economics," in *Communication in International Politics*, Richard L. Merritt, ed. (Urbana, Ill., 1972), pp. 413, 415-16.

York in recent years have come to determine not only monetary conditions in the United States, but in Europe as
well.[17] "When America sneezes, Europe catches cold" has
become a saw in the conventional wisdom about our international monetary system—at least as it is perceived to have
operated in the 1960s.[18]

While few observers deny America's monetary hegemony in
the 1960s, projecting this American position of the 1960s back
to the British role before 1914 greatly strains the historical
imagination. This particular imperial hypothesis about financial history suffers from a fundamental flaw: It confuses the
gold standard with the British Empire. To be sure, Britain's
role in the prewar international economy was immense. Britain formed the political and economic center of both a formal
empire and an array of informal dependencies. Monetarily,
this imperial system was doubtless on a sterling standard.
Monetary reserves of the colonies, dominions, and informal
dependencies were held in sterling balances rather than gold,
and London's actions did certainly weigh heavily upon the
domestic money supplies throughout the empire. Unques-
tionably, London was the major source of capital for peripheral savings. Nevertheless, this imperial system, with

[17] The Eurodollar market, a vast pool of expatriate dollars, is the
key mechanism for American monetary influence over Europe during the past decade. For example, if the Federal Reserve tightens the
U.S. money supply, which it did in 1966, 1969, and 1971, U.S. banks
tend to borrow from their branch banks abroad, raising Eurodollar
interest rates and attracting European funds. This serves to restrict
European money supplies. Likewise, when easy money returns, U.S.
bank borrowings are paid back, flooding the Eurodollar market and
lowering interest rates, thus thwarting possible European restrictive
monetary policies by providing European borrowers with a lake of
relatively cheap funds. See Herbert V. Prochnow, *The Eurodollar*
(Chicago, 1970).

[18] Aside from its objectionable political features, the hegemonic
system is said to be highly inflationary. Since the dollar deficits

London as its center, was a bloc within the world system rather than the world system itself.

It therefore seems perverse to describe this imperial sterling network, however vast, as the gold standard. For the gold standard had to do not with the monetary relations between Britain, and say, Australia or Argentina, but among Britain and the other center countries—France, Germany, Austria, and, later on, the United States. The other major financial powers admired the British system and tried to imitate it. The French had an imperial bloc, which extended to Russia, whose large borrowings from Paris were kept, in great part, as franc balances in French banks. The Germans, in a similar fashion, sought to extend their monetary bloc throughout Eastern Europe. In short, the gold-standard system was composed of a number of currency blocs, within each of which a particular reserve currency held sway. The network among these blocs constituted the world system. While the principal members were interdependent to some degree, Britain's position among them was far from comparable to the monetary hegemony exercised by the United States in the 1960s. While sterling was the most important vehicle currency used for trading purposes, and was, as we have stressed, the reserve currency within the formal and informal empire, its use as a reserve among the major centers is much more doubtful.

---

automatically accepted by foreign countries are then reinvested in the United States as interest-bearing instruments, the contraction of the American money supply which should occur to correct the deficit fails to occur. The United States thus continues its deficits. What correction occurs is likely to be made by the surplus countries. Dollars exchanged for domestic currencies there will end up in central banks and contribute to the monetary base. Dollars retained as dollar balances in domestic banks can add to inflation if they become the source of credit pyramiding. Continued U.S. deficits lead to a weakened dollar, and attempting to maintain fixed exchange rates under speculative conditions by buying up dollars merely fans the fires of inflation. See Rueff, op. cit.

The critical historical issue is whether the system was plural—in that the major centers were in equilibrium with each other, according to the classic idea of the gold standard, or whether the system was "hegemonic," with London running deficits as the controlling center of a common system. Specifically, did Paris and Berlin hold sterling as a reserve, and, in so doing, finance a continuing British deficit? If it could be shown that Britain ran a persistent large deficit with Paris and Berlin, and that they financed the deficit by holding sterling, then it could indeed be argued that the gold standard was a sterling-exchange standard. Then, it might also be said that Paris and Berlin—or New York—were really part of an imperial sterling bloc. But the assertion runs counter to what everyone believed to have been true at the time, and the evidence for it is not decisive. The traditional view, upheld by several distinguished scholars, believes the imperial system to have been in basic balance until World War I. In other words, before World War I, Britain is said to have had sufficient income from trade, investment, and services, plus the Indian milk cow, to remain in balance with the other major centers.[19] However,

---

[19] Although Britain ran continual trade deficits before the war, "invisible earnings"—especially returns on overseas investments—sustained a highly favorable current account balance. After the war, however, British exports increased only slightly in value whereas imports jumped by almost 50 percent. A £525 million export earnings in 1913 averaged £742 million (1924-29), while imports increased from £659 million (1913) to over £1,000 million annually (1924-29). Postwar invisibles earnings did not increase enough to cover the trade deficit by any substantial amount. In the pre-1914 period, returns on foreign investment often exceeded total foreign investment and were usually sufficient to produce a healthy current account surplus. Moreover, foreign investment outlays almost invariably returned to Britain in the form of increased demand for British exports, first of capital goods, then consumer goods. Before 1914 foreign investment thus helped the trade position, but in the interwar period the rise of competing centers as well as a decline in the British competitive position largely obliterated this effect. In

the central banks of France and Germany did, in fact, hold substantial sterling balances. A good deal more sterling is believed to have been held privately. The question remains whether these sterling assets were held against corresponding liabilities in sterling. In other words, were these foreign sterling balances held in place of gold, or merely to cover debts in sterling?

Not only are the facts elusive, especially for the private holdings, but their significance is questionable. Would large and uncovered private sterling holdings indicate British financial hegemony over Paris and Berlin, in the American fashion since World War II? In other words, to what extent can it be said that London controlled the money supply in the other major centers? London was certainly the world's largest

---

fact, during the post-World War I years, net capital exports were generally in excess of the current account surplus. Although no figures exist on pre-1914 short-term capital movements, it is clear that Britain's ability to influence them via monetary measures contributed greatly to maintaining sterling stability. This influence derived from Britain's investment and trade position, not from a so-called sterling-exchange standard. In 1860 Britain absorbed 30 percent of the rest of the world's exports and in 1913 the amount was still 17 percent. British overseas assets by 1914 totaled nearly £4,000 million. It is clear that fluctuations in Britain would influence overseas economies. Still, this influence did not come about via foreign government or central bank holdings of sterling. The ratio of bullion to foreign exchange was quite high (6:1) compared to the post-World War II ratio of 2:1. The dollar's position after World War II is much closer to a dollar-exchange standard. See P. M. Oppenheimer's "Monetary Movements and Position of Sterling," pp. 90, 95-96, and Alexander G. Kemp's "Long Term Capital Movements," pp. 138-42, in D. J. Robertson and L. C. Hunter, *The British Balance of Payments* (Edinburgh and London, 1966); see also A. K. Cairncross, *Home and Foreign Investment, 1870-1913* (Cambridge, 1953), p. 180.

capital market. When the Bank of England raised its discount rate, great attraction was exerted on foreign funds. Does this mean that a hegemonic Bank of England could command foreign money at will? Other central banks were, it seems, prepared to counter London's moves. Some retaliated by following London with equally high rates. Some scholars argue, however, that London's leading position in world business gave the City a disporportionate attraction for short-term funds, even if other central banks did raise their discount rates to counter a rise in London.[20] Nevertheless, the Bank of England's discretionary power to raise rates was, it would seem, severely limited by its own character as a profitmaking private business. Bagehot, in his classic description of the City as it worked around 1870, energetically dismissed the notion that the Bank of England could control interest rates. The Bank's position, he argued, was that of the major supplier of a commodity in a "Dutch" auction. The Bank could set a price for its commodity, but buyers would always hope to do better with the lesser suppliers.[21] And, as a private corporation, profit was, after all, the Bank of England's business—even if it did

[20] See above, note 8.

[21] In a "Dutch" auction the largest seller of a commodity (in this case the Bank of England) sets the maximum or upset price, which, if too high, would fall in competition with other lesser sellers. Thus, although the Bank of England had the power to affect the marginal value of money, it could not affect its average, long-run value. Even if the Bank wanted to sell at a subnormal price, Bagehot argued, subsequent inflation would create an additional demand for money, which, in the long run, would reestablish the money rate to the average rate. Other banks, in fact, held larger private deposits than the Bank of England. Its issuing department, it should be remembered, was entirely separate from its discount department and was, in any event, severely constrained by Peel's Act of 1844, which forbade the issuing of currency over £14 million not backed by bullion. This amount was increased periodically and the law itself suspended during the crisis of 1866.

have half-conscious public responsibilities as lender of last resort.[22]

Bagehot's analysis suggests the profound changes which World War I brought to banking, money, and economic life in general. After the war, government was thoroughly mixed in the management of economies, despite often heroic attempts to disengage. Unprecedented domestic disruptions, plus the general progress of collectivist and revolutionary ideas, profoundly challenged the informal public and private arrangements which characterized economic management in the era of laissez-faire. Money had been "politicized." The issues of inflation and currency stabilization were, clearly, political questions, upon which seemed to depend the fate of the bourgeoisie itself.[23]

Money had not only become a political issue domestically, but, in the era of war debts and reparations, international financial transactions had obviously also become intensely political. The collapse of German and Austrian power, moreover, opened up Eastern Europe to competition between Britain and France. Each, using financial stabilization as part of its diplomatic armory, competed to bring the Eastern countries into its political-economic orbit. In short, it was a different world after 1914. Money, international and domestic, had become far more consciously political—a fact which might seem too obvious to mention, but for the growing tendency to ignore it.

Because it was a different world, it seems unhistorical to

[22] See Walter Bagehot, *Lombard Street* (New York, 1902), Chaps. VII, XII. Bagehot was deeply concerned by the Bank's lack of institutional structure and conscious responsibility for its managing role, critical, he believed, in view of the extremely extended position of London's financial institutions.

[23] For an exhaustive analysis of the domestic politics of monetary stabilization in Europe, see Charles S. Maier, *Recasting Bourgeois Europe* (Princeton, 1975).

equate Britain's position before World War I with its position in the 1920s, let alone with that of the United States in the 1960s. Mixing the prewar gold standard with the later Anglo-American hegemonies confuses two quite different roles—one, the leading position in the highly automatic prewar system, under rules which a group of autonomous and roughly equal powers accepted in their own self-interest, the other, a hegemonic pretension to be exempted from the rules which govern the others. Put in political terms, Europe before World War I was not part of the British Empire. After World War II, it had become part of the American.

We can perhaps understand the pre-1914 system better if we consider the position of Paris. Until 1870, Paris was an active rival to London as the principal international capital market. After the Franco-Prussian War, Paris nevertheless remained the world's second banking center and is said to have been gaining on London after 1900.[24] In any event, little evidence suggests that French firms felt constrained to go to London to find capital. France, of course, had much larger gold reserves than Britain, even if French banks were not permitted to pyramid credit in anything like the British fashion. The Bank of France was so well endowed with precious metals that it was able not only to finance French domestic needs, but also large loans to Russia and Austria. The French money market, moreover, would not appear to have been particularly responsive to London rates. Indeed, the French

[24] Lindert notes "the relative rise of France and Germany as reserve centers." The franc as a foreign exchange asset grew in amount by over 1,000 percent during the years 1900-13 (from $27.2 to $275.1 million). Sterling grew by over 300 percent (from $121 million to $441.4 million). See Lindert, op. cit., pp. 22, 25. See also Rondon E. Cameron, *France and the Economic Development of Europe, 1800-1914* (Princeton, 1961). Periods of unusually large capital exports coincided with prosperity and rapid domestic capital formation.

almost never changed their low discount rate. If capital began to flow out excessively, they altered the gold points, or began paying in silver rather than gold—an early form of devaluation. In short, before 1914, Paris would seem to have been amply protected from London's hegemony.[25]

The Interwar Collapse: Hegemony Lost?

If there was no British financial hegemony before World War I, then the failure of the interwar monetary system cannot so easily be explained either by Britain's failure to sustain hegemony or America's refusal to take over. In fact, a more sensible view would see the interwar system breaking down not from the absence of a hegemon, but because the major centers could no longer sustain a stable equilibrium with one another. A brief look at each major center will remind us of the reasons.

The United States had aquired immense claims through the

[25] Variations of discount rates in France averaged less than half those of England or Germany. France had a large metallic reserve and little pyramiding of credit. Bank of France bullion reserves averaged better than 70 percent of liabilities, whereas Bank of England bullion reserves averaged less than 50 percent of liabilities. The French also had a successful technique of frustrating sudden gold outflows. According to Harry Dexter White, *The French International Accounts, 1880-1913* (Cambridge, 1933), p. 185, placing a premium on the price charged for gold "constituted a formidable barrier (when the exchange rate was 'unfavorable') to the outward movement of short-term funds, and rendered the French gold holdings insensitive to movements of discount rates in foreign money markets." After 1900, the premium was little used, and loans to other reserve centers were made at times of high foreign discount rates. Still, from 1900 to 1913, French discount rates remained much lower than comparative British rates, signaling a continued ease in obtaining funds in Paris. For example, in 1908, when rates were approaching 5 percent at the Bank of England, Bank of France rates were scarcely above 3 percent.

war, but unlike Britain in the prewar era, America was unwilling to provide a market for her debtors. As a huge state which spanned a continent, and a self-sufficient economy which exported both food and manufactures, the United States was ill-suited to take on Britain's international role. Indeed, much of the trouble with the international economic system throughout this century can be laid to the unpromising attempt, promoted by the elites of both countries, to fit America for Britain's role.

But if America was unsuited for Britain's traditional economic role, so was Britain after World War I. As Robert Skidelsky points out, the war had finally broken the old trade pattern by which dependencies provided the raw materials and Britain the manufactures. The shortages and blockades had accelerated industry in the periphery and encouraged agriculture in Britain. Readjustment proved difficult. Britain, moreover, had lost her huge overseas investments and could no longer afford to live as the world's *rentier*. But just as the Americans could not adjust to being rich, neither could the British adjust to being poor. Instead, they sought to keep up the old establishment by borrowing. The City, having lost its own savings, hoped to employ those of others. London, having lost its capital, would capitalize its prestige. If Britain lacked gold, she would use sterling instead. Hence, as Reuff points out, the Genoa Conference of 1922 and the birth of the ill-fated gold-exchange standard. With Germany defeated and France ruined, Britain, in partnership with America, made a bid for financial hegemony. But sterling's prestige could not survive the increasingly evident decline of Britain's economic base. The decline was hastened, of course, by Churchill's restoring the pound to prewar parity, a decision taken, ironically, to sustain the City's prestige as a safe repository for foreign savings. An overvalued pound, sustained by high interest rates, weakened British industry further and made a current account equilibrium all the more remote. As Britain's foreign lending continued nonetheless, and her debts became larger, bankruptcy grew inevitable.[26]

This is not the place to recount the familiar story of Weimar Germany's doomed attempt to restore its own international financial equilibrium; nor of France's anguished early policies, a story well told in Judith Kooker's essay. In effect, a bankrupt France looked to relief from a bankrupt Germany. In the end, of the former major European centers only France, battered but still richly self-sufficient, pulled herself together, stabilized the franc at a reasonable parity, and returned to the discipline of the prewar gold standard—only to discover that no one else would join her.[27]

[26] Structural changes in world industry and trade made costs higher in older British plants and weakened British competitiveness in world markets. Deflationary policy discouraged shifts to more profitable industries. Sticky wages helped keep costs high. The result was that British export share in world markets declined by 10 percent in the latter half of the 1920s while world trade rose 7 percent. Britain's ultimately failing attempt to remain a large international lender was frustrated by America's (and France's) sterilization policy. Thus, in 1928, when British gold reserves were at their maximum of £172 million, short-term liabilities amounted to between £270 million and £300 million.

[27] Even France's limited success is often said to have rested on Britain's unwillingness to undertake a comparable devaluation. It seems more reasonable, however, to blame the British for deliberately overvaluing the pound in order to preserve London as a financial center. The common British view that the franc was deliberately and unreasonably undervalued is not sustained by a recent close study using newly available official papers. The franc was stabilized at its actual market value, which was not officially manipulated, and so was not undervalued except relative to an overvalued pound sterling. The French were eager to stabilize and saw no reason to promote or await further appreciation, which they realized would mean deflation, further addition to the already heavy state debt, and for a franc that had depreciated 80 percent, take much too long to accomplish in any significant degree. See Judith Kooker, "French Financial

Thus, the quarrel between France and Britain throughout the 1920s occurred. France piled up more and more reserves; Britain went even deeper into debt. Britain complained of a lack of world "liquidity"; France lectured London on living beyond its means. British bankers, avid for Paris gold, found France "inward looking." The French bourgeoisie, mourning the loss of Czarist bonds, kept their capital at home.

In the end, French and American opposition doomed Britain's attempt to transform the gold standard into the sterling standard. Neither France nor the United States was willing to accumulate sterling balances indefinitely. Both realized that Britain's attempt constituted a qualitative change in world financial relations—from pluralism to a hegemonic imbalance. Neither would accept such a subordinate position within a British-run system. As a result of Britain's attempt and failure, the gold-exchange standard collapsed and the system broke up into blocs.

Such a view of the 1920s undermines the belief that hegemony represents the optimum state of the international monetary system. Instead, it would seem to lead to the contrary opinion: Attempting an exploitative hegemony inevitably breaks up a plural world financial system. But even if Britain's ill-fated ambition was a sufficient cause for breakdown, the system was bound to collapse in any event. No interdependent system of autonomous states is likely to hold together without the requisite conditions for equilibrium among them. No one, except perhaps the French, was sufficiently adapted to the postwar world, either internally or externally, to participate in an open international system

---

Diplomacy: The Interwar Years," unpublished doctoral dissertation, The Johns Hopkins University, Washington, D.C., 1975, Chap. 2. For the common British view, see The Royal Institute of International Affairs' *The International Gold Problem* (Oxford,1931), p. 213.

based on rules of the game observed by all. The structural adjustments required after the war were too great for a liberal system to manage. In the circumstances, the system was bound to break up into discrete blocs. Isolationism was the consequence of universal weakness.

The Blocs of the 1930s

Our essays, Brittain's in particular, by taking a close look at the "breakdown" itself, suggest a major new insight into the later interwar period. The bloc system, in fact, worked relatively well, at least as a phase of economic recuperation and adjustment. Great Britain, by limiting and consolidating her external commitments and concentrating on domestic growth, enjoyed a domestic industrial rejuvenation not seen since the later nineteenth century. The unattractive character of the Nazi regime should not blind us to the remarkable recovery of the German economy under Hitler, an achievement which came, to a greater extent than is usually admitted, without the stimulus of rearmament. Moreover, as Brittain's paper indicates, these recuperating national blocs were not as conflicting, or even as monetarily isolated from each other, as the usual view has it.

What emerges from our researches, in short, is not the collapse of an interdependent international economic system into beggar-thy-neighbor policies of economic warfare, but a system of negotiated relationships among recuperating national economies. A considerable degree of world integration was, in fact, preserved—although not permitted to threaten the internal recovery of the major national units. It is difficult not to find this negotiated system superior to the superficial liberalism of the 1920s—a system which, because its major participants were incapable of achieving equilibrium, headed inevitably toward breakdown.

With the Tripartite Agreement of 1936, the bloc system reached a new degree of consciously organized cooperation which appeared to lead toward a resumption of liberalism among reconstituted partners. It becomes grotesque, of course, to consider economic arrangements in the later 1930s in isolation from general international conditions. The renewal of cooperation among Britain, France, and the United States in 1936 took place under rather special circumstances. France, menaced by a resurgent Germany, had to a great extent become a prisoner of British policy. Britain, finding the appeasement of Germany more and more distasteful, expensive, and uncertain, conceded America's economic demands in the hope of securing an alliance. In other words, the bloc system, in its later stages, seems not so much the natural evolution of a negotiated economic system, as the beginnings of America's postwar hegemony over Europe.[28]

Consideration of these general conditions leads to a fundamental historical issue: the relation between interwar economic blocs and the war that followed. As Robert Skidelsky points out about the gold standard before World War I, a system which eventually blew up in a holocaust of unprecedented proportions must have had some deficiencies. The same may be said of the bloc system in the 1930s. The question, of course, is whether the nature of the blocs, and the economic recovery which they fostered, was itself conducive to war—or whether the causes for conflict have to be found elsewhere. In particular, was the nature of the Nazi recovery such that rearmament and war were its inevitable conclusion? [29]

[28] For a close analysis of Britain's growing strategic dependence upon the United States and its economic consequences, see Benjamin M. Rowland, "Commercial Conflict and Foreign Policy: A Study in Anglo-American Relations, 1932-38," unpublished doctoral dissertation, The Johns Hopkins University, 1975.

[29] The same point, of course, is sometimes made about the economic policies of the democracies; the depression—massive unemployment in particular—it is often said, never really ended in Britain, and especially the United States, until rearmament restored flagging demand.

Clearly, Hull's simple-minded and rather self-serving view that blocs led to war can no longer be accepted at face value. At the very least, the historical record shows a more complex picture. What then caused the war? Why were the major powers unable to accommodate each other? The causes would seem to lie in their political relations rather than in the character of their economic nationalism.

Obviously, the particular character of the Nazi regime greatly increased the difficulties of mutual accommodation. It is incorrect, however, to regard that regime as a product of economic nationalism. If anything, it was the result of the catastrophic instability of the 1920s, when Germany tied herself faithfully to a convulsing liberal world economic order. Germany's experience from that liberal era destroyed the traditional checks on domestic power, ruined and embittered much of the population, and installed a gangster regime whose vicious domestic practices and abusive international style probably made accommodation with it impossible. Had Weimar turned resolutely to economic nationalism, Germany might have avoided Nazism. Ultimately a more stable, tractable, "appeaseable" regime might conceivably have obtained satisfaction of Germany's grievances and ambitions without going to war.[30]

In any event, it is difficult to see the character of the Nazi economy, or even of the German economic bloc in Eastern Europe, precluding economic accommodations with other

---

[30] Briand and Streseman may have had some such view during their discussions in the 1920s on the formation of a European bloc. As it turned out, however, Bruening pursued a policy of deflation which only worsened Germany's economic problems until the Nazis took power and Schacht instituted (in the "New Plan") a comprehensive exchange control program in conjunction with the general expansionary plan. See W. Kendall Myers, "Economic Blocs in Historical Perspective," unpublished paper for the Washington Center of Foreign Policy Research, 1975.

capitalist countries. Historical scholarship denies that German economic recovery depended upon rearmament.[31] Nor, on the whole, do the relationships with Eastern Europe seem to have been exploitative.[32] Was Germany's Eastern economic bloc, in itself, an intolerable threat to British, French, and American economic security—and, therefore, in itself, a prime cause of the war? To reverse the question: Would the concession of such an economic bloc to Germany have sated her ambitions? The historian will doubtless always remain skeptical of the

[31] By 1935 unemployment had fallen to 2.2 million workers from the peak level of 5.6 million in 1932. A year later some labor shortages began appearing. Production had recovered well by 1935 with GNP (92 billion Reichsmarks) surpassing predepression levels (1928—91 billion Reichsmarks). Rearmament itself was largely a myth until German reoccupation of the Rhineland in the spring of 1936. In the three years before March 31, 1936, only 5 percent of the total national production went for war production. Clearly, recovery did not depend on rearmament, but was well under way even as rearmament geared up. See Burton H. Klein, *German's Economic Preparations for War* (Cambridge, 1959), Chap. 1.

[32] Germany's role in Eastern Europe was certainly dominant. But with the exception of Rumania, the East European countries needed Germany much more than the reverse. Their trade with Germany amounted to £72 million, five times that of their next largest trading partner, Britain. They provided a scant market for German industrial goods and their agricultural products complicated Germany's domestic agricultural development program. German intentions were perhaps long range: to develop the region for a future trade relationship while putting up with some present drawbacks. Of course, if it is assumed that Germany aimed at self-sufficiency in preparation for war then the Eastern bloc becomes more sensible. A bloc, in any event, cannot be judged merely on its immediate economic results, particularly in an uncertain world where access to markets, food, and other raw materials is precarious. Over a long period of time, a complementary economy can doubtless be created, particularly where overriding political conditions are more important than short-term economic efficiency. In any event, if an Eastern

possibility that Hitler's Germany would have been appeased by any conceivable British concessions. Yet it must be confessed that the attempt was never made. A recent study of British foreign policy, based on Cabinet papers, shows how little the British were willing to concede Germany in Eastern Europe, even though the British economic interests were trivial, whereas the interest in direct trade with Germany was substantial.[33] Britain's reluctance is complex to explain. In the early 1930s, Chamberlain, hoping to restore Britain's domestic economy while limiting and consolidating her international bloc, seems to have been willing to consider conceding Germany a sphere of her own. Why were the British so recalcitrant? Chamberlain's failure to follow through cannot easily be explained by economic differences with Germany, let alone by the inherent failings of a world of blocs. Instead, in refusing accommodation with Germany, the British sacrificed their most cherished economic interests to the United States, a

European bloc was of doubtful economic use to Germany, it was certainly of even less economic significance to Britain and France. Whereas Germany's imports from the East European countries grew from 12 percent to 16 percent of her total imports, and her exports grew from 11 percent to 15 percent of total exports, British and French trade with East Europe remained static at around 2.5 percent and 4 percent of total trade, respectively. See Simon Newman, "March 1939: Chamberlain's Diplomatic Revolution? The Origins of the British Guarantee to Poland," unpublished doctoral dissertation, The Johns Hopkins University, 1974, to be published by Oxford University Press.

[33] Newman, op. cit. pp. ix, 46. Newman's researches in official papers suggest that "Britain never intended Germany to have a free hand in Eastern Europe at all." British trade with Eastern Europe totaled £16m. in 1938, whereas Anglo-German trade was much more important, almost £60m. Britain hoped to thwart any attempt by Germany to form a self-sufficient trading bloc with the East European countries and thus cut out Anglo-German trade.

development which Chamberlain himself appears long to have anticipated and feared.[34]

Politics rather than economics explains British and French resistance to a German Eastern sphere. As long as Germany seemed still determined to become a world power, a process which necessarily would give Germany hegemony over Europe and reduce France to a satellite, whatever strengthened Germany was unacceptable to France.[35] The British could only appease the Germans at the expense of their French allies—a policy followed fitfully in the interwar period, but never to an extent necessary for Anglo-German accommodation. In the end, as Chamberlain seems to have feared, another European war destroyed Britain's world position and gave America and Russia domination over Europe.

World War II, like World War I, came from the failure of Europe's major powers to accommodate each other. But any stable accommodation among the three was probably impossible, as A. J. P. Taylor argues, as long as they continued to believe Europe the center of world power.[36] Accommodation, to the limited extent that it has occurred in recent years, springs from the double realization: first, that with Germany divided, no one of the three Western European powers is likely to achieve hegemony over the others; and second, that a disunited Europe is fated to remain partitioned and controlled from the outside.

After thirty years of a benevolent American hegemony, our present era will witness perhaps another critical round in the European game. Hegemony has gradually been bankrupted; economic nationalism will hope to restore a viable economic

[34] See Myers, op. cit., p. 16; and his *Neville Chamberlain and Britain's Choices*, forthcoming. See also Rowland, op. cit.

[35] See Ludwig Dehio, *Germany and World Politics in the Twentieth Century* (New York, 1959).

[36] A. J. P. Taylor, *The Origins of the Second World War* (London, 1961), pp. 127-28.

order on a national basis.[37] Perhaps Europe will this time build its own regional system, as a prelude to a reintegrated and balanced world system. Or perhaps Britain, France, and Germany will find it easier to endure a renewed external hegemony than to accommodate each other.

The Imperial View Reconsidered

Whatever may happen in the coming decades, the history of the interwar era does not appear to support the imperial view. To review our argument: first of all, the prewar sterling standard was not hegemonic, in any sense which suggests a parallel with the British and American gold-exchange standard which followed. Instead, as everyone believed at the time, the gold standard was a multilateral system designed to preserve equilibrium among a few powerful centers. In a premercantilist world, where even central banks were still constrained to make profits, whatever managerial role the central banks played, including the Bank of England, accorded with accepted rules of the game among equal sovereign systems. The system collapsed into World War I because Germany was no longer content to limit her power within a European scale, and Britain, France, and Russia preferred war to accommodation. The postwar era could not reestablish the gold standard because the general destruction and disruption of economic patterns, the loss of Britain's inheritance, and the war debts and reparations tangle made it impossible for the old centers to return to equilibrium. In particular, Britain, determined to retain her old world financial position, tried to substitute a sterling standard for the gold standard. Inevitably the pound, and international finance with it, collapsed for the same technical reasons which have enfeebled the dollar in our own era.

After both wars, France has appeared to play a critical role

[37] This is the general thesis of Calleo and Rowland, op. cit., Chap. 5.

in bringing down Anglo-Saxon pretensions to financial hegemony. From the beginning, British and American economists
have tended to give the French position short shrift. Dispassionate examination of the historical record suggests it ought
to have been taken more seriously. Since World War I, the
French would seem to have lacked any pretension to general
financial hegemony, but felt strong enough to resist domination from others. From the Anglo-American view, this puts the
French in the role of irresponsible wreckers. But the French
position in the 1920s, as in the 1960s, was more complex. It
Rueff is to be credited, the French in the 1920s believed
themselves the defenders of the classic liberal system which
they believed was, par excellence, a plural, nonhegemonic
order. They genuinely believed that the gold standard, if
faithfully obeyed, would adjust international transactions according to those hidden laws of measure which govern so many
of nature's phenomena. The British, in their view, were the
real destroyers of the liberal order. By insisting upon lending,
but without the resources, the British brought down themselves and the world. The bourgeois French perhaps had a
more social view of money than the British. Capital was sacred
because it was tied up in the preservation of the family. Inflation was a disease, not of the economy but of the society. The
French, of course, were also more self-conscious about the
political dimension of money. While the British saw vital
international needs for credit being filled by the expert mechanisms of the City, the French saw British power, financed
by other people's money, reaching out to control economic
life throughout the globe. For the French, British pretensions
were not only politically insupportable, but financially self-
destructive for the system as a whole. The hegemonic order
would lead to inflation followed by collapse. For whatever the
reasons, French prognostications in both the 1920s and the
1960s have borne a remarkable resemblance to the actual
events which have followed.

Once the system had collapsed in the 1930s, all the major

centers withdrew into economic nationalism in hopes of putting their own houses in order—a task which had become
hopeless while participating in a general international system
lacking the preconditions for an acceptable equilibrium. Inas-
much as the blocs, by restoring the major national economies,
gradually reestablished the conditions for international economic equilibrium, they paved the way for reinstituting a
stable new world economy. There is no reason, prima facie,
to believe economic nationalism, in itself, prevented that cooperation. On the contrary, it would seem to have been its
necessary precondition. What made a cooperative order impossible subsequently was not Germany's isolationism, but
the threat that she would gain hegemony over the rest of
Europe. That general geopolitical issue was settled by World
War II. The American financial hegemony which followed
has persisted for thirty years, in recent years under severe
challenge. The world system, once more resisting pretensions
to hegemony, again appears to be disintegrating into nationalist blocs. History, of course, never repeats itself exactly. Nevertheless, the historian may perhaps be forgiven if the present
crisis suggests a certain sense of déjà vu.

If the historical record does not support the interpretation
suggested by an imperial theory of world financial order,
neither, it must be admitted, does it support the view that
only a plural balance-of-power system can succeed. First of all,
hegemony need not fail if it is firmly imposed and accepted.
The Russians, after their fashion, achieve a tolerable degree of
monetary cooperation within their own imperial system.
What does not succeed, it would seem, is weak hegemony
under challenge. Must a weak hegemony always be challenged? The answer obviously depends upon the general political ambitions and perceptions of the major states within the
system. one thing, however, seems relatively certain: States
will resist hegemony when it seriously disrupts that managing
of their domestic economies which, in this modern mercantilist era, seems essential to sustaining political and social stabil-

ity. Both the British and American imperial episodes strongly suggest that the hegemonic power, absolved from general discipline, cannot long resist yielding to those excesses which are soon exported throughout the imperial system as a whole. From the perspective of the lesser members, imperialism becomes synonymous with their exploitation. When the imperial power is not strong enough to compel others to go on accepting these imperial costs, economic nationalism is the natural result.

For better or for worse, no single power among the modern Western capitalist nations has been able to sustain a prolonged hegemony over the others. Britain's preeminence in Europe was strictly limited and rested upon rather special circumstances. Germany's drive for world power, and thus continental hegemony, provoked a prolonged European civil war. Among its other consequences, that war accelerated the American advance toward Western hegemony, a force already strongly felt by the later nineteenth century. In the era after World War II, American hegemony over the West seemed firmly established, at least until it became exploitative. If the United States had inherited Britain's position, or rather what we imagined Britain's position to have been, Russia had perhaps become successor to Germany, the head of a growing rival imperial bloc. Like the British in the interwar period we have toyed with appeasement, a stable accommodation with our rival by conceding each other an imperial sphere. But however cordial our relations with the rival imperium, our problems grow more intense with a Europe supposedly within our sphere. The old French position reminds us why hegemony is seldom stable in the West. Today, Western Europe as a whole seems to have inherited that interwar French position. Europe demands not hegemony for itself, but equality within an interdependent system of rules.

If interwar history offers no proof that hegemony is essential to world order, neither, of course, does it inspire great faith in the universal validity of the balance of power. Tranquillity, no doubt, is typical only of ages where either hegemony is so overwhelming or balance so obvious as to be unchallenged. The interwar period would appear to demonstrate the unhappy effects of pretensions either to hegemony or to independence, when those who assert them lack the strength or will to sustain their ambitions.

Index